T0329953

Management Perspectives on the Covid-19 Crisis

Management Perspectives on the Covid-19 Crisis

Lessons from New Zealand

Edited by

Kenneth Husted

The University of Auckland Business School, New Zealand

Rudolf R. Sinkovics

The University of Auckland Business School, New Zealand and LUT University, Finland

Edward Elgar
PUBLISHING

Cheltenham, UK • Northampton, MA, USA

Published by
Edward Elgar Publishing Limited
The Lypiatts
15 Lansdown Road
Cheltenham
Glos GL50 2JA
UK

Edward Elgar Publishing, Inc.
William Pratt House
9 Dewey Court
Northampton
Massachusetts 01060
USA

A catalogue record for this book
is available from the British Library

Library of Congress Control Number: 2021939241

This book is available electronically in the **Elgar**online
Business subject collection
http://dx.doi.org/10.4337/9781800882096

ISBN 978 1 80088 208 9 (cased)
ISBN 978 1 80088 209 6 (eBook)

Printed and bound by CPI Group (UK) Ltd, Croydon, CR0 4YY

Contents

Contributors

Maureen Benson-Rea (PhD, University of Auckland, NZ) is an Associate Professor in Management and International Business at The University of Auckland Business School, where she is currently also Associate Dean Postgraduate Research. Maureen has held academic positions in the UK as well as several international policy roles with a major UK business organisation, the Confederation of British Industry. There she advised companies, developed policy and represented the views of British business, with a focus on the EU, in Whitehall, Westminster and Brussels. Maureen was the founding co-director of the University of Auckland's Europe Institute, and was recently elected President of the Academy of International Business Oceania Chapter. A company director and board chair, Maureen's research covers international business, marketing and strategy. She has supervised over 100 postgraduate students and her research has appeared in *Academy of International Business Insights, Management International Review, International Business Review, European Management Journal, Industrial Marketing Management, Marketing Theory, Public Administration, Journal of Business Research* and *Multinational Business Review* among others.

Peter Boxall (PhD, Monash University, AU, CFHRINZ) is Professor in Human Resource Management at the University of Auckland Business School. His research is concerned with strategic HRM and employee well-being and has appeared in such journals as *Human Resource Management Journal, International Journal of Human Resource Management, Economic and Industrial Democracy, Journal of Management Studies, British Journal of Industrial Relations* and *Work, Employment and Society*. With John Purcell and Patrick Wright, he co-edited the *Oxford Handbook of Human Resource Management* (Oxford University Press, 2007) and, with Richard Freeman and Peter Haynes, he co-edited *What Workers Say: Employee Voice in the Anglo-American Workplace* (Cornell University Press, 2007). He is the co-author with John Purcell of *Strategy and Human Resource Management* (Palgrave Macmillan), now in its fourth edition.

Jose Brache (PhD, Adolfo Ibañez University, CL) is the Director of the Huizenga Business Innovation Academy at the Wayne Huizenga College of Business and Entrepreneurship of Nova Southeastern University. His research highlights the mechanisms present within inter-firm cooperation projects, pinpointing how certain forms of collaboration lead to an increase in firm performance. His interests include: Inter-firm cooperation in innovation and internationalization, cooperation in entrepreneurial networks, SMEs' internationalization, industrial clusters and international entrepreneurship. His work has been published in journals such as *International Business Review* and *Journal of Business Research*. He actively participates in entrepreneurial and innovation networks, assisting in the promotion of business startups and the commercialization of novel and disruptive technologies.

Brigid Carroll (PhD, University of Auckland, NZ) is a Professor at the University of Auckland Business School and holds the Fletcher Building Employee Educational Fund Chair in Leadership there. Her research is in the areas of leadership as practice, collective and distributed leadership, theory and practice of leadership development and the relationship between leadership, identity, power and resistance. She has co-edited three books: *Leadership: Contemporary, Critical Perspectives*, *Responsible Leadership: Realism and Romanticism* and *After Leadership* and has published in journals such as *Organization Studies*, *Human Relations*, *Management Learning* and *Organization and Leadership*. She has designed and delivered extensive leadership development intervention and programmes across private, public and community sectors and specialises in the development of leadership mindset, identity and practice within a system, cross-organisational and collaborative context.

Charl de Villiers (DCom (PhD-equivalent), University of Pretoria, ZA) is Professor of Accounting at the University of Auckland, New Zealand, where his research interests include Integrated Reporting, Integrated Thinking and Sustainability Accounting. He is also an adjunct professor at the University of Cape Town, University of Pretoria and University of the Western Cape, in South Africa; and Universiti Teknologi Mara, in Malaysia. Charl has over 150 research based publications, including more than 90 articles in refereed journals, and two Routledge published edited books, namely *Sustainability Accounting and Integrated Reporting* (2018) and *The Routledge Handbook of Integrated Reporting* (2020). He has published in journals such as *Accounting, Organisations and Society*, *Journal of Management* and *Accounting, Auditing & Accountability Journal*.

Ruth Dimes is a PhD candidate at the University of Auckland, researching in the field of Integrated Reporting and Integrated Thinking using computer-aided text analysis. She is also a Professional Teaching Fellow, teaching financial analysis on the University of Auckland Business Masters and Executive Education programmes. Ruth has published articles in *Meditari Accountancy*

Research and *Journal of Management and Governance*. Prior to her career in academia, Ruth worked as a Chartered Accountant in senior financial management roles in the UK FMCG industry, subsequently specialising as a consultant in executive education. Ruth is a Fellow of the ICAEW and the HEA. She holds an MCom in Accounting from the University of Auckland and a BA (Hons) in Modern Languages and Linguistics from Durham University (UK).

Lina El-Jahel (PhD, University of London, UK) is an Associate Professor of Finance at the University of Auckland Business School. She was previously at Imperial College London Business School where she acted as director of the MSc Finance Programme and was awarded the Economic & Social Research Council (ESRC) New Scholars Fellowship. Her current research interests are in the fields of corporate and sovereign credit risk, term structure modelling, derivatives pricing, risk management and regulation of financial institutions. Lina's work has appeared in finance journals such as *Journal of Money Credit and Banking*, *Journal of Banking and Finance* and *Journal of Financial Markets*, and in more mainstream practitioner publications such as *Risk and Professional Investor*. She is currently an associate editor for the *European Journal of Finance*.

Ljiljana Eraković (PhD, University of Auckland, NZ) is Associate Professor at the University of Auckland Business School. Her research focuses on corporate governance and boards of directors. Ljiljana is particularly interested in exploring board–management relationships and the interface of governance and leadership processes in organisations with different ownership structures. Her research has been widely published in scholarly books and international academic journals, including *Public Administration, British Journal of Management, Journal of Business Ethics* and *Industrial Relations Journal.* Ljiljana has co-authored two books: *Corporate Governance and Leadership: The Board as the Nexus of Leadership-in-Governance* (Cambridge University Press, 2020) and *Stepping through Transitions: Management, Leadership and Governance in Not-for-Profit Organisations* (CGO Transitions Ltd, 2013).

Benjamin Fath (PhD, University of Auckland, NZ) is Senior Lecturer at the University of Auckland Business School. He has researched innovation, internationalisation and growth of NZ businesses for over a decade. Ben teaches Research Methods on the MBA programme. He has facilitated workshops across New Zealand for practitioners on partner strategy in Asia in collaboration with the Asia New Zealand Foundation and ExportNZ. His work has been published in journals including *Australian Journal of Management, Human Relations, International Small Business Journal* and the *European Journal of Industrial Relations.*

Antje Fiedler (PhD, University of Auckland, NZ) is Senior Lecturer at the University of Auckland Business School. Her research interests include growth and internationalisation of firms, with a focus on emerging Asia, and employment relations. Antje is a member of the New Zealand Asia Institute and the Director of the China Studies Centre of The University of Auckland. She is a member of the Academic Advisory Team of the Southeast Asia Centre of Asia-Pacific Excellence. Her work has been published in international journals, such as *New Political Economy, Human Relations, International Small Business Journal* and the *Industrial Relations Journal*.

Nigel Haworth (PhD, University of Liverpool, UK) is Emeritus Professor of Human Resource Development. Trained as an economist, he specialised in Latin American Studies and the international labour market, and focused his research in part on the Pacific Rim in the areas of national policy towards internationalisation, the role of WTO and the development of the ASEAN economies. He was Chair of the Partnership Resource Centre, located in the Department of Labour, and its successor, the High Performance Work Initiative, and was Chair of the Centre for Housing Research, located in the Housing Corporation of New Zealand. He was National President of the Association of University Staff for three years between 2005 and 2008. In 2018, Professor Haworth retired from the University, returning on a part-time contract to complete PhD supervisions, whilst continuing in the role of President of the New Zealand Labour Party.

Carla Houkamau (PhD, University of Auckland, NZ) is an Associate Professor at the University of Auckland Business School where she holds roles as Associate Dean Māori and Associate Dean Faculty. Her research is concerned with the impact of intergroup relations on identity, and she holds deep personal interest in the multiple facets of the complex inter group relations between Māori and Pākehā (New Zealand Europeans). Her publications typically examine how ethnicity helps reproduce socio-economic inequalities but can be leveraged to address them. She has been published in a wide range of journals including *Personality & Social Psychology Bulletin, Psychological Science, Social Indicators Research, Personality and Individual Differences* and *Cultural Diversity and Ethnic Minority Psychology*. Carla currently leads the most extensive longitudinal study of Māori identity, financial attitudes and behaviour (Te Rangahau o Te Tuakiri Māori me Ngā Waiaro ā-Pūtea | The Māori Identity and Financial Attitudes Study) for which she received a Marsden Award from the Royal Society of New Zealand in 2015.

Kenneth Husted (PhD, Copenhagen Business School, DK) is a Professor of Innovation and Research Management at the University of Auckland Business School, New Zealand. He has been the Head of Department, Management and

International Business since 2018; in 2020 he was also the Acting Director of the Graduate School of Management at the University of Auckland Business School. His research covers Innovation (R&D collaboration, science and innovation policy, innovation in low-tech industries) and Knowledge Management (knowledge sharing, knowledge protection, knowledge governance). Kenneth's current research projects focus on knowledge sharing as a microfoundation of technology roadmapping, early-stage financing and the embeddedness of new technology-based ventures, Industry 4.0 and innovation, development of innovation practices in traditional industries, AI and innovation. His academic work has appeared in, among others, *Journal of Management Studies, California Management Review, Technovation, Journal of World Business, Organizational Dynamics, International Journal of Technology Management, Journal of Knowledge Management* and *R&D Management*. Kenneth is the Regional Editor for the *Journal of Knowledge Management* and Associate Editor of *Technology Innovation Management Review*.

Deepika Jindal (PhD, University of Auckland, NZ) is Professional Teaching Fellow at the University of Auckland Business School. She teaches human resource management on the Business Masters programme. Prior to that, she worked in the industry for more than a decade in the areas of strategy and human resource management. Her research interests include work engagement, job crafting and the future of work. Deepika is President of Academic Branch and committee member of Auckland Branch of Human Resources New Zealand (HRNZ).

Peter Lee (PhD, University of Auckland, NZ) is Adjunct Professor at the University of Auckland Business School. He teaches technology commercialisation in the MBA programme. He has been the CEO and member of the senior management teams for several large corporations in the US and New Zealand. He currently consults with and is a director of several high technology companies and investment boards. The Royal Society of New Zealand awarded Peter the Thomson Medal for his outstanding contribution to the commercialisation of scientific research. Peter serves as New Zealand's Chief Defence Technologist.

Tyron Love (PhD, Massey University, NZ) is Senior Lecturer in Management at the University of Auckland Business School. His research interests lie at the intersection between Indigenous peoples and organizations/institutions. He is interested in the kind of research which considers Indigenous people at the centre and at the periphery of managing and organizing. In 2019 he published *Indigenous Organization Research* and he has had papers published in journals such as *Accounting, Auditing & Accountability Journal, Media International Australia, Public Relations Inquiry, Qualitative Research in Organizations* *and Management* and *Corporate Social Responsibility and Environmental Management.*

Sholeh A. Maani (PhD, University of Illinois at Urbana-Champaign, US) is Professor of Economics at the University of Auckland. She is a specialist in applied microeconomics, in particular the economics of the labour market. She has held visiting professor positions at Harvard, NBER, Oxford, Cornell and Melbourne Universities. She has served as a member of the Royal Society of New Zealand, Social Science Advisory Committee and as the President of the New Zealand Association of Economists. She is an editor of the *Australian Journal of Labour Economics* and serves as a research advisor on economic research and policy in New Zealand and overseas including the OECD. Among her publications, her work has been published in *Applied Economics*, *Papers in Regional Science, Economics of Education Review, Economic Record, Land Economics* and *ILR Review.*

Robert MacCulloch (PhD, University of Oxford, UK) holds the Matthew S. Abel Chair of Macroeconomics at Auckland University. A native of New Zealand, he worked at the Reserve Bank of NZ before travelling to the UK to complete a PhD in Economics at Oxford University. Robert was awarded a Royal Economic Society Junior Fellowship and pursued research interests at London School of Economics and Princeton University. He joined Imperial College London Business School as Director of their PhD Program, where he was awarded Best Teacher prizes and the Rector's Award for Distinguished Research Excellence. Robert subsequently returned to his alma mater in NZ. He has published in journals including *American Economic Review, Review of Economic Studies, Review of Economics and Statistics, Journal of Economic Perspectives* and *Brookings Papers on Economic Activity.*

James Metson (PhD, Victoria University of Wellington, NZ) is a Professor and Deputy Vice Chancellor (Research) at the University of Auckland. He is a materials scientist with research interests in surface science and particularly applications in the international aluminium industry. He was founder of the Light Metals Research Centre at the University of Auckland and a founding member of the MacDiarmid Institute for Materials Science and Nanotechnology. He has served in a range of national and international roles, most recently as the Chief Science Advisor to New Zealand's Ministry of Business Innovation and Employment. He is an author of more than 200 publications.

Snejina Michailova (PhD, Copenhagen Business School, DK, 1997) is a Professor of International Business at the University of Auckland, New Zealand. Her research is in International Business, Management and Knowledge

Management and her academic work has appeared in the prime journals of all three disciplines. Journals where she has published include: *Academy of Management Review*, *Academy of Management Executive*, *California Management Review*, *critical perspectives on international business*, *Global Strategy Journal*, *International Journal of Management Reviews*, *Journal of International Business Studies*, *Journal of International Management*, *Journal of Knowledge Management*, *Journal of Management Studies*, *Journal of World Business*, *International Business Review*, *Long Range Planning*, *Management International Review*, *Management Learning*, *Organizational Dynamics*, *Organization Studies*, *Technovation* and others. She has also co-edited and co-authored six books. Her three main current research projects are on modern slavery, host country nationals and talent management. She served as Editor Europe for *Journal of World Business* (2001–2007) and as Co-Editor-in-Chief of *critical perspectives on international business* (2017–2019). She is currently Consulting Editor at *Journal of International Management*.

Deanna Norgrove (BSc, University of Auckland, NZ) is currently completing her Masters in Bioscience Enterprise at the University of Auckland and is a Business Development Executive at Auckland UniServices Ltd, the technology transfer office for the University of Auckland. Her research interests include innovation and entrepreneurship, particularly in the health sciences sector.

Dana L. Ott (PhD, University of Auckland, NZ) is a Lecturer in International Management at the Otago Business School – University of Otago. Her research interests lie in the areas of International Management and International Human Resource Management. In particular, she examines cultural intelligence, international experiences, global mobility and talent management. Dana is the Director of the Postgraduate International Business Programmes at the University of Otago. Her work has been published in the *International Journal of Management Reviews*, *Journal of Global Mobility*, *critical perspectives on international business* and *European Journal of International Management*, among others. She has also co-authored *Talent Management in Small Advanced Economies*.

Barbara Plester (PhD, Massey University, NZ) is currently Senior Lecturer in the Department of Management and International Business at the University of Auckland. Her research explores workplace humour, fun, play, organizational culture, food rituals and critical perspectives of organizational life. Barbara belongs to the Organization Studies group and teaches Organizational Behavior, Organizational Theory and HRM infused with humour stories, at both undergraduate and postgraduate levels. She serves on the University of Auckland Education Committee – concerned with teaching and learning in her university. Prior to her academic career, Barbara worked in publishing and information technology companies and has practical experience in sales, marketing and HRM.

Cate Roy (Gribble) (PhD, University of Melbourne, AU) is a Senior Policy Analyst in the Office of Research Strategy at the University of Auckland. Prior to moving to New Zealand, she held academic positions at both RMIT University and Deakin University and remains an Adjunct Principal Fellow in the Science Engineering and Health Education Research (SHEER) Centre, RMIT University. Her research focusses on international student mobility, migration and employability. She has worked extensively with international students, employers, professional organisations, government and universities. Many of her projects have had considerable national and international significance, informing government policy, curriculum design and university strategy. Between 2010–2014, she was co-investigator on an Australian Research Council Linkage Project, Investigating Stakeholder Responses to Changing Skilled Migration Policies for Australian International Graduates. This national project identified the issue of international students and post study employment as a critical issue and led to multiple projects and government consultancies on the topic. In recognition of her expertise in graduate employability, she was invited to give evidence to the 2016 Australian House of Representatives Standing Committee on Education and Employment inquiry into innovation and creativity: a workforce for the future economy.

Noemi Sinkovics (PhD, University of Manchester, UK) is Senior Lecturer in Management and International Business at the University of Auckland Business School. Prior to that she worked at Alliance Manchester Business School, University of Manchester, UK. Her research interests are theoretical and practical issues around entrepreneurship (including international and social entrepreneurship) and social, environmental and economic sustainability and upgrading in global value chains. Her work has been published in *International Business Review, International Marketing Review, Journal of Business Research, Journal of World Business, Management International Review, Journal of International Management, European Journal of International Management, Journal of Interactive Marketing, critical perspectives on international business* and as chapter contributions to edited volumes.

Rudolf R. Sinkovics (PhD, WU-Vienna, AT) is Professor of International Business at the University of Auckland Business School and Visiting Professor at LUT University, Finland. His research writing covers issues of inter-organizational governance and the role of ICT, with a current focus on responsible business. His work has been published in journals such as *Journal of International Business Studies, Management International Review, Journal* *of World Business, International Business Review, Journal of International Management, Journal of Business Research, Journal of International Marketing* and *International Marketing Review.* He is co-editor-in-chief for *critical perspectives on international business,* Consulting editor for *Journal of World Business* and Associate editor for *Transnational Corporations* and serves on a number of editorial boards.

Susan Watson (LLB(Hons), MJur, University of Auckland, NZ) holds a joint chair in Law at the University of Auckland Law School and at the University of Auckland Business School where she is the Dean. She has been a visiting Professor at the University of Oxford, Tilburg University and Vanderbilt University. Her research focuses on corporate law and corporate governance with a focus, through an interdisciplinary lens, on the structure, development and role of the modern company. She is currently writing a book for Hart Publishing on these themes. She has published over 100 journal articles and book chapters with her work published in leading law and business law journals such as *Law Quarterly Review, Journal of Business Law* and *Journal of Corporate Law Studies,* as well as law treatises and edited collections. In 2015 she won the Legal Research Foundation prize for best article or book chapter by a New Zealand author and she has been cited by the Supreme Courts of the UK and New Zealand. She is a past co-editor for the *New Zealand Business Law Quarterly* and is on its editorial board.

Rachel Maunganui Wolfgramm (PhD, University of Auckland, NZ), (Te Aupouri, Ngai Takoto, Whakatōhea, Vava'u, Kingdom of Tonga). Rachel is an author, consultant and systems artist. She holds formal positions at the University of Auckland Business School as Director/Manutaki of the Dame Mira Szászy Research Centre and Senior Lecturer in the Department of Management and International Business. Her research investigates social innovations designed to advance pro-social and pro-environmental outcomes. She is currently Lead Principal Investigator of a Nga Pae o te Maramatanga Project (NZCoRE) focused on Māori Leadership and Economies of Wellbeing. Her research has been published in *Human Relations, Journal of Business Ethics, Leadership, AlterNative: An International Journal of Indigenous Peoples, Journal of Management Learning, Journal of Corporate Citizenship, Māori and Indigenous Review* and *International Journal of Sustainability* and in books published by Cambridge University Press, Routledge, Chicago University Press, Information Age and Edward Elgar Publishing. As an experienced public speaker and facilitator, she leads, designs, collaborates and delivers works of interest with international teams in multiple forums.

Foreword by Rt Hon Helen Clark[1]

New Zealand's management of the COVID-19 pandemic is of global interest. The country's approach of zero-tolerance towards transmission of the disease in the community has enjoyed wide public support and, notwithstanding the small number of occasions when the virus has spread beyond the border since the end of the major national lockdown from March to May, has been remarkably successful.

This book, which offers management perspectives on the handling of the crisis in New Zealand, is very timely, not only because many countries are still battling major outbreaks of COVID-19 and are looking for examples of what has worked elsewhere, but also because there will be a need to maintain vigilance against COVID-19 for the long term. The disease looks set at some point to move from being pandemic in nature to being endemic. That means we cannot relax our guard. International interest will be as strong in how New Zealand plans to keep the disease at bay for the foreseeable future as it has been in its success in curbing transmission to date. Continued public buy-in to ongoing public health measures is essential.

New Zealand's success has been scoffed at in some circles because of the protection which our geography provides us. Yet, we could all too easily have blown that advantage with an economy-first, rather than a health-first approach. A key factor in New Zealand's approach was to put people's health first, and to recognise that having a fearful, insecure public traumatised by the loss of family, friends, and colleagues would be destructive of the well-being of both the society and the economy.

While the country has taken an economic hit, with the international tourism and education-related sectors suffering disproportionately, the availability of social protection, retraining and job placement services, and business support schemes have all helped to cushion the blows. As there is unlikely to be a return to the status quo ante, a repositioning of the economy and workforce to enable it to thrive in the new normal will be vital.

The New Zealand approach was also based on accepting the best scientific and public health advice on how to manage a pandemic. This too distinguishes it from that of a range of countries where the disease was downplayed and health systems quickly became overwhelmed. It is not possible to hospitalise or treat one's way out of a pandemic: transmission just has to be curbed. In many respects there is nothing new about how to do that. Capacities have to be built and sustained for testing, tracing, quarantine, and consistent messaging and engagement with the public around the need for physical distancing, mask wearing, and hygiene. Many countries are still struggling to develop those capacities.

The rapid development of vaccines is a welcome development, but their rollout is not a panacea. The next campaign must be to achieve a high level of acceptance of vaccination in the community. Then, much continues to be unknown about the impact and evolution of COVID-19. Variants of it which have already emerged are causing justified concern. It remains to be seen how effective current vaccinations will be as populations encounter new variants, and if and whether there will need to be periodic revaccination. Continued research and development to ensure ongoing protection through immunisations will be vital, as it will be for innovations in testing and diagnosis and treatments.

Central to building resilient health systems, societies, and economies is being prepared to review how these have responded to a severe shock. The World Health Assembly mandated such a review of the internationally co-ordinated response to COVID-19, with a view to distilling lessons learned and identifying areas for improvement. Every country should be prepared to do the same, regardless of its success or otherwise in managing the crisis. Being prepared to reflect and learn, and committing to continual improvement equips countries to do better next time. This publication is an important contribution to such a review, and its chapters written from a range of perspectives deserve serious consideration.

29 January 2021

NOTE

1. Former Prime Minister of New Zealand and former UNDP Administrator. Co-Chair of The Independent Panel for Pandemic Preparedness and Response.

Introduction

Kenneth Husted and Rudolf R. Sinkovics

The Covid-19 pandemic has a wide-ranging impact across almost all areas of activities in our societies. Because of the disruptive and complex nature of the impact, governments and organisations across all sectors had to urgently and proactively rethink their approach to decision making and management of critical processes and activities (Verma and Gustafsson, 2020).

Faced with a need for remedial action to deal with the global pandemic's largely unknown territory, a wide variety of management approaches has been explored and tested by governments, companies, civil society organisations, and citizens. Many of these approaches are with far-reaching ramifications. They are also characterised by inherent uncertainty about both the immediate outcomes and the long-term consequences. Some of these management approaches rely on, for example, extending well-established management knowledge and research. In contrast, others have been breaking new ground in implementing innovative strategies tailored to their particular context.

The pandemic has also spotlighted strengths and weaknesses in contemporary management theory and some of the fundamental assumptions that frame our understanding of organisations and their impact on stakeholders. One prominent example of this is the call for rethinking organisations' role in creating inequality (Munir, 2020) as evidence is mounting that Covid-19 has a disproportional impact across socio-economic groups in society.

New Zealand (NZ) offers an astonishing story in how the response from various constituents is situated in the broader societal and political discourse.

1. THE RISE OF COVID-19 RELATED MANAGEMENT RESEARCH

The Covid-19 pandemic has triggered significant collaborative science, technology, engineering, and mathematics (STEM) research efforts to come to terms with the clinical and biomedical issues of the virus. This has resulted in an unprecedented volume of papers published related to the disease and placed extraordinary pressure on the academic peer-review system (Teixeira da Silva et al., 2020).

STEM disciplines inarguably are instrumental in addressing the clinical and biomedical issues associated with the Covid-19 crisis. However, social sciences are critical for providing cutting-edge insight into how communities, institutions, and people deal with the pandemic (Reisz, 2020). Management research is one social science discipline that has responded to this call.

There have been similar efforts to fast-track Covid-19 related special issues, perspective papers, and scoping studies in the business and management disciplines to highlight implications of the pandemic on business actors, consumers, civil society actors, and governments. A Web of Science literature review of the search terms 'Covid' and 'Pandemic' for top tier articles and Advance online journal publications of 2020 in major business and management domains delivers 485 outputs. As it can be seen in Table 1, most of the management-related outputs are in the general management category (98 papers), with sizeable outputs related to public sector and health journals (93 papers), economics (69 papers), and various social science and sector studies, which includes tourism (53 and 47 papers, respectively). Organisational psychology (39 papers) and general psychology journals (32 papers) capture another big slice of the overall business and management outputs, with regional studies, marketing, entrepreneurship, international business and operations management following suit.

Using bibliometric mapping approaches (Sinkovics, 2016; Sinkovics et al., 2019) six broad themes emerged from the identified sample of management research on Covid-19. These are: (1) public policy and institutional administration issues; (2) development and policy implementation challenges; (3) grand challenges and the futures of management areas (HRM, leadership, supply chain, CSR); (4) gender struggles and family issues; (5) hospitality and travel sector issues; (6) critical issues (psychological, power-related, social media polarisation).

A sizeable body of work deals specifically with Covid-19 matters in hotspots such as, for example, Italy, the USA, and the UK, but a closer thematic analysis of the papers reveals that management perspectives on the Covid-19 crisis from regions with more successful strategies to keeping Covid-19 at bay such as Australia, NZ, and Taiwan are underrepresented. This book intends to make a specific contribution in this space, and interrogate the learnings from the specific NZ context. As the crisis is still unfolding elsewhere, it is becoming clear that the economic and social aftermath will be felt in the years to come. NZ offers an astonishing story in how the response from various constituents is situated in the wider societal and political discourse. In fact, drawing on the chapters in the book we argue that NZ offers lessons for management actors across various institutional, geographical, and political contexts in the world.

We categorise the learnings into three distinctive sets of dichotomies. The first dichotomy is around proximity and distance, a key feature of the NZ

Table 0.1   *Covid-19 related papers, published in selected business and management domains*

AJG (CABS) 2018 subject areas	No. of papers
General Management	98
Public Sector and Health	93
Economics	69
Social Sciences	53
Sector Studies	47
Psychology (Organisational)	39
Psychology (General)	32
Regional Studies	20
Marketing	12
Entrepreneurship	7
International Business	6
Operations Management	6
Human Resource Management	3
Innovation	3
Management Development	2
Total	485

Note: Web of Science search terms: Covid and Pandemic, applied to journals within the AJG/CABS 2018 subject areas (CABS, 2018) at 3 and 4 star levels, drawing on journal names and ISSN data from Tüselmann et al. (2016).

geographical and economic position in its regional and global networks. The second dichotomy is what we call the 'dichotomy of centralisation and decentralisation in decision making'. The NZ government has quickly embraced a top-level expert group around leading scientists and public-health authorities and adopted a centralised response action plan. Key actions include a four-tier alert system introduced in March 2020, closed borders – except for NZ citizens and residents, and a small number of limited critical worker exceptions – prioritised testing and a Covid-19 compliance checking system. In other countries, the private sector and decentralised influencers have made a coordinated government-led response more difficult. The third dichotomy is a function of collective versus individual learning. It relates to NZ's disaster preparedness (e.g., Orchiston, 2013) and its national focus on health and well-being (OECD, 2019), which has allowed the unfolding of a 'go hard, go fast' approach and a significant buy-in to this approach from the NZ population.

2.   TENSIONS AND DICHOTOMIES

2.1   Proximity and Distance

The international business and management literatures have placed a keen interest on the concept of 'distance', both geographical, cultural and psychic (Ambos and Håkanson, 2014; Beugelsdijk et al., 2018). The effect of distance on firms' performance when entering, operating, and orchestrating business in and across foreign markets is broadly considered negative and more pronounced with increasing distance. In the political economy literature, the focus has been more along the lines of institutional distance and business systems differences (Hall and Gingerich, 2009; Hotho, 2009) and NZ's island nation in the southwestern Pacific Ocean is characterised as a free-market 'liberal market economy' (LME) (Nicholls, 2018). Despite institutional distance measures similar to the UK, the US, and European economies, and particularly the notion of a 'happy variety of capitalisms' (Bergheim, 2007), whereby health and well-being is now at the heart of a NZ governmental policy agenda (OECD, 2019), the key trading partners in 2019 were – using a continental lens – Asian countries, led by China with fellow Oceanian countries, particularly Australia, North America, and European countries. With the distance from Auckland, the major business hub in NZ, to Shanghai being around 9000km and its antipodean distance located at around 20,000km in Spain, it is evident that 'barriers' to international expansion and growth are primarily related to the geographical distance dimensions above. Except for Australia, which is 'only' 4000km away, this 'tyranny of distance' (Blainey, 2001) has shaped the engagement of NZ firms with international partners in major ways and, arguably, diminished the potential of NZ to develop and upgrade towards a robust knowledge-based industrial sector (Nicholls, 2018, p. 161).

However, in the context of the Covid-19 pandemic, the remoteness and insularity of the NZ economy and its relationships with trading partners have been serendipitously transformed into an advantage. As container shipments continued unfettered through the crisis and NZ emerged extraordinarily well connected from the upgrades to undersea fibre-optic cable infrastructures ('Hawaiki cable') connecting NZ, Australia, American Samoa, Hawaii, and the US mainland (Starosielski, 2015; Hawaiki, 2020), the management of distant relationships through virtual means became more competitive than other Asian countries and vastly outperformed several OECD countries (FOSN, 2019).

2.2   Centralisation and Decentralisation in Decision Making

In theory, all of us are vulnerable to coronavirus, but in practice how well we fare has to do with what you could call pre-existing conditions that are not only medical but economic, social, political, and racial – and the pandemic, which is also an economic catastrophe, has made these differences glaringly clear. (Solnit, 2020)

Covid-19 triggers many questions regarding the resilience of the liberal international order in the face of global shocks and also questions regarding the liberal international order to survive in a 'rudderless world' (Norrlöf, 2020). Emergent literature on Covid-19 refers to 'socially distanced capitalism' which transforms neoliberal capitalism in previously unimaginable ways (Cline-Cole, 2020), radically rearranges power structures in our societies and there is an argument that refers to and empirically examines Covid-19 as a 'liberal democratic curse' (Norrlöf, 2020). Curiously, NZ has withered this curse and gone against the trend of other liberal market economies, as it managed to stamp out community transmissions with its 'go fast, go hard' approach and sports low death rates.

The NZ experience showcases that through high centralisation of power in government, whereby a small group of people and scientific advisors adopted a science-based approach, they were able to short-circuit an otherwise long and traditionally more complex consultation process. Despite numerous interacting factors, the NZ government thus managed to get a sophisticated grip on the situation and avoid overload and decision paralysis through human and clear communication (c.f. Foss, 2020). Interestingly, many private firms and public organisations in NZ chose – like many governments across OECD – to decentralise key processes in order to unleash the innovative ability of their organisations in search for appropriate responses to Covid-19.

2.3　　Preparedness – Collective and Individual Learning

The NZ Government has taken its 5 million inhabitants on a collective learning journey which started prior to the Covid-19 pandemic and thus contributed to a high level of crisis preparedness and resilience. The countries' high seismic risk and disasters such as the Christchurch earthquake (2011) and the White Island eruption (2019) have triggered significant science-informed learning. The Government has funded the science, provided platforms for scientists to share their knowledge, and assigned credibility to both scientific knowledge and scientists. Out of such experience, community-based efforts were developed, to prepare specific sectors such as tourism or specific townships, lending support to the concept of collective, community-led disaster planning (Ritchie, 2008; Orchiston, 2013).

Education and individual learning has also propelled NZ towards high levels of disaster preparedness (Johnson et al., 2014) and crisis management capabilities, both at corporate levels (Laufer, 2012, 2015) and country level (National Science Challenges, 2020). Evidence further suggests that participation and individual levels of compliance to responses to crises are high (Cretney, 2016). Thus, it is not surprising that NZ's response to the coronavirus pandemic has been cited by Joseph Stiglitz, one of the world's top economists, as one of the best in the world (Satherley, 2020).

> If the United States represents one extreme, perhaps NZ represents the other. It's a country in which competent government relied on science and expertise to make decisions, a country where there is a high level of social solidarity – citizens recognize that their behavior affects others – and trust, including trust in government. (Stiglitz, 2020, 17)

3. SETUP AND STRUCTURE OF THE BOOK

Contributions are structured around three parts. The first part offers a theoretical framing and socio-political background that situates the Covid-19 pandemic within the country context. We conceptualise the Covid-19 crisis as one of the turning points at the intersection of the economic, socio-demographic geopolitical and political gearboxes (Guillén and Ontiveros, 2016). A return to the world that we have lived in before (Gray, 2020), while desired socio-psychologically, is increasingly unlikely. We are witnessing a redefinition of the 'new normal' in terms of social, cultural, and business practices and the challenges that this may prompt.

The second part offers contributions that look at the Covid-19 pandemic from a functional management and organisational perspective. With more and more information unearthed about the immediate consequences of this latest pandemic via news and online media, we witness the intricate complexity of globalised supply chains, the consequences of low levels of buffer in optimised outsourcing and offshoring agreements, and the criticality of 'non-critical' labour for the seamless functioning and organisation of society. At the same time, the powerful force of creative destruction is eroding the foundation for well-tested business models and resource uses to create place for new innovative solutions and organisations. In this part, we draw attention to problems and challenges in specific functional and organisational areas.

The concluding part is devoted to implications of the Covid-19 pandemic for business and management in other countries and the NZ Covid-19 response's geopolitical significance beyond the Pacifica/Oceania region. The Covid-19 experience in NZ has been a cathartic one, redefining the notion of civic partnership (Goddard et al., 2016), where the close interaction of university, policy, and private actors has helped to understand pathways for pivotal and transformative change experiences. Chapters in this part illuminate how the NZ experience can offer insights and learning for other countries.

Based on the parts outlined above, the book and its chapters unfold in a flowering structure, as depicted in Figure 0.1. The central connection and core of the flower is the notion of Covid-19 and the NZ country perspective. The petals represent keywords that cover the themes in the various chapters. Some chapters deal with personal characteristics of managers and leaders; expert leadership is a dimension that stands out in a chapter dealing with the government response. Several chapters address the notion of economic growth, well-being on a national level and on a personal level, for example through laughter as a coping and response strategy, one chapter deals specifically with the notion of talents and the potential of Covid-19 reversing the brain drain of the past. A further topic represented in one of the topic petals of the flowering structure is the notion of business recovery and how NZ's exporting and internationalisation strategies have been affected by Covid-19. Innovation, labour market implications, and commercialisation issues as well as economic policy topics are more frequently mentioned in the chapters in the book. Finally, another key theme and associated keywords in the book are related to sustainable value creation. The keywords are interrelated and make connections between the various parts of the book.

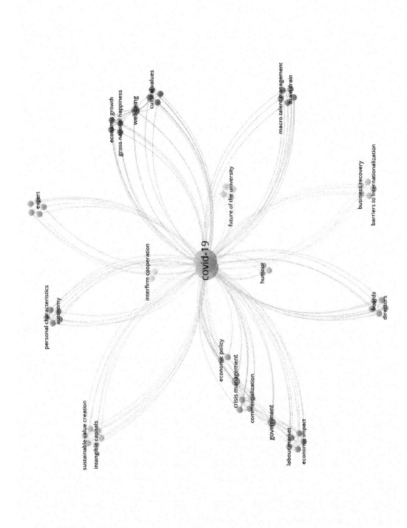

Figure 0.1   The flowering structure of the book and its chapters

REFERENCES

Ambos, B. and L. Håkanson (2014), 'The concept of distance in international management research', *Journal of International Management*, **20** (1), 1–7. doi: 10.1016/j.intman.2013.10.003

Bergheim, S. (2007), *The Happy Variety of Capitalism*, Deutsche Bank Research, pp. 1–24.

Beugelsdijk, S., T. Kostova, V.E. Kunst, E. Spadafora and M. van Essen (2018), 'Cultural distance and firm internationalization: A meta-analytical review and theoretical implications', *Journal of Management*, **44** (1), 89–130. doi: 10.1177/0149206317729027

Blainey, G. (2001), *The Tyranny of Distance: How Distance Shaped Australia's History*, London: Macmillan.

CABS (2018), 'Academic journal guide', Retrieved June 13, 2019, from https://charteredabs.org/academic-journal-guide-2018/

Cline-Cole, R. (2020), 'Socially distanced capitalism in a time of coronavirus', *Review of African Political Economy*, **47** (164), 169–196. doi: 10.1080/03056244.2020.1814627

Cretney, R.M. (2016), 'Local responses to disaster: The value of community led post disaster response action in a resilience framework', *Disaster Prevention and Management*, **25** (1), 27–40. doi: 10.1108/DPM-02-2015-0043

FOSN (2019), 'Asian countries lead the ftth-fttb global ranking', Retrieved Dec 26, 2020, from https://www.fomsn.com/market-research/sobhana/asian-countries-lead-the-ftth-fttb-global-ranking/

Foss, N.J. (2020), 'Behavioral strategy and the Covid-19 disruption', *Journal of Management*, **46** (8), 1322–1329. doi: 10.1177/0149206320945015

Goddard, J.B., E. Hazelkorn, L. Kempton and P. Vallance (2016), *The Civic University: The Policy and Leadership Challenges*, Cheltenham, UK and Northampton, MA, USA: Edward Elgar Publishing.

Gray, J. (2020, 2020/04/05/), 'Why this crisis is a turning point in history', Retrieved Apr 5, 2020, from https://www.newstatesman.com/america/2020/04/why-crisis-turning-point-history?utm_source=pocket-newtab

Guillén, M.F. and E.B. Ontiveros (2016), *Global Turning Points: The Challenges for Business and Society in the 21st Century*, Cambridge, UK: Cambridge University Press.

Hall, P.A. and D.W. Gingerich (2009), 'Varieties of capitalism and institutional complementarities in the political economy: An empirical analysis', *British Journal of Political Science*, **39** (3), 449–482. doi: 10.1017/S0007123409000672

Hawaiki (2020, 2020/12/26/), 'Hawaiki cable – the power of greater connectivity in the Pacific', Retrieved Nov 15, 2020, from https://www.hawaiki.co.nz

Hotho, J.J. (2009), 'A measure of comparative institutional distance', *SMG Working Paper*, **7**, 1–54. https://research-api.cbs.dk/ws/portalfiles/portal/58953388/SMG_WP_2009_07.pdf

Johnson, V.A., K.R. Ronan, D.M. Johnston and R. Peace (2014), 'Implementing disaster preparedness education in New Zealand primary schools', *Disaster Prevention and Management*, **23** (4), 370–380. doi: 10.1108/DPM-09-2013-0151

Laufer, D. (2012), 'Incorporating a global perspective in teaching crisis management', *AIB Insights*, **12** (2), 13–17. https://documents.aib.msu.edu/publications/insights/archive/insights_v012n02.pdf

Laufer, D. (2015), 'Emerging issues in crisis management', *Business Horizons*, **58** (2), 137–139. doi: 10.1016/j.bushor.2014.10.002

Munir, K.A. (2021), 'Inequality in the time of corona virus', *Journal of Management Studies*, Advance online publication. doi: 10.1111/joms.12674

National Science Challenges (2020, 2020/12/26/), 'Resilience to nature's challenges', Retrieved Dec 26, 2020, from https://resiliencechallenge.nz

Nicholls, K. (2018), 'Economic outcomes in New Zealand: A varieties of capitalism lens', *Australian Journal of Political Science*, **53** (2), 160–175. doi: 10.1080/10361146.2017.1416581

Norrlöf, C. (2020), 'Is Covid-19 a liberal democratic curse? Risks for liberal international order', *Cambridge Review of International Affairs*, **33** (5), 799–813. doi: 10.1080/09557571.2020.1812529

OECD (2019), *OECD Economic Surveys – New Zealand, Focus Well-being*, Paris: OECD.

Orchiston, C. (2013), 'Tourism business preparedness, resilience and disaster planning in a region of high seismic risk: The case of the Southern Alps, New Zealand', *Current Issues in Tourism*, **16** (5), 477–494. doi: 10.1080/13683500.2012.741115

Reisz, M. (2020), 'Post-pandemic future: What does Covid-19 mean for HE?', *Times Higher Education*, **2**, 456.

Ritchie, B. (2008), 'Tourism disaster planning and management: From response and recovery to reduction and readiness', *Current Issues in Tourism*, **11** (4), 315–348. doi: 10.1080/13683500802140372

Satherley, D. (2020, 2020/09/03/), 'Coronavirus: Nobel prize-winning economist praises NZ's handling of Covid-19, slams United States', Retrieved Sep 3, 2020, from https://www.newshub.co.nz/home/new-zealand/2020/09/coronavirus-nobel-prize-winning-economist-praises-nz-s-handling-of-covid-19-slams-united-states.html (VPN)

Sinkovics, N. (2016), 'Enhancing the foundations for theorising through bibliometric mapping', *International Marketing Review*, **33** (3), 327–350. doi: 10.1108/IMR-10-2014-0341

Sinkovics, N., R.R. Sinkovics and J. Archie-Acheampong (2019), 'An overview of social responsibility dimensions in international business', in L.C. Leonidou, C.S. Katsikeas, S. Samiee and C.N. Leonidou (eds), *Socially-Responsible International Business: Critical Issues and the Way Forward*, Cheltenham, UK and Northampton, MA, USA: Edward Elgar Publishing, pp. 29–72. doi: 10.4337/9781788114127.00009

Solnit, R. (2020, 2020/07/01/), 'Coronavirus does discriminate, because that's what humans do', *The Guardian*. Retrieved April 17, 2020, from https://www.theguardian.com/commentisfree/2020/apr/17/coronavirus-discriminate-humans-racism-sexism-inequality

Starosielski, N. (2015), *The Undersea Network*, Durham: Duke University Press.

Stiglitz, J. (2020), 'Conquering the great divide', *Finance & Development* (September), 17–19.

Teixeira da Silva, J.A., P. Tsigaris and M. Erfanmanesh (2020), 'Publishing volumes in major databases related to Covid-19', *Scientometrics*. doi: 10.1007/s11192-020-03675-3

Tüselmann, H., R.R. Sinkovics and G. Pishchulov (2016), 'Revisiting the standing of international business journals in the competitive landscape', *Journal of World Business*, **51** (4), 487–498. doi: 10.1016/j.jwb.2016.01.006

Verma, S. and A. Gustafsson (2020), 'Investigating the emerging Covid-19 research trends in the field of business and management: A bibliometric analysis approach', *Journal of Business Research*, **118**, 253–261. doi: 10.1016/j.jbusres.2020.06.057

PART I

National and institutional perspectives on
Covid-19

1. Crashing down from a blue sky: the political management of COVID-19 in New Zealand

Nigel Haworth

Everybody knows that pestilences have a way of recurring in the world; yet somehow we find it hard to believe in ones that crash down on our heads from a blue sky. There have been as many plagues as wars in history; yet always plagues and wars take people equally by surprise.
Albert Camus, *The Plague*

1. INTRODUCTION

In December 2019, a mysterious pneumonia-like outbreak was reported in Wuhan, People's Republic of China. By the time New Zealand re-elected a new government in October 2020, the world was facing a global second wave of COVID-19. Since its appearance, more than 50 million cases have been identified internationally. New Zealand has weathered both first and second waves, having just overcome a second small wave of community transmission and, overall, experiencing a modest 1886 cases and 25 deaths. This brief analysis offers, first, a heuristic model against which to compare the New Zealand approach to the pandemic; second, a brief explanation of national political governance in New Zealand; third, the rationale of the government's response to COVID-19, with some commentary on related matters; fourth, some conclusions about short- and long-term consequences of COVID-19 for political governance in New Zealand.

2. A FRAMEWORK FOR THE ASSESSMENT OF PRACTICE

Janssen and van der Voort (2020) provide a helpful framework for the subsequent discussion. In particular, the 'adaptive governance' model (Bronen and Chapin, 2013) is consistent with the key features of New Zealand's management of the COVID-19 crisis. Here, I am particularly interested in Janssen and van der Voort's (2020) 'lessons for practice' derived from their study of the Dutch management of COVID-19. They conclude:

- There is no 'one best response' and, indeed, there is great value in having available a variety of response strategies. Thus, national responses, as in the case of New Zealand, will tend to the eclectic, contingent and location specific;
- Responses will change over time. The mix and intensity of government interventions will vary as the pandemic flows and ebbs;
- Adaptation (change) in the mix and intensity of responses is best accompanied by stability, that is, effective change is supported by populations continuing to enjoy a sense of stability in society;
- Government must mobilize society in support of its pandemic strategy. People must feel confident and respected in the implementation of interventions. Hence, communication is important as is its perceived authenticity. Equally, I suggest, the nature and quality of national leadership is important in societal mobilization.

Subsequent discussion will show that these lessons for practice conform closely to the New Zealand experience, particularly in terms of, first, contingency in response planning driven by the scale of the crisis and, second, the importance of community support for government actions.

3. NATIONAL POLITICAL GOVERNANCE IN NEW ZEALAND

New Zealand's three-year electoral cycle is short, with two modalities. An established government, re-elected, usually comes to power with one or more cycles of governance in hand, and is able to build on existing personnel and legislative initiatives. The second modality arises when a government takes office after a significant period in opposition. In 2017, the Labour-led government took power somewhat unexpectedly, after nine years in opposition, with few seasoned senior politicians and an unwieldy dependence on three political parties, two of which (Greens and New Zealand First) were not happy bedfellows.

Labour was last in government in 2008, contributing to its relative inexperience in 2017, and owed much of its success in the 2017 election to a strong popular response to Jacinda Ardern, who ascended to party leadership a matter of weeks before the election. New Zealand First offered one of the most experienced (and iconoclastic) politicians in New Zealand in Winston Peters. The Greens were inexperienced in government and grappling with strong internal currents around political focus – environment versus radical social change – and willingness to make the compromises necessary in government.

In this second modality, inexperience, combined with a somewhat unexpected rise to power, resulted in an inevitable period of adjustment to power as, for example, freshly minted ministers grappled with the mechanisms of authority. Simultaneously, the breadth of the governing coalition had a constraining effect on policy implementation as policy differences intruded.

Against this background of constrained policy implementation, the 'rhythm' of government provided an overlay. That rhythm is in general bi-modal. Government is a skein of activities, some focused on policy and its implementation, and others on day-to-day political management. In the first mode, government is bound by established rules and norms, both formal and informal, laid down by the Speaker, Parliamentary Service, party whips, political party constitutional requirements, security requirements, to name but some. In general, much of this is understood and managed with little significant disruption.

The second mode – rarer and of a different order – is illustrated primarily by the impact of global economic disruption, war or similar 'shocks' which lie unquestionably outside the usual expectation of government. Post 2017, the Labour-led government has faced one other crisis approaching this order of events – the terrorist attack in Christchurch in 2019. Arguably, however, despite the appalling nature of that attack, the COVID-19 challenge is substantially greater in impact, akin to that of the Great Depression, and, perhaps, the Second World War. The defining characteristic of this mode is a level of disruption such that orthodox government management practices are insufficient to manage the scope and scale of events. When COVID-19 struck, neither politicians nor officials had first-hand experience of a shock of this order and did not possess a 'play book' to consult.

The COVID-19 pandemic drove a disrupted order. COVID-19 plunged national governance into an unheralded and comprehensive challenge to political management. As we see below, the New Zealand government was fortunate to grasp the implications of the crisis relatively early and configured itself institutionally and strategically equally early. It followed an adaptive governance model of response to a disrupted order.

4.   DEVELOPING THE RATIONALE: GO HARD, GO EARLY

The essence of the New Zealand government strategy was to 'go hard, go early', combining a strong social cohesion focus with complementary legal backing. This has proved to be a successful approach, with New Zealand implementing an early and strict lockdown, ahead of much of the OECD, coupling that urgency with, for example, a broad and simple wage subsidy for both employees and the self-employed, full-time and part-time, which rapidly supported over 1.6 million people in the workforce.

4.1   Why 'Go Hard, Go Early'?

The structural advantage of New Zealand's political model is immediately apparent. The unicameral arrangement with effective national oversight unimpeded by powerful state or provincial political arrangements permitted a strong centralized unitary response. Authority to act rested unequivocally in central government.

The tradition of a Cabinet-led government, itself led by the Prime Minister, created a ready-made crisis management executive, in principle able to oversee a whole-of-government approach to the pandemic. In practice, this model was rapidly refined during the practice of crisis management. In practice, the Prime Minister and Minister of Finance formed a very tight core group, immediately supported by two other senior ministers with specific COVID-19-related charges. Other ministers were brought into the mix as needed, but a core political executive, supported by core government officials and other extra-official advisers, emerged as a crisis management executive.

Executive control of this order has both management and political/messaging dimensions. Paramount in government thinking was the need to lead New Zealand through this crisis at minimum human cost. However, it was also a political challenge, in which a general election in October 2020 loomed large. However intense a crisis may be, a weather eye on electoral prospects will also inform policy implementation and messaging.

4.1.1   Using and managing technical expertise

Another factor in the executive management mix is the role of technical expertise. The government has access to advice from ministries and their officials, but, equally, in highly technical matters such as the pandemic, it calls on specialist knowledge, especially from medical experts. Such expertise is not bound by the disciplines attached to civil service status, and is also deeply centred in a broader professional world in which political considerations take second place to professional standards. In turn, external technical voices have in general been measured and supportive of government action, creating an environment in which public technical disagreement has been rare and in which both sides have been responsive. In the New Zealand context, personal networks have played an important role in this accommodation.

Managing technical inputs and commentary also raises the issue of data management. This had two major dimensions. The first was to involve the public in data generation, especially by means of the NZ COVID-19 Tracer app (the mobile phone app distributed to allow people to track their where-abouts). The second was to manage the public dissemination of data about cases and government initiatives. The flagship event in this was the daily briefing in which the status of the Prime Minister was coupled with that of the Director-General of Health. Those briefings were something of a masterclass in the public presentation of often technical and complex, and usually politically sensitive, data. Their aim was simultaneously informative – for example, how many new cases; educative – for example, wash your hands frequently; and political – generally, we have this crisis in hand, our strategy is working, the 'team of 5 million' will vanquish the threat.

4.1.2   Government intelligence sources

The government acted in response to a wide variety of information flows along multiple channels. Notably, there were four particular sources, which, together, informed both understanding of the crisis and the need for early, rapid and effective action. The first source derived from close commercial ties with China. A fall-off in trade early in the crisis led to, for example, lay-offs in the New Zealand logging industry, in part driven by the COVID-19 outbreak in China. The government became aware early of this dislocation. Second, the networks linking the Chinese diaspora were very quick to signal the gravity of the Wuhan outbreak. Private commercial and political networks were rapidly appraised of these concerns by New Zealand's Chinese community. Third, there is a corps of New Zealand specialists involved with trade and business matters linking New Zealand and China, some resident in China, others in New Zealand, who also signalled the scale of the crisis in China. They networked with ministers and officials, emerging as important sources of data analysis of events and consequences. Fourth, the government's own political antennae – official and unofficial – were receiving confirmatory messages about the Chinese situation.

4.1.3   The challenge of 'whole of government response'

The scale of the crisis required a whole-of government response, which in turn required the imposition of overall political control of decision making. The advantages of whole-of-government decision making in New Zealand government have been considered for at least two decades, but its practice is impeded in part by the institutional impact of leadership and culture in ministries, and in part by the political sensitivities of ministers. It often becomes simply too hard to achieve, despite valiant efforts. The New Zealand government managed this challenge by imposing strong, central political leadership. By lodging strategy determination and consequent decision making in a small group of ministers, it overcame substantially the potential for inter-agency differences, whilst also creating a strong central performance appraisal mechanism overseeing agency performance.

4.1.4   The nature of leadership

The emergence of a tight leadership cadre within the government was not a fortuitous coincidence, but the conscious building on an established political order within government. The Prime Minister sat at the apex of the response, unassailed in any way by internal political challenges, and able to counter challenges from the political opposition. As the 2020 election results have shown, the political reach of the Prime Minister is commanding. The political victory in 2017, the response to the Christchurch attack and the White Island volcanic eruption, the international focus on her premiership, all came together to empower her leadership. It is clear that her standing resulted in challenges to the government's management of the crisis being more easily explained and banished.

Even before the crisis, the government's leadership mode tended towards attenuation, that is, a clear distinction between the Parliamentary Caucus and Cabinet-level ministers, and a further distinction in influence between ministers. Indeed, all prime ministers have an 'inner group' of ministers and advisers with greater access to information and impact on decisions. That attenuation was increased during the crisis by the need to integrate political decisions with technical advice on a day-to-day, sometimes hour-to-hour basis. In the event, primary political leadership settled in a group of four ministers in which two had primacy. The rationale for this lay in performance factors – for example, ministerial performance, skillsets and judgement – and personal factors – for example, long-established trust relationships. Labour as a party is not factionalized, so there is little, if any, factional pressure on such roles. Where a prime minister commands support as does the incumbent, her writ is strong.

4.2   The Rationale for the Government's Approach to COVID-19

Early in the COVID-19 crisis, the government determined to build on high levels of social cohesion within New Zealand as the foundation for action. The notion of the 'team of 5 million' came to reflect this approach. A key dimension of the team was social cohesion – the skein of beliefs, norms and practice which allowed New Zealand to operate broadly around the pandemic on a unitary basis. Central to this was trust and its legacy built up through the Christchurch and White Island events, embodied in the person of the Prime Minister. She was the lynchpin of the unitary response, the 'necessary but not sufficient' condition for successful management of the crisis.

The government understood early the need to gain mass support for its strategy so the role of the Prime Minister was complemented by a powerful communications strategy emphasizing a unitary approach grounded in a vision of 'kindness'. Confidence in the technical advice used by the government was built round regular communication with increasingly respected commentators, especially the Director-General of Health and a core group of epidemiologists and other medical experts. The economic support packages introduced were similarly understood to be a response on behalf of the team. Benefit increases and compassionate responses to the homeless reflected unitary social interventions.

The government also understood that, whilst voluntary compliance was always preferable, there would be a need to discipline some citizens into compliance. Here, again, the 'team' traditionally displays a strong commitment to the 'rule of law', an advantage that would support the need for compulsion in some circumstances. Thus, the government consciously sought the 'sweet spot' between voluntarism and compulsion, emphasizing the former but unequivocal in its willingness to use the latter if necessary. Clearly, this was a matter for constant assessment and management, and inevitably an unremitting concern – achieving the optimum balance was the goal, with an understanding that failure to do so would result in greater levels of compulsion, and the probable loss of social commitment to the government's COVID-19 strategy. The spectre of events in, for example, the USA and the UK loomed large in this concern.

4.3   Legislative Management

The scale of COVID-19's challenge raised legislative and constitutional challenges. At a simple functional level, Parliament found its essential functions disrupted by COVID-19 measures. One response by government was to establish a Select Committee of Parliament, chaired by the Leader of the Opposition, to meet virtually during lockdown, between 25 March and 26 May. The purpose of the committee was to consider and report to the House on matters relating to the government's management of the COVID-19 epidemic. This committee had a two-fold function – to give practical meaning to parliamentary oversight of the handling of the crisis and to confirm for civil society that the democratic process still functioned. The nomination of the Leader of the Opposition as chair of the committee was politically astute.

In August 2020, a panel of three High Court judges issued findings in relation to a claim raised by Anthony Borrowdale to the effect that, first, the initial nine days of lockdown were illegal; second, three Orders made by the Director-General of Health relating to social gatherings and other matters exceeded the powers permitted under the relevant parts of the Health Act 1956; third, the Director-General had unlawfully delegated the definition of 'essential services' used in COVID-19 management to the Ministry of

Business Innovation and Employment. The High Court found fault only in the first matter, and, even then, it stated: 'While there is no question that the requirement was a necessary, reasonable and proportionate response to the COVID-19 crisis at that time, the requirement was not prescribed by law and was therefore contrary to s 5 of the New Zealand Bill of Rights Act' (*Borrowdale v Director-General of Health* [2020] NZHC 2090 [292]).

In May 2020, the COVID-19 Public Health Response Act was passed, illustrating the government's requirement for urgent legislative management of the crisis. The need for special legislation to deal with Level 2-type lockdowns is interesting. On the one hand, it shows that the Health Act 1956 in general continues to be an effective measure for dealing with many of the circumstances that arise in a pandemic. On the other, the need for specific legislation to permit previously unlegislated degrees of lockdown, and the willingness of opposition parties in Parliament to oppose such legislation, captures the emerging politicization of the anti-COVID-19 campaign as a general election approached and as the merits of the 'Go fast, go hard' approach were subjected to political scrutiny.

4.4   Managing Key Interest Groups: Business, Labour

Business sentiment throughout the crisis has been guardedly positive. Criticism has arisen in relation to, for example, the timing and configuration of government support for business, the perceived limited role of senior business people in developing the COVID response, and the impact of stringent lockdowns on business activity. However, the scope and size of government financial support for business as the pandemic developed was such as to mute criticism. That support was generous and easy to access. As BusinessNZ (2020) said in relation to the 2020 General Election:

> This year's [election] survey shows a clear view by business that the Government has done well in its initial response to the COVID-19 situation. There are mixed feelings about whether the Government has spent the right amount on business support, but there is strong support for the wage subsidy and leave schemes. (para. 3)

BusinessNZ is making a distinction also made by the New Zealand Council of Trade Unions (CTU). This is between the immediate response to the pandemic's dislocation and longer-term recovery initiatives. The CTU has been equally positive about the government's short-term measures but also sees the need (especially post-2020 General Election) for the much-heralded legislation of Fair Pay Agreements and further reform of the employment relation legislation, coupled to industry planning.

In sum, in terms of the social partners – unions and employers – relations with the government have been active and substantive. Ministers have gone some way to ensure that communication channels are open and receptive. However, both social partners are now focused on the post-COVID-19 recovery phase, which promises to be a more challenging engagement around the configuration of recovery.

4.5   Managing the Media

Messaging has been central to the government's COVID-19 strategy. The government, and particularly the Prime Minister and Minister of Finance, have a complement of internal and external advisers, press secretaries and strategists supporting press–government relations. Contacts with the media exist on and off the record. From the government's side, management of relations with the media is, in general, effective. From the media perspective, shortened news cycles, reductions in resources and funding and the emergence of new social media platforms produce a richer texture of both informed and uninformed comment, and a move away from in-depth extended analysis.

Against this background, the government has shared news management between the four core ministers, the Director-General of Health and a small number of officials. Media engagement has been tightly managed. The focus of the government's media strategy has been fourfold – to inform the public of developments on a daily basis, impart important behavioural messages, promote the unitary national strategy and publicly anchor decisions in technical advice, rather than political requirements. This approach has been sustained and successful.

5.   IT'S THE ECONOMY, STUPID: BUDGETS AND COSTS

Government economic management of the crisis is an important measure of popular, media and expert commentary. This is inevitably a highly charged political matter, which came to figure large in the 2020 General Election. Traditionally, management of the economy is an area in which, rightly or wrongly, the National Party eclipses Labour in polls. Hence, the government laid great stress on both its generosity (that is, the extent and size of expenditure), the success of the expenditure (that is, the jobs and firms supported) and its grasp of the consequences of such expenditure (that is, how debt consequent on expenditure would be managed). This was, clearly, a delicate and crucial balancing act. To give perspective, by April 2020, the government had committed $41.9 billion to the COVID-19 response, with $20.2 billion in hand for further allocation. Net core Crown debt was 19 per cent of gross domestic product year ending June 2019; it is projected to rise to 53.6 per cent in years ending June 2023 and 2024. Notwithstanding these challenging figures, one can sum up a generally positive business commentary in a quote from PwC New Zealand's (2020) budget commentary: 'This is a big, bold Budget. The government has sent a strong signal that they are committed to economic recovery from COVID-19, and are ready to keep spending to speed up the recovery' (para. 1).

A Newshub-Reid Research poll published in July 2020 suggested that, given the question of which party would run New Zealand's economy better through the COVID-19 crisis, 62.3 per cent of respondents said Labour and 26.5 per cent National (Lynch, 2020). In support of this, Grant Robertson (Minister of Finance) was chosen by the *NZ Herald*'s 'Mood of the Boardroom' CEOs as the top-performing Cabinet Minister (O'Sullivan, 2020).

6.   INTERNATIONAL DIMENSIONS

At the time of writing (December 2019), the World Trade Organization (2020) is forecasting a 9.2 per cent drop in world merchandise trade in 2020, followed by a 7.2 per cent increase in 2021. These data are more tentative than is usually the case, but certainly more positive than some earlier forecasts of COVID-19's impacts on global trade. Some New Zealand trading sectors have been hard hit, especially education and tourism. Other sectors have been significantly less disrupted. In New Zealand, the government reacted to this trade challenge with a Trade Recovery Strategy (Parker, 2020). The core components of this are direct support to exporters, a focus on a reformed international trade regime and an upgrading of key international trade links. The emphasis lies in a trading system that rebuilds quickly and better as a result of COVID-19.

Migration issues are also important, in particular in relation to regular and anticipated movements of labour into New Zealand. Such movements – be they seasonal agricultural workers from the Pacific Region, fishing crews from the Caucasus or international performers for New Zealand-based film productions – carry with them risks of reintroduction of COVID-19 (as was seen in the case of some migrant fishers, who, upon arriving in New Zealand to crew New Zealand-based fishing vessels, in some cases tested positive for COVID-19). The government has carefully monitored this demand for access, recognizing economic imperatives but refusing to subordinate medical advice to economic considerations.

Geo-politically, COVID-19 has thrown up myriad challenges. For example, how may travel between China and New Zealand be managed when the Chinese claim the defeat of COVID-19? What should be the status of travel between New Zealand and Australia? Or New Zealand and the Pacific Islands?

Suffice it to say that in both international economic and diplomatic terms, COVID-19 has been severely disruptive.

7.   CONCLUSIONS AND DISCUSSION

7.1   Reflecting on Janssen and van der Voort

The relevance of the Janssen and van de Voort (2020) discussion of 'lessons for practice' should be clear. New Zealand neither chose nor developed a 'one best response'. The scale of the pandemic drove something akin to a 'just-in-time' response to the crisis, contingent on particular circumstances as they emerged in New Zealand. The success of a just-in-time approach was made possible by a number of factors – for example, the capacity to drive a unified national response, the quality of science-based advice, the commitment of the population to an effective response and the quality of national political leadership.

The just-in-time element of the response was also a source of flexibility in, and nuancing of, intervention. Whilst flexibility did lead on occasion to uncertainty in policy delivery, in general it allowed national leadership to adjust policy in a timely fashion.

A hallmark of the New Zealand experience was the dialectic between changing policy responses to COVID-19 and stability in messaging and policy delivery. Stability was enshrined in the use of a handful of 'talking heads' in the media, messaging around the unity of the '5 million' and the persona of the Prime Minister and her carefully crafted and consistent presence. The government positively counterposed the unity and coherence of society to the pandemic-related uncertainties.

The mobilization of the '5 million' against COVID-19 built on the impact of the earlier Christchurch terrorist attack. The New Zealand population has displayed to date high levels of discipline and adherence to pandemic-related regulations. There is a chicken-and-egg dimension to this – early discipline proved effective and permitted later freedoms barely constrained domestically by regulation.

7.2   Thinking Ahead

For the New Zealand government, COVID-19 promises an uncertain future. Government sources are sanguine about COVID-19 vaccine development and anticipate its availability in early 2021, with substantial supplies flowing in mid-2021. Much depends on that outcome. The government remains hopeful that the social cohesion displayed since the pandemic arrived will continue to support effective counter-COVID-19 measures. Furthermore, there is hope amongst government economists (and others) that the economic recovery from COVID-19 will be 'v-shaped'.

Budget 2020 in large part rested on these assumptions. Key themes of the Budget – jobs, training and infrastructure – were predicated on not just maintaining workforces and skills for a rapid recovery, but also on using the disruption of the crisis as an impetus to improved economic performance. The business community and many economic commentators are sympathetic to this approach. Interestingly, the more radical suggestions emerging are from the government's own supporters, such as an interest in modern monetary theory.

Let us assume that a vaccine is available from mid-2021, a reasonable assumption given news of vaccine development success in early November 2020. At some point thereafter, government performance will be subject to a post-COVID-19 reckoning. As Camus writes, plagues and wars do seem to take people by surprise, but they are also rapidly consigned to history as the immediate takes precedence over the past. The government will have only so long in which it can blame COVID-19 for its challenges.

Domestically, the government will be expected to have managed a variety of matters well. Unemployment is one; growth rates and their impact on inequality and investment will be another. The question will be asked: has the trading system recovered sufficiently to support the needs of a strong trade-based economy? Will financial support through the crisis have contributed to the transformation of the economy to a high-performance model? To what extent will COVID-19 have 'crowded out' essential economic changes driven by climate change, or will the government have grasped the opportunity to rebuild with climate at the centre of its policy thinking? Is there social partnership, which is committed jointly to a transformed New Zealand? Such questions are many, but they point to the opportunity to change New Zealand for the better – the silver lining of the crisis to be acknowledged and seized. Hence, all eyes are on a government with an extraordinary mandate after the 2020 General Election. To what extent will it be transformational?

Internationally, the government has the potential to play a major role in re-energizing the international trade system and contributing to global diplomatic arrangements that rebuild, rather than fragment. New Zealand has been a powerful voice, far more effective than its economic presence might suggest, in international councils on trade and diplomatic collaboration. One obvious context in which New Zealand counsels are heard is Asia-Pacific Economic Cooperation (APEC), which China and the US are also members of. An economic rapprochement between China and the US in a post-Trump world would be an important building block for the post-COVID-19 international economy.

REFERENCES

Borrowdale v Director-General of Health [2020] NZHC 2090.

Bronen, R. and F. Chapin (2013, June 4), 'Adaptive governance and institutional strategies for climate-induced community relocations in Alaska', *PNAS*, **110** (23), 9320–25. https://doi.org/10.1073/pnas.1210508110

BusinessNZ (2020), 'Business Covid and the 2020 election', accessed 27 Nov 2020 at https://www.businessnz.org.nz/news-and-media/media-releases/2020/business, -COVID,-and-the-2020-election

Janssen, M. and H. van de Voort (2020), 'Agile and adaptive governance in crisis response: Lessons from the COVID-19 pandemic', *International Journal of Information Management*, **55**, 102180.

Lynch, J. (2020), 'Newshub-Reid Research poll: Kiwis trust Labour more than National to run the economy', *Newshub*, 27 July, accessed 27 Nov 2020 at https://www.newshub.co.nz/home/politics/2020/07/newshub-reid-research-poll-kiwis-trust -labour-more-than-national-to-run-the-economy.html

O'Sullivan, F. (2020), 'Mood of the boardroom: Grant Robertson impresses the business leaders', *NZHerald*, 28 September, accessed 27 Nov 2020, at https://www .nzherald.co.nz/business/mood-of-the-boardroom-grant-robertson-impresses-the -business-leaders/T2FSWAHSHDY74F5723BELTI3AA/

Parker, D. (2020), 'Trade strategy for the recovery from the impacts of Covid-19', 8 June, accessed 27 Nov 2020, at https://www.beehive.govt.nz/speech/trade-strategy -recovery-impacts-COVID-19

PwC New Zealand (2020), 'Budget 2020', accessed 27 Nov 2020, at https://www.pwc .co.nz/insights-and-publications/budget/nz-budget-2020.html

World Trade Organization (2020), 'Trade shows signs of rebound from COVID-19, recovery still uncertain', accessed 27 Nov 2020, at https://www.wto.org/english/ news_e/pres20_e/pr862_e.htm

2.   It's (not) the economy, stupid: New Zealand's targeting of gross national happiness during the coronavirus crisis

Lina El-Jahel and Robert MacCulloch

1.   INTRODUCTION

> [It] does not allow for the health of our children, the quality of their education, or the joy of their play. It does not include the beauty of our poetry or the strength of our marriages, the intelligence of our public debate or the integrity of our public officials. It measures neither our courage, nor our wisdom, nor our devotion to our country. It measures everything, in short, except that which makes life worthwhile.
> Senator Robert Kennedy on GDP (cited in Mankiw, 1999)

A striking feature of the New Zealand policy reaction to the coronavirus pandemic was the strict initial 'Level 4' government lockdown, initiated on 25 March 2020. It was praised by Nobel laureate, Joseph Stiglitz (2020), who declared that 'New Zealand has managed to bring the disease under control and is working to redeploy some underused resources to build the kind of economy that should mark the post-pandemic world: one that is greener and more knowledge-based, with even greater equality, trust, and solidarity' (para. 3). A study in the Lancet has recently stated how 'the speed and intensity of the national response to limit the epidemic is unprecedented internationally … It is likely this early, intense response, which also enabled relatively rapid easing while maintaining strict border controls, prevented the burden of disease experienced in other high-income countries with slower lockdown implementation' (Jefferies et al., 2020, n.p.).

The Oxford University Blavatnik School of Government Stringency Index shows only six out of 185 countries in the world had (slightly) more severe sets of rules as of 26 March 2020. Figure 2.1 compares NZ's stringency with three other countries, namely the US, UK and Sweden, as prominent examples.

Great debate still rages as to whether this has been the optimal policy. Some commentators have questioned the approach on the grounds that it does not accord with a rational weighing of costs arising from lost output compared to health benefits.[1] For example, Gibson (2020) estimates that at least $NZD 10 billion worth of output (or 3.3 per cent of GDP) was lost during the stringent Level 4 lockdown, compared to staying at Level 2. He states that 'the ineffectiveness of lockdowns implies New Zealand suffered large economic costs for little benefit in terms of lives saved' (p. 1).

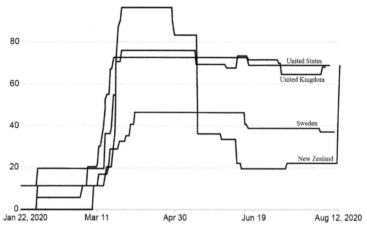

Note: This index is a composite measure based on nine indicators including school closures, workplace closures and travel bans, rescaled to a value between 0 and 100 (100 = strictest response). Creative Commons Attribution CC BY standard. This data is provided free of charge.
Source: Hale et al. (2020).

Figure 2.1   COVID-19: Government Response Stringency Index

On the other hand, Davies and Grimes (2020) argue that there was an objective basis for the strict lockdown, since it preserved the option of eliminating the virus that may otherwise have been lost. This view is strengthened by the fact that when NZ entered its Level 4 lockdown in March 2020, much about the microbiology of the virus was still not known.

This chapter instead looks for an explanation for NZ's reaction drawn from well-being economics. Although NZ has ranked extremely highly in global surveys of happiness, its GDP per capita lies below the OECD average.[2] Consequently, the country appears to have been relying on other (non-materialistic) factors to maintain such impressive levels of 'gross national happiness'. For example, NZ has long been characterized as a place that enjoys low inflation, low corruption, high levels of social trust and a comprehensive welfare state, including universal healthcare and pensions systems.

However, there have been growing concerns that some of the quality-of-life dimensions underpinning NZ's high ranking have been in decline. Congestion has grown greatly in several of our biggest cities, housing affordability has deteriorated and pressures on the public healthcare system, not to mention the natural environment, have been increasing. Many public and private goods have experienced soaring demand as the population of the country has grown from around 4 million to 5 million people over the past 17 years.

We check for whether subjective well-being measures have been stagnant, or even falling, in NZ, over the past one and a half decades, notwithstanding the strong upward trend in total GDP, using the Gallup World Poll. The evidence suggests that a re-emphasis and prioritization of well-being goals may indeed lie behind the policy reaction of the current government to the pandemic. We also discuss how the ultimate success of the approach in terms of future long-run outcomes remains an open question.

In other words, the thesis of this chapter is that a national-level prioritization of health and well-being over other outcomes helps account for the decision by the NZ government to close borders and embark on one of the world's most stringent lockdowns as the pandemic exploded in the early part of 2020.

2.   AN EXPLANATION FOR NZ'S APPROACH

2.1   A National Focus on Health and Well-being

Why did NZ explicitly put health and well-being goals ahead of a narrower focus on the economy and the maximization of GDP during the onset of the coronavirus pandemic? The policy background to the approach is the development of the 'living standards framework', by the Chief Economist of the Treasury, Dr Girol Karacaoglu, which began in 2008. The ultimate objective of the framework was: 'on increasing the freedoms of NZers at large to live the kinds of lives they want and choose to live' (Karacaoglu, 2012, para. 5).

The living standards framework found a basis in law after the election in 2017 of the new Labour government. For example, an amendment to the Reserve Bank of NZ Act (1989) passed the following year giving the Bank a new aim to promote: 'the prosperity and well-being of New Zealanders and contribute to a sustainable and productive economy'.

Furthermore, the Public Finance (Well-being) Amendment Act passed in 2020 now requires: 'the Government to report annually on its well-being objectives in the Budget and for the Treasury to report periodically on the state of well-being in NZ'.

Political rhetoric also shifted in the direction of promoting a gross national happiness perspective. For example, the Prime Minister distinguished her government from the previous one by arguing that: 'after nine years of a singular focus on GDP and surplus, the actual result was … too many NZ'ers suffer-ing from poor mental health' and that instead 'people and their well-being' (Ardern, 2020, n.p.) would be the new focus.

In the year before the pandemic, in 2019, the NZ government delivered the world's first 'well-being budget'. It received widespread international atten-tion from the likes of Cass Sunstein (2019), the Harvard legal scholar, whose column for Bloomberg noted: 'New Zealand's Labour coalition government has done something that could prove historic. Led by Prime Minister Jacinda Ardern, it has produced the world's first "well-being" Budget, focused explic-itly on a single goal: using its limited funds to promote the well-being of its citizens' (para. 1).

The founder of well-being economics, Professor Richard Easterlin, who we interviewed about NZ's response, argued: 'If you look at the concerns that are most important for people's well-being, it is three things: their job, family circumstances and their health. The NZ approach involved a composite of attention to health and a job' (quoted in Robertson, 2020).

More deeply, this approach appears to draw on a cultural disposition of Kiwis to emphasize factors important to achieving a high overall quality of life. Before the formal adoption by the incoming government of the Treasury's framework, NZ already regularly ranked near the top of surveys of well-being. For example, the World Happiness Report (2020) placed it in the top ten of 156 countries on this basis.

2.2   The New Zealand Approach in an International Context

The approach of NZ policy-makers continues a tradition of questioning the appropriateness of using GDP as an indicator of development. The Kennedy quote at the beginning of this chapter shows the enormous political appeal of this logic. Indeed, a variety of authors and organizations have advocated more comprehensive measures of well-being, capturing other elements of modern life besides income, in particular environmental degradation.[3]

In 1973, William Nordhaus and James Tobin asked, 'Is Growth Obsolete?' Their answer was a partial yes, and they argued in favour of adjusting GDP so that leisure and household work were valued. Some costs to urbanization were also included. They constructed a Measure of Economic Welfare for the United States and observed that it grew like GDP over the period under study, albeit more slowly.

In 2008, the President of the French Republic, Nicholas Sarkozy, created The Commission on the Measurement of Economic Performance and Social Progress. The primary authors of the Commission's report were Nobel Laureates Joseph Stiglitz and Amartya Sen, as well as Jean-Paul Fitoussi. Its aim was to identify the limits of GDP as an indicator of economic performance and social progress as well as to consider what additional information might be required for the production of more relevant indicators (see Stiglitz et al., 2009).

A number of social observers have also pointed out that the large increases in GDP experienced by many countries over the last several decades do not appear to have been associated with increases in mental well-being. In a seminal paper, Richard Easterlin (1974) showed that one could approach these issues using 'happiness data', namely the responses that individuals give concerning a simple well-being question. The most common form comes from a survey question that asks, 'How would you say things are these days – would you say you're very happy, fairly happy, or not too happy?' Using data for the United States, Richard Easterlin showed that happiness responses in any particular year rose with an individual's income. However, over time, average happiness scores were untrended, in spite of strong increases in average income levels (see also Di Tella and MacCulloch, 2008).[4]

More recently, other authors have showed a similar pattern for the period following the publication of Easterlin's paper. The same kind of findings, or with very slight detectable trends, have been observed in a variety of countries (see, for example, Blanchflower and Oswald, 2000).

2.3   Had NZ been Experiencing Rising GDP but Not Well-being Before the Virus?

A national decision to emphasize health and well-being and willingly sacrifice GDP has not been without much controversy, given that the three main drivers of NZ economic growth between 2012 and 2018 were international tourism, immigration and residential construction (Reserve Bank of New Zealand, 2016). External demand has played an important role in each one of these drivers.

In the case of residential construction, the country has attracted strong inflows of foreign capital aimed primarily at the purchase of real estate in Auckland, the country's largest city. Combined with a shortage of supply due to local council regulations, together with high demand from immigrants, NZ began experiencing one of the world's sharpest increases in property prices, further fuelling the inward flow of capital and exacerbating a housing affordability crisis. These factors led to strong growth in GDP in NZ, which ran at close to 3 per cent per annum between 2015 and 2019.

A question this chapter seeks to address is whether mental well-being was also rising over the past decade. To provide an answer, we use the Gallup World Poll that has surveyed residents in more than 150 nations, using representative samples. Around one thousand individuals undertook interviews each year in each country, allowing us to determine trends in NZ using a relatively long annual time series.[5]

We use two Gallup World Poll questions. The first captures the thoughts people have about their life as a whole when they evaluate it:

> Please imagine a ladder with steps numbered from zero at the bottom to ten at the top. Suppose we say that the top of the ladder represents the best possible life for you and the bottom of the ladder represents the worst possible life for you. If the top step is ten and the bottom step is zero, on which step of the ladder do you feel you personally stand at the present time?

The second question relates more to the emotional quality of a person's everyday experience. It asks: 'Did you experience the following feelings during a lot of the day yesterday? How about enjoyment?'

Figures 2.2 and 2.3 plot the average responses to the 'ladder of life' and 'enjoyment' questions, respectively, from 2006 to 2019. Whereas GDP per capita had a sharp upward trend, both of these well-being measures fell.

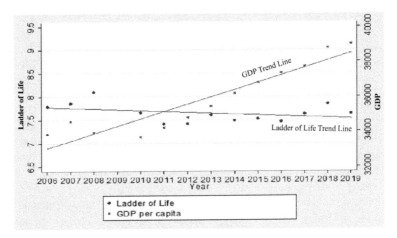

Figure 2.2   Ladder of life, NZ: 2006–2019

Table 2.1 estimates the size of the time trend after controlling for a set of personal characteristics that include one's income, age, gender, marital status and number of children. Column 1 shows that the ladder of life dropped by 0.6 units (on a 10-point scale) between 2006 and 2019. By contrast, GDP per capita rose by 15.1 per cent over this same period. On the other hand, within NZ, people in higher income quintiles reported a monotonically increasing

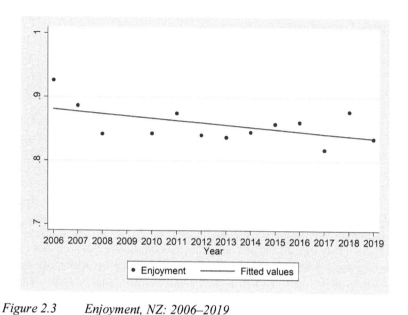

Figure 2.3   Enjoyment, NZ: 2006–2019

Table 2.1   Trends in well-being for New Zealand: 2006–2019, Gallup World Poll

	(1)	(2)
Dependent variable	*Ladder of life*	*Enjoyment*
Time trend	−0.05˙ (0.004)	−0.01˙ (0.001)
Personal income quintile: Second	0.23˙ (0.05)	0.01 (0.01)
Third	0.43˙ (0.03)	0.04˙ (0.01)
Fourth	0.58˙ (0.07)	0.04˙ (0.01)
Fifth	0.90˙ (0.07)	0.04˙ (0.01)
Other personal characteristics:		
Gender, age, marital status, number of children	Yes	Yes
Year dummies	Yes	Yes
R-squared	0.08	0.02
Number of observations	12 448	11 448

Note: Bold is significant at 5 per cent level and star-bold at 1 per cent level. Column 1 is an ordinary least squares regression and Column 2 is a probit regression with marginal probabilities reported.

ladder of life score. For example, a rise from the bottom quintile to the top quintile added 0.9 units.

Column 2 shows that the chances of experiencing enjoyment decreased by 14 percentage points, on average, between 2006 and 2019. Within NZ, people in higher income quintiles reported greater levels of enjoyment. For example, a rise from the bottom to the top quintile increased the chances of reporting this particular emotional state by 4 percentage points.

These results are consistent with the 'Easterlin Paradox', whereby increases in GDP in many countries have not been associated with rising well-being. The within-country gradient is often explained by appealing to 'relative income' effects, whereby individuals who are comparatively better off than those with whom they compare their fortunes, report higher levels of well-being.

To summarize, although GDP had been increasing in NZ in the decade leading up to the coronavirus pandemic in early 2020, self-reported levels of well-being had not been rising and appear to have even fallen. Starting in 2018, the newly elected Labour government, even before the virus had made an appearance, declared a new emphasis on improving broader measures of well-being, in line with the living standards framework that had already been developed by the NZ Treasury. This shift toward a gross national happiness approach and away from a more narrow focus on GDP growth appears to have been a significant factor in influencing the reaction of the government to the initial outbreak of the pandemic, particularly in terms of the stringency of the national lockdown.

2.4   Compliance with Rules and the Role of Social Capital

The second distinguishing feature of NZ's response was the remarkable degree of compliance and cooperation amongst its citizenry. Effective implementation of the particularly stringent lockdown required a great deal of trust, especially since most individuals were not closely monitored by the government. Furthermore, penalties for noncompliance had not been firmly established.

How did this situation come about? The country has historically enjoyed one of the highest levels of social capital in the world. The Legatum Prosperity Index in 2019, for example, ranked NZ seventh out of 167 countries in terms of the 'strength of its personal and social relationships, social norms and civic participation' (Legatum Institute, 2019). Social capital is important for promoting coordination and collaboration between people and groups in society. Since catching coronavirus involves an 'externality' whereby one person can hurt another by infecting them, prosocial, responsible behaviour rooted in altruism becomes an important factor in limiting its spread.

3.   CONCLUSION AND THE FUTURE

New Zealand has appeared to target gross national happiness as a response to the coronavirus pandemic and after experiencing a decade of falling well-being, as measured by the ladder of life. Most other nations were reluctant to shut down large parts of their economies to such an extreme degree in order to prioritize health and well-being outcomes. A high level of social capital led to widespread compliance and cooperation with the initial stringent lockdown. In the short run, the approach has met with significant success.

However, the implementation of a national objective focused on health and well-being in favour of GDP is fraught with problems. For example, the measurement of well-being remains controversial. Nobel laureate Daniel Kahneman emphasizes the distinction between experiencing life and thinking about it (Kahneman and Deaton, 2010). He regards questions like 'Are you happy now?' as measuring an emotional experience that is different from evaluations like 'How close are you to the best possible life?'. Which type of question better captures human well-being, or whether they capture different aspects, is still unresolved. The NZ government has already erred in terms of using too many different types of measures (over 50) as part of its living standards framework, many of which are moving in opposite directions. Commentators like Nobel laureate Angus Deaton (2010) argue that until we understand this issue better, it is too soon to give up on economic growth, and 'to try to deny to our children and grandchildren the increase in opportunities that we ourselves have been fortunate enough to experience'.

Furthermore, although there is a view that good health and well-being outcomes will align over time with better economic outcomes in the context of the coronavirus, the prospect that a trade-off exists poses significant risks for a small, isolated island like NZ. Whether the nation can maintain tight border controls whilst simultaneously addressing its longstanding problem of weak productivity growth is still an open question. This past decade, economic growth has relied heavily on external drivers such as attracting foreign tourists and immigration. To the extent that the virus persists, internally focused structural reforms will be required. The local skill base needs to be improved and the small capital base increased.

Most pertinently, the pandemic revealed that the country's health-care system, already struggling with the demands of an ageing population, would have been quickly overwhelmed had the number of virus cases ever risen to significant levels. A radical overhaul of that system, consequently, has become long overdue.

NOTES

1. See Heatley (2020) who argues that a shift from Level 4 to 3 strictness would have outperformed the actual NZ government decision on 20 April 2020 to stay 5 more days at Level 4 on cost–benefit grounds. He estimates the net cost of the extra days was NZ$741 million.
2. For example, NZ was placed 8th out of 156 countries by the World Happiness Report in 2019. A GDP per capita ranking of OECD countries can be found at: https://data.oecd.org/gdp/gross-domestic-product-gdp.htm
3. There are many such indicators of welfare. Perhaps the most famous one is the human development index in the Human Development Report produced by the United Nations. Considerable impetus to develop a national environmental indicator set occurred following the 1989 G-7 Economic Summit Leaders' request to the OECD to develop indicators in the context of improved decision making. Canada is one of the most advanced in this sense, after passing the Well-Being Measurement Act (Bill C-268) with the purpose of developing and regularly publishing measures to indicate 'the economic, social and environmental well-being of people, communities and ecosystems in Canada'. Its key provisions require a Standing Committee of the House of Commons to 'receive input from the public through submissions and public hearings' so that they can identify 'the broad societal values on which the set of indicators should be based'.
4. For a literature review see Di Tella and MacCulloch (2006).
5. Face-to-face interviews were approximately 1 hour in length, whereas telephone interviews were about 30 minutes. The coverage region is the entire country, including rural areas, and the sampling frame represents the whole civilian, non-institutionalized, population who are aged 15 years and over. Most World Gallup Poll questions have a simple dichotomous ('yes or no') response set to minimize contamination of data because of cultural differences in response styles and to facilitate cross-cultural comparisons.

REFERENCES

Ardern, J. (2020), 'Election campaign launch speech', 8 August 2020, accessed at https://www.labour.org.nz/news-speech-campaignlaunch
Blanchflower, D. and A. Oswald (2000), 'Well-being over time in Britain and the USA', *Journal of Public Economics*, **88** (7–8), 1359–86.
Davies, B. and A. Grimes (2020), 'COVID-19, lockdown and two-sided uncertainty', *New Zealand Economic Papers* (forthcoming). doi:10.1080/00779954.2020.1806340
Deaton, A. (2010), 'Book: In pursuit of happiness', *The Lancet*, **376** (November 20), 1729.
Di Tella, R. and R. MacCulloch (2006), 'Some uses of happiness data in economics', *Journal of Economic Perspectives*, **20** (1), 25–46.
Di Tella, R. and R. MacCulloch (2008), 'Gross national happiness as an answer to the Easterlin Paradox?', *Journal of Development Economics*, **86** (1), 22–42.
Easterlin, R. (1974), 'Does economic growth improve the human lot? Some empirical evidence', in P. David and M. Reder (eds), *Nations and Households in Economic Growth: Essays in Honour of Moses Abramovitz*, New York: Academic Press, pp. 89–125.

Gibson, J. (2020), 'Government mandated lockdowns do not reduce Covid-19 deaths: Implications for evaluating the stringent New Zealand response', *Working Papers in Economics*, University of Waikato, accessed at https://ideas.repec.org/p/wai/econwp/20-06.html

Hale, T., N. Angrist, E. Cameron-Blake, L. Hallas, B. Kira, S. Majumdar, A. Petherick, T. Phillips, H. Tatlow and S. Webster (2020), *Oxford COVID-19 Government Response Tracker*, Oxford, UK: Blavatnik School of Government.

Heatley, D. (2020), 'A cost–benefit analysis of 5 extra days at COVID-19 Alert Level 4', Research note, May, Wellington, NZ: New Zealand Productivity Commission, accessed 14 December 2020, at https://www.productivity.govt.nz/assets/Documents/cost-benefit-analysis-covid-alert-4/92193c37f4/A-cost-benefit-analysis-of-5-extra-days-at-COVID-19-at-alert-level-4.pdf

Jefferies, S., N. French, C. Gilkison, G. Graham, V. Hope, J. Marshall, C. McElnay, A. McNeill, P. Muellner, S. Paine, N. Prasad, J. Scott, J. Sherwood, L. Yang and P. Priest (2020), 'COVID-19 in New Zealand and the impact of the national response: A descriptive epidemiological study', *The Lancet*, **5** (11), E612–E623, accessed 14 December 2020, at https://doi.org/10.1016/S2468-2667(20)30225-5

Kahneman, D. and A. Deaton (2010), 'High income improves evaluation of life but not emotional well-being', *Proceedings of the National Academy of Sciences*, **107** (38), 16489–93.

Karacaoglu, G. (2012), 'Improving the living standards of New Zealanders: Moving from a framework to implementation' [Speech], The Treasury, accessed 14 December 2020, at https://www.treasury.govt.nz/publications/speech/improving-living-standards-new-zealanders-moving-framework-implementation

Legatum Institute (2019), *The Legatum Prosperity Index 2019*, accessed 14 December 2020, at https://li.com/reports/2019-legatum-prosperity-index/

Mankiw, N. G. (1999), *Macroeconomics* (4th ed.), New York: Worth Publishers.

Nordhaus, W. and J. Tobin (1973). 'Is growth obsolete?', in M. Moss (ed.), *The Measurement of Economic and Social Performance*, New York: National Bureau of Economic Research, pp. 509–64.

Reserve Bank of New Zealand (2016), *Monetary policy statement for August 2016*, accessed 14 December 2020, at https://www.rbnz.govt.nz/-/media/ReserveBank/Files/Publications/Monetary%20policy%20statements/2016/mpsaug16.pdf?revision=b4ff30ea-be8c-4a1e-a954-17886af6a43a

Robertson, G. (2020), 'Govts to consider wider measures of success as Well-being Amendment Bill passes' [press release], June, accessed at https://www.beehive.govt.nz/release/govts-consider-wider-measures-success-wellbeing-amendment-bill-passes

Stiglitz, J. (2020), 'Conquering the great divide', *Finance and Development*, **Fall**, 17–19, accessed 14 December 2020, at https://www.imf.org/external/pubs/ft/fandd/2020/09/COVID19-and-global-inequality-joseph-stiglitz.htm

Stiglitz, J., A. Sen and J.-P. Fitoussi (2009), 'The measurement of economic performance and social progress revisited: Reflections and overview', OFCE Working Documents. Observatoire Français des Conjonctures Economiques.

Sunstein, C. R. (2019), 'Bloomberg analyst: NZ's Well-being Budget worth copying', *NZ Herald*, June 10, accessed 14 December 2020, at https://www.nzherald.co.nz/business/bloomberg-analyst-nzs-wellbeing-budget-worth-copying/XISLFO2GMFKHNYOJNAMYSOJ7XA/

World Happiness Report (2020), accessed 14 December 2020, at https://worldhappiness.report/ed/2020/

3. Covid-19: government responses to labour market disruptions and economic impacts

Sholeh A. Maani

1. INTRODUCTION

What shape would the employment and the economic environment take if all social and work contact is potentially deadly? The idea that, one day, almost the entire workforce of a country would be confined to quarantine at home may at first appear as the setting of a dystopian science fiction movie. But this is precisely what New Zealand and many other countries have experienced in 2020, in response to the Covid-19 pandemic. How has such an event changed the economic landscape? What lessons have we learned from this experience? The Covid-19 crisis created significant shifts in the operations and fortunes of several sectors within New Zealand. The economic fallout happened immediately. Yet, the full impacts continued to evolve through the recovery periods – and are expected to continue into the foreseeable future. The international flow of people and products stopped or was severely disrupted, significantly impacting the tourism and hospitality industries. This changed the expected short- to long-term viability of some industries, compared to others. Changes to employment opportunities had a significant role in the economic landscape. In many sectors, the production of goods and services was reduced (on the supply side). From an earnings perspective, incomes were significantly reduced. Isolation in quarantine in New Zealand and overseas also reduced consumer demand for products and services, leading to further losses in employment and income. A reinforcing feedback loop of underemployment, reduced incomes and reduced demand for products and services created a vicious cycle.

The onset of the pandemic in New Zealand was slightly later than in the US and Europe. This fortuitous timing helped New Zealand to prepare for and avoid an exponential growth of the virus – 'flattening the curve'. New Zealand's response to the pandemic was, in many ways, different from the responses in other countries, providing an interesting case study. Specifically, the government adopted the ambitious goal of eliminating the virus. The quarantine measures proved to curb the virus from overtaking the population, which made normal life and work possible for 102 consecutive days, and again after a second shorter resurgence and elimination period.

Given the unknown and highly contagious nature of the virus, the key trade-off between public health and economic activity proved to be a daunting international challenge. A growing number of international studies relating to the epidemiological and economic response to the Covid-19 pandemic have highlighted the trade-off between these objectives (e.g., Adda, 2016; Eichenbaum et al., 2020; Glover et al., 2020; Guerrieri et al., 2020; Hur, 2020; Mendiola et al., 2020; Verelst et al., 2016).

As part of the elimination strategy, the government introduced an economic package to support businesses and employment. The logic behind this strategy was to keep the population safe, while protecting livelihoods and economic activity to the greatest extent possible (Robertson, 2020; Robertson and Sepuloni, 2020). The package included the designation of essential workers – those who worked in food, medical supplies and other essential production and service industries. In addition, a wage subsidy scheme was swiftly enacted to stop mass unemployment. The New Zealand government moved its own operation to online work performed by staff working at home. Many businesses followed suit.

This chapter focuses on major changes in the economic landscape and employment during and in the aftermath of the Covid-19 response. The chapter evaluates the impact of three important components of the policy that have affected economy and employment. First is the contribution of essential workers to maintaining the operation of the economy. Second is the successful large-scale move to contactless work and production. Third is the wage subsidy that was, in many respects, unique to the New Zealand policy. These three employment-related examples of the policy response in New Zealand provide an interesting case, with lessons that can guide our understanding in the future. The chapter concludes by examining both the question of whether Covid-19 will change the New Zealand economic landscape forever and the learning from the New Zealand experience.

The experience of New Zealand, and many other countries, during the pandemic has highlighted that manoeuvring the competing goals of public health and economic activity is impossible without trade-offs. In the case of New Zealand, border closures and lockdowns resulted in contractions in economic activity, and government economic stimulus expenditures and safety-net expenditures resulted in a government budget deficit – a change from a budget surplus before the pandemic. These trade-offs are addressed in greater detail in other chapters of this volume. This chapter focuses on positive aspects of the New Zealand response on employment.

2.   THE PRE-PANDEMIC ECONOMIC LANDSCAPE

In considering the impacts of the pandemic, it is useful to briefly note some of the features of the New Zealand population and economy prior to the pandemic's onset.

First, since the recovery from the global financial crisis, the New Zealand economy had seen a decade of steady positive economic growth (an average of 2 per cent per annum). At the time of the onset of the pandemic, the economy enjoyed a high employment rate, with unemployment at an historically low(est) rate of around 4 per cent – signifying a strong economy at the time.

Second, and importantly, New Zealand had a fiscal budget surplus – among the privileged few in the OECD. This proved to be imperative in allowing the government to provide relief policies, including wage subsidies and tax deferments, with speed.

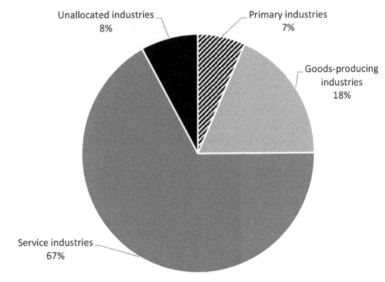

Source: Stats NZ (2020a).

Figure 3.1   *The shares in GDP and a significant service industries sector, followed by goods and services industries, March 2020*

Third, the workforce had been upskilled significantly in the past three decades, with one of the highest percentages of the population with higher education in the OECD (2020). As a result, a greater proportion of the workforce has been engaged in professional occupations that use technology platforms.

Fourth, New Zealand can be classified as a service economy, with a productive agricultural sector. Service industries (Figure 3.1) made up about 67 per cent of the country's Gross Domestic Product (GDP), goods-producing industries accounted for about 18 per cent, and primary industries 7 per cent.[1]

In addition, international demand for New Zealand's agricultural and dairy products has been developed to a strong and stable market. The fact that New Zealand could provide food for her trade partners during the pandemic was a key component of economic policy prior to and during the pandemic. Tourism had grown to contribute significantly to the New Zealand economy (about 5 per cent of GDP in 2019) and the sector was on the rise prior to the pandemic.

Finally, New Zealand has a large proportion of small and medium-size enterprises (SMEs). SMEs can show significant flexibility and agility to market shifts. However, capital shortage can put SMEs at a greater risk, which proved to be important during lockdown periods.

3.   UNFORESEEN DISRUPTIONS

The pandemic-induced disruptions in employment markets are attributable to three key sources: (1) a decrease in domestic and international demand; (2) the fear of contagion itself – the effect of these two factors was greatest for jobs that required face-to-face or physical contact; and (3) quarantine compliance, which necessitated further isolation and reduced business activity, exacerbating the feedback effect of decreased demand due to diminished and uncertain earnings.

However, consumer demand and employment for 'necessities' continued. This was also true of essential services that were deliverable in contactless settings. A surprising result was that, with remote work from home, productivity did not drop in many firms, and it increased in some cases. While the sectors reliant on travel were heavily hit, international trade provided a welcome relief for the economy.

Some skills proved more resilient and compatible with this landmark shift – notably, farming, legal, financial, technical support, government and most high-skilled jobs that could be conducted online. In contrast, employment in tourism, hospitality and retail could not effectively shift to online platforms. In addition, many small businesses were caught unprepared for digital operations, and their premises were required to stay closed during lockdown periods. As a result, they found it difficult to establish an online presence and payment systems with short notice.

4.   GOVERNMENT ECONOMIC RESPONSE

Since the onset of the pandemic, the trade-off between saving lives and having a functioning economy emerged as a key challenge for the government and New Zealanders alike. While these two imperatives were clearly at odds in the short term, the long-term links between stamping out the virus and normalized economic activity were fully congruent.

The approach ventured by the New Zealand government was to prioritize lives, while accepting lower economic activity in the short term, with the aim of recovered and sustained economic activity in the long term. This entailed a leap of faith, as dealing with a new and unknown virus it was not possible to know exactly when and how the virus could be eliminated.

The early and stringent quarantine system adopted in New Zealand was a four-stage system, with varying degrees of restrictions. The initial and longest stage of quarantine (Level 4) through March and April of 2020 required people, with few exceptions, to stay at home in their defined 'bubbles'! The government also implemented travel bans for both international and domestic travel. The quarantine system was later moved to less stringent levels (3 and 2). The return to normal activity of Level 1 occurred in May 2020. By early June, domestic travel had resumed, which was followed by an immediate increase in economic activity in both increased consumption and production.

However, a resurgence of cases – albeit on a much smaller scale – in August 2020 resulted in a second but shorter lockdown period. This second wave lasted until 21 September, with easing for Auckland delayed until 8 October.[2]

The quarantine restrictions required companion programmes to secure the operation of the economy, population well-being and preservation of work and earnings to the maximum extent possible. The designation of essential workers, remote work and contactless trade, and a wage subsidy system to keep people at work, comprised important features of New Zealand's policy response.

4.1   Designation of Essential Workers

Government allowed essential workers, those working in diverse sectors including healthcare, aged care, security, education (primary, secondary and tertiary education), food transport for supermarkets, cleaners of essential services, medical and other essential supplies to continue to operate. International trade was made possible by essential workers. New Zealand's primary products, especially food and dairy, continued to flow to her trade partners.

New Zealand's designation of essential workers (released on 23 March) was set earlier than other countries after the onset of the first Covid-19 case in the country. The unified national designation and its clear communication reduced much confusion. The European Commission's designation of essential workers, albeit released later (on 30 March), was also accepted as a clear baseline for member countries. But its implementation proved problematic, as it allowed movement of essential workers across the EU. In the US, the Cybersecurity and Infrastructure Security Agency (CISA)'s definition of essential workers was followed by less than half of the US states. The inconsistency in the definition of essential workers is plausibly one of the reasons that prevented the US from containing the Covid-19 outbreak.

4.2   Remote Work and Contactless Retail

Remote work and contactless business activities, including in retail, were among important features of the pandemic response. The government itself moved its own operations and services to remote modes through its technology platforms. Both local and national government departments continued to function uninterrupted. This included civil defence, customs, education, health and welfare, payrolls, emergency management functions and overseeing of primary products. Many government departments showed flexibility and prompt expansion of services. Other businesses which could adapt, such as the financial sector and teaching institutions, followed suit.

A notable response of the market to the disruption – caused both by the pandemic and government restrictions – was the remarkable agility, flexibility and willingness by organizations and the workforce to adapt, cooperate and adopt new technologies within a short span of time.

4.3   Wage Subsidy Scheme

As part of the government response package, a wage subsidy to firms was provided which reduced labour costs for employers and helped preserve jobs. The wage subsidy scheme, introduced swiftly in March 2020, provided financial assistance to businesses that were significantly impacted by the pandemic. The employer eligibility criteria for receiving the wage subsidy required that the business's revenues had to be at least 30 per cent lower in the previous 30 days compared to a similar time period in the previous year (Employment New Zealand, 2020). The scheme paid out weekly per-employee rates of $585.80 for full-time workers (working for more than 20 hours per week), and $350 for part-time workers, for a period of 12 weeks. To put these figures in context, the full-time rate was equivalent to 57.6 per cent of the median weekly earnings in New Zealand in the year 2019.

5.   IMPACT ON ECONOMIC SECTORS

By March 2020, the New Zealand economy was growing at an annual rate of 1.5 per cent. This was a significant drop from the previously projected growth rate of 3.7 per cent. During the first quarter of 2020, the New Zealand economy shrunk by 1.6 per cent (Stats NZ, 2020a). This was the single largest decrease in New Zealand's GDP in 29 years – and a greater decline than during the global financial crisis. Per capita GDP also decreased by 2.2 per cent during the same quarter. Figure 3.2 shows changes in GDP by industry during the 4-month period of December 2019 to March 2020, representing effects in the initial stages of the pandemic compared to the pre-pandemic period in December 2019.

By June 2020, the economy had contracted at an annual rate of 2.0 per cent since June 2019 (Stannard et al., 2020; Stats NZ, 2020b). A more significant drop of about 12.2 per cent in GDP production occurred during Quarter 2, compared to the first quarter of 2020. This represents the largest decrease in economic activity in New Zealand in decades. The measure also reflects the substitution of some government-sponsored economic activity and services in place of previous production by the private sector.

On an annual basis, New Zealand's GDP had decreased by a similar drop of 12.4 per cent, compared to Quarter 2 of 2019. Likewise, New Zealand's trade partners had also reported contractions in their annual GDP growth by the end of Quarter 2 of 2020: The European Union, −3.9 per cent; OECD average, −11.7 per cent; Australia, −6.3 per cent; US, −9.1 per cent; UK, −21.7 per cent; and Canada, −13 per cent (OECD, 2020; Stats NZ, 2020).

Figure 3.2 provides a comparison of the contractions in economic activity (GDP) by industry in the first and second quarters of 2020. As seen in Figure 3.2, 13 out of 16 industries showed decreases in GDP, with construction, manufacturing, retail and accommodation being hardest hit. SMEs were highly represented among the latter two groups and were disproportionately affected. Energy, business services, wholesale trade, public administration, safety and defence experienced more modest impacts. In contrast, information, media and the telecommunications industry, healthcare and mining showed continued positive changes in their industry GDP.

Figure 3.2 further shows that by June 2020, no industry was unscathed by the pandemic. Retail, transport, construction and business services continued to shrink significantly in the June quarter. The large impacts in Quarter 2 of 2020 reflected the combined impacts of the pandemic itself, loss of tourism and the lockdown periods that caused the closure of many businesses. These combined forces had unequal impacts across industries.

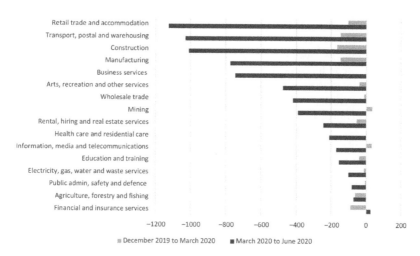

Source: Figure based on Stats NZ (2020a, 2020b) data.

Figure 3.2   *Gross domestic product by industry, changes from December 2019–March 2020, and March 2020–June 2020*

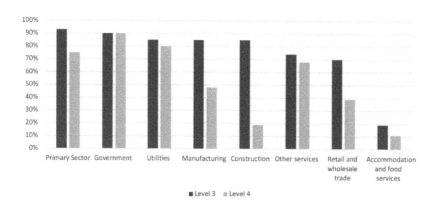

Source: Figure based on data in Stannard et al. (2020).

Figure 3.3   *GDP production by industry during lockdown as percentage of pre-pandemic production*

Figure 3.3 highlights the impact of the lockdown on capacity utilization for different industries. Notably, during the Level 4 alert, construction, retail, accommodation, food services and manufacturing were operating below 50 per cent of their usual pre-pandemic levels, representing one of the main reasons for the reduced GDP.

In addition to the reduction of GDP, the share of GDP components had also changed by June 2020, in comparison with June 2019 (Stats NZ, 2020b). Private investment's share of GDP had decreased (from 24 per cent to 18 per cent), and the share of government spending and net exports had increased (respectively from 19 per cent to 22 per cent and from −0.1 per cent to 3 per cent). The relative share of private consumption in the GDP had remained almost unchanged (about 57 per cent). The increased share of public spending reflected the amplified government administrative support required for the response to Covid-19, and economic stimulus spending to generate economic activity. Increased net exports partly reflected the impact of reduced imports.

6.   IMPACT ON THE WORKFORCE

Despite the reduced economic activity by June 2020, a key positive outcome of the New Zealand strategy was the preservation of jobs, while minimizing the loss of lives.

New Zealand experienced a modest change in the unemployment rate of 0.2 per cent in the first 6 months from December 2019 to June 2020 (New Zealand Parliament, 2020; Stats NZ, 2020c). Stats NZ (2020a, 2020b) data placed New Zealand in 5th ranking among OECD countries on employment engagement in both March and June 2020. Sweden had the 6th ranking, UK and Finland were ranked 8th equal. Australia's position had deteriorated from 13th to 18th, while the US dropped from 20th to 31st place during the same period.

6.1   Essential Workers

As mentioned earlier, essential workers made a significant contribution to the success of New Zealand's response, both in terms of the population's well-being, and in providing essential goods and services. This included doctors, nurses and medical staff, aged-care workers, security and border control employees, those working in supermarkets and related supply chains, bus and transport drivers, delivery and courier workers, police force and cleaners in sensitive operations. Without these workers, the impact on the economy would have been severe.

The Ministry of Health's (2020) list of essential workers under the Covid-19 isolation alert systems ensured provision of physical and mental health, education, government and financial services. In addition, many

Table 3.1   *Essential service and other work under Alert Levels 3 and 4 (year 2020)*

		Essential Service	Non-Essential Service	Total
Alert Level 4	Going to work	529 000	NA	529 000
	Working from home	139 000	501 000	640 000
	Unable to work	457 000	1 019 000	1 476 000
	Total	1 125 000	1 520 000	2 645 000
		Operational Service	Non-Operating Service	Total
Alert Level 3	Going to work	1 172 000	NA	1 172 000
	Working from home	507 000	NA	507 000
	Unable to work	829 000	137 000	966 000
	Total	2 508 000	137 000	2 645 000

Source: MBIE (2020).
Note: Non-Operating services were specifically restricted from opening.

front-line workers for the production and distribution of food, essential construction, running of utilities and the manufacturing and distribution of essential items were designated as essential workers. Statistics from the Ministry of Business, Innovation and Employment (MBIE, 2020), summarized in Table 3.1, show the number of individuals who were designated as essential workers under Alert Level 4, and who worked for the population's well-being during lockdowns.

As shown in Table 3.1, more than half a million (529 000) people were identified as critical service workers. In addition to this group, another 139 000 essential workers worked from home. This combined group comprised about 25 per cent of the New Zealand workforce. Without the operation of this group of workers, the economy would have been paralyzed.

On the impact of the alert systems on work, as Table 3.1 (Column 1) shows, the percentage of active workers moved up to 63.4 per cent under Level 3 compared to 25 per cent under the lockdown. This comparison clearly demonstrates the significant increase in employment activities made possible during Level 3. Further analysis confirms employment gains across all industries with greatest increases in construction and retail (MBIE, 2020).

Under Alert Level 3, gatherings of up to ten people with social distancing were possible, allowing several more people to go to work. This, combined with 'contact tracing', prevented a more severe adverse economic impact.

Throughout the lockdown and alert levels essential workers continued to work regardless of the risks involved. The recognition of the significant role that these members of the workforce play created a major shift in public recognition of what constitutes 'essential work' for the operation of the economy and the well-being of its population. It is interesting that if a survey were to have been conducted prior to the experience from the pandemic, asking individuals to identify essential workers in our economy, a different list would have been very likely to emerge – assigning higher value to jobs with greater influence, earnings and prestige. This lesson and awareness from the experience with the Covid-19 pandemic may indeed endure.

6.2   Remote Work and Contactless Business

The notion of working from home, although a partial practice in the past by many professional firms, was not considered as a viable option by the majority of businesses. The experience of the pandemic altered those assumptions, by demonstrating that this mode of work can be viable and effective for both organizations and workers.

Recent statistics from MBIE (2020; see Table 3.1) confirm that under the lockdowns, close to a quarter of the workforce (24.2 per cent) was able to work remotely from home and further remote work became possible as digital and contactless systems improved. This sudden major change is indeed likely to have created an impetus for long-lasting changes in remote work arrangements as a norm in labour markets. Bick et al. (2020) find a similar surge in working entirely from home following the pandemic (35 per cent of the workforce), in particular among highly educated employees.

The relatively high level of remote and digital work done in New Zealand, including by the government, was made possible through its significant digital infrastructure – in particular the high-speed fibre and broadband infrastructures that had started a decade earlier. Figure 3.4 demonstrates the significant increase in the country's number of high-speed fibre-optic broadband installations during the period prior to the pandemic. Indeed, had the pandemic occurred even five years earlier, the possibility of remote work from home in New Zealand cities would have been much more restrained.

It is important to note that back in 2009, the New Zealand government collaborated with Crown Fibre Investment Co to work on the Ultra-Fast Broadband programme with the objective of delivering high-speed broadband for New Zealanders. At the cost of approximately 1.5 billion dollars, this programme aimed to speed the connection up to 100 megabits per second, which was 50 times faster than the speed in 2009. Phase 1 of the programme commenced in the same year, focussing on areas that had higher populations

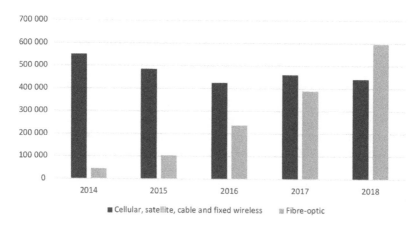

Source: Figure based on Stats NZ (2019) data.

Figure 3.4   *Broadband internet connections infrastructure*

ranging from 1.2 million people (Auckland) to 12 600 people (Oamaru; Stats NZ, 2019).

By 2019, high-speed internet connections were available to 79 per cent of New Zealanders, exceeding initial expectations. As of Quarter 2 of 2020, the number of active connections had increased to 83 per cent with more than 1 million households using it (Crown Infrastructure Partners, 2020).

A Harvard Business Review study that evaluated several countries in terms of their readiness for remote work (Chakravorti and Chaturvedi, 2020) placed New Zealand in the top category of readiness at the time of the onset of the pandemic. The analysis incorporated three dimensions of internet availability (robustness of digital platforms, the resilience of internet infrastructure to traffic surges and proliferation of digital payment systems). Other countries in the top readiness group included Singapore, Netherlands, US, Canada, Germany and South Korea.

This underscored the importance of internet and other digital infrastructures for continued economic activity across several professional services, financial, government, health and education as well as wholesale and retail.

6.3   Hybrid Remote and Flexible Work Hours

Since the onset of the pandemic, a number of interesting and hybrid models of flexible work arrangements that combine a mixture of remote and in-office work have proven workable and even desirable across New Zealand private and public sector organizations.

An unintended but welcome outcome of the remote work was the significant digital upskilling and capacity building for organizations and their workforce. This included a noticeable increase in the uptake of digital and contactless transactions to operate across different alert levels. Online ordering and payment system capability for small and medium-sized businesses and their workforces was an important part of this enhancement.

This was highlighted during Auckland's resurgence of Covid-19 cases which caused the second quarantine period in August 2020. This shorter period demonstrated that the businesses that were unprepared during the earlier quarantine period had learned to adopt contactless or online sales, pick-up and payment systems, allowing them to operate under the quarantine restrictions. This is a major shift that could affect the nature of future work operations and service delivery in New Zealand.

A central learning from the remote work experience was that worker productivity could in fact remain unchanged in the remote mode. This was a major shift in long-held assumptions regarding the importance of monitoring of employees at work places to ensure high productivity. Further, the efficiency gains by saving travel time and more focused and flexible work hours at home were also recognized.

The recognition of the feasibility of remote work is a major unintended consequence and learning from the response to the pandemic. In addition, flexible work-hour arrangements have proven viable and productive in many work places, while improving work–life balance. It is likely that this change will continue to shape employment and work relations in this decade. Economic history has other interesting parallels, such as the labour force participation of women during World Wars I and II, which, later, was recognized as a major impetus for the significant and irreversible increase in the economic activity of women in the post-World War II period (Goldin, 1991).

6.4   Wage Subsidy

The wage subsidy was made available in the latter part of Quarter 1, 2020, under significant time pressure, as the pandemic had started to take hold in New Zealand. Speed in rolling out the policy in connection with imposed stringent social distancing and lockdown systems was imperative before mass job losses took hold.

An important feature of the 12-week subsidy scheme – and the Wage Subsidy Extension Scheme (WSES) – was that employers were required to retain the staff members for whom the wage subsidy was received, and they were urged to pay them their regular wages. The wage rate paid to employees could, however, be renegotiated between the employer and the employee, at levels not below 80 per cent of the employee's regular wage.

The WSES was rolled out for a period of eight weeks beyond the initial 12-week period. To qualify for the extension, employers had to demonstrate an earnings loss of more than 40 per cent of their regular earnings during the previous month. The cumulative number of applications received was just below 1 million (982 194), of which 77.3 per cent were approved (Ministry of Social Development, 2020).

By mid-October 2020, the wage subsidy schemes had cost $14 billion (about 4.5 per cent of GDP), and the programme had supported 76 000 employees. According to the Ministry of Social Development (2020), 11 billion dollars of the expenditure on the scheme was used in the first 12 weeks of the programme.

It was recognized that the administrative cost of scrutinizing the applications process on a case-by-case basis would be costly and time consuming. The government's compromise was to make the scheme available within broad criteria for eligibility. This naturally resulted in some teething issues, including an over rather than undersubscription of the scheme. For example, the number of complaints received by the government about misuse of the scheme was as high as 4000. Some 10 500 recipients of the scheme also returned the subsidy received to the government as either their income losses proved not to be severe, or they were unable to maintain employment for their employees. Some of these returns of the subsidy were initiated voluntarily.

Despite the cost, the policy was successful in preventing possible mass unemployment across the country and a domino effect of losses of output, which would have been further caused by lost earnings and spending.

By September 2020, the unemployment rate reached 5.3 per cent as wage subsidy eligibility ended for many businesses, and with Covid-induced economic downturn in affected industries. Jobs that were secure and productive in the pre-pandemic periods were painfully lost across the skill spectrum. In the absence of the wage subsidy, the job losses would have initially resulted in an estimated additional increase of around 3 per cent in the unemployment rate, to rates of around 7 per cent of the labour force, followed by higher rates with secondary impacts due to lost earnings and lower consumer spending. Job losses that were averted in the first two quarters due to the wage subsidy would have been costly for the economy in the form of unemployment income-support payments. Job losses would have had further costs for the business community due to reduced production and the loss of skills and talent.

7.   CONCLUSION

The New Zealand Covid-19 pandemic experience has provided many lessons for both the government and the private sector. The government's early and stringent approach to combating the pandemic succeeded in eliminating the spread of the virus and saw a return to 'normality' for 102 consecutive days. However, despite closed borders, New Zealand experienced a second wave of contagion in August, which was addressed swiftly in a similar way, returning to freedom of movement in Quarter 4 of 2020. In addition, with returning citizens, flight staff and transport workers, the risk of a new contagion at the border has necessitated diligent isolation monitoring of new arrivals on a regular basis. This New Zealand experience has shown the complexity of fully stamping out the virus, if borders are to be opened, even to a limited extent. Yet it also shows the exceptional success of the response in relation to health outcomes.

Some of the successes of the New Zealand experience may have been facilitated due to its lower population density, geographical isolation, the structure of the economy and the high level of social coherence. However, much of its approach as a case study in relation to the very early lockdown, the designation of essential service workers, remote work and the wage subsidy has relevance to other countries.

New Zealand's response also featured the government's provision of some safety nets for businesses and employees. The wage subsidy played an important role in keeping workers employed, avoiding an alternative of mass unemployment and business bankruptcies in the wake of the pandemic itself and the consequent quarantine. The policy reduced or delayed the impact of the lockdowns. However, the haste with which the scheme had to be rolled out, showed that it requires adjustments in assessing eligibility for targeting the wage subsidy to employers and businesses in need. Extended border closures continued to result in reduced economic activity and job losses in certain industries.

During the height of the pandemic, essential workers played a key role in keeping the economy moving. These workers made it possible for the population to stay safe, and for the economy to continue to function at a difficult time, when both the fear of illness and the need for necessities plagued the nation. This also highlighted that, ironically, some of these workers have earnings that are at the lower end of the wage scale. This begs the question of whether, beyond the current pandemic, a living wage would be considered more favourably for this group of workers in the lowest earnings decile, recognizing their role and contribution to the population's critical needs and economic vitality.

Another key learning is that remote work could prove to be productive in many organizations and allow superior work–life balance for staff. Future historians may note that, in a similar way that the experience of women's work during World War II provided the impetus for greater workforce participation of women, the Covid-19 pandemic may have already provided the impetus for many more organizations to embrace remote working modes, more flexible work arrangements and the possibility of a four-day work week. The remote work experience further demonstrated older workers' willingness and aptitude to upskill with technology when it is called for.

New Zealand's Covid-19 response with expanded and amplified remote work has allowed many businesses and individuals to continue their operations with less disruption over the course of the pandemic. This has placed New Zealand in a strong position for economic recovery in her post-pandemic period. Overall, the New Zealand experience provides a plausible case study for other countries on the positive effects of its policy responses, in evaluating response options or should future pandemics arise.

NOTES

1. These percentage allocations were similarly 66 per cent of GDP for service industries, and 19 per cent for goods-producing industries in March 2019.
2. Public opinion is divided on whether or not the stringent second lockdown was necessary, given the very small number of cases in the second wave. With hindsight, the less stringent Australian response suggests that a less strict alert level (Level 3) with less impact on the economy may have been justified.

REFERENCES

Adda, J. (2016), 'Economic activity and the spread of viral diseases: Evidence from high frequency data', *The Quarterly Journal of Economics*, **131** (2), 891–941.

Bick, A., A. Blandin and K. Mertens (2020), *Work from home after the Covid-19 outbreak*. CEPR Discussion Paper No. DP15000, July.

Chakravorti, B. and R.S. Chaturvedi (2020), 'Which countries were (and weren't) ready for remote work?', *Harvard Business Review*, Retrieved 27 November 2020, from https://hbr.org/2020/04/which-countries-were-and-werent-ready-for-remote-work.

Crown Infrastructure Partners (2020), 'Quarterly connectivity update Q2: to 30 June 2020', accessed at https://www.crowninfrastructure.govt.nz/wp-content/uploads/CIP-Quarterly-Rep-June_FINAL.pdf.

Eichenbaum, M.S., S. Rebelo and M. Trabandt (2020), *The Macroeconomics of Epidemics. Technical Report*, Cambridge, MA: National Bureau of Economic Research.

Employment New Zealand (2020), 'Wage subsidy schemes', accessed 12 November 2020, at https://www.employment.govt.nz/leave-and-holidays/other-types-of-leave/coronavirus-workplace/wage-subsidy/.

Glover, A., J. Heathcote, D. Krueger and J.-V. Ríos-Rull (2020), *Health versus Wealth: On the Distributional Effects of Controlling a Pandemic, Technical Report*, Cambridge, MA: National Bureau of Economic Research.

Goldin, C.D. (1991), 'The role of World War II in the rise of women's employment', *American Economic Review*, **81** (Sept.), 741–56.

Guerrieri, V., G. Lorenzoni, L. Straub and I. Werning (2020), *Macroeconomic Implications of Covid-19: Can Negative Supply Shocks Cause Demand Shortages? Technical Report*, Cambridge, MA: National Bureau of Economic Research.

Hur, S. (2020), *The Distributional Effects of Covid-19 and Mitigation Policies*. Globalization and Monetary Policy Institute Working Paper 400. Dallas: Federal Reserve Bank Dallas. https://doi.org/10.24149/gwp400

Mendiola, S., O. Stavrunova and O. Yerokhin (2020), *Determinants of the Community Mobility during the Covid-19 Epidemic: The Role of Government Regulations and Information*. Bonn, Germany: Institute of Labor Economics.

Ministry of Business Innovation and Employment (2020), 'Essential services workforce fact sheet', accessed at https://www.mbie.govt.nz/assets/essential-services -workforce-factsheet.pdf.

Ministry of Health (2020), 'Covid-19: Essential services in the health and disability system', accessed at https://www.health.govt.nz/our-work/diseases-and-conditions/ covid-19-novel-coronavirus/covid-19-current-situation/covid-19-essential-services -health-and-disability-system.

Ministry of Social Development (2020), 'Covid-19 Report', accessed at https://www .msd.govt.nz/about-msd-and-our-work/publications-resources/statistics/covid-19/ index.html#IncomeSupportandWageSubsidyWeeklyUpdate2.

New Zealand Parliament (2020), 'Monthly economic review – July', accessed at https:// www.parliament.nz/en/pb/library-research-papers/monthly-economic-review/ monthly-economic-review-july-2020/.

OECD (2020), 'Quarterly national accounts: Quarterly growth rate of real GDP, change over previous quarter', accessed at https://stats.oecd.org/index.aspx?queryid=350 %20.

Robertson, G. (2020), '\$12.1 billion support for New Zealanders and business' [Press release], 17 March, accessed at https://www.beehive.govt.nz/release/121-billion -support-new-zealanders-and-business.

Robertson, G. and C. Sepuloni (2020), 'Govt takes significant economic decisions as NZ readies for Alert Level 4 in COVID-19 fight' [Press release], 23 March, accessed at https://www.beehive.govt.nz/release/govt-takes-significant-economic-decisions -nz-readies-alert-level-4-covid-19-fight.

Stannard, T., S. Gregorius and C. McDonald (2020), 'Economic impacts of COVID-19: Containment measures', Wellington, New Zealand: Reserve Bank of New Zealand.

Stats NZ (2019), 'Fibre uptake by businesses doubles in four years', March, accessed at https://www.stats.govt.nz/news/fibre-uptake-by-businesses-doubles-in-four-years.

Stats NZ (2020a), 'Gross domestic product (March quarter)', accessed at https://www .stats.govt.nz/information-releases/gross-domestic-product-march-2020-quarter #gdp.

Stats NZ (2020b), 'Gross domestic product (June quarter)', accessed at https://www .stats.govt.nz/information-releases/gross-domestic-product-june-2020-quarter.

Stats NZ (2020c), 'Labour market statistics (March quarter)', accessed at https://www .stats.govt.nz/information-releases/labour-market-statistics-june-2020-quarter.

Verelst, F., L. Willem and P. Beutels (2016), 'Behavioural change models for infectious disease transmission: A systematic review (2010–2015)', *Journal of The Royal Society Interface*, **13** (125), 20160820. doi:10.1098/rsif.2016.0820.

4.   'Listen to the wise': expert leadership in the Covid-19 crisis

Brigid Carroll

1.   INTRODUCTION

The Covid-19 crisis has heightened the significance and profile of the expert leader – those we could consider as *the wise* and *the seer(s)* of the Covid-19 crisis ('Oh oh children of the earth […] listen to the wise' (c.f. Queen, 1975)) – the epidemiologists, immunologists and health professionals who have not just steered our health systems, but who have been front of stage in the safety, security and protection of entire nations. Such figures have been variously celebrated, scorned, elevated and dismissed by the different political cultures around the globe. What they share, in this pandemic era, is unusual leadership prominence, profile, status and visibility regardless of the contexts in which they are operating in. They also share a relative invisibility in terms of leadership research with the assumption that such figures are advisers, policymakers and bureaucrats rather than leadership actors in their own right. This chapter not only seeks to expose such invisibility, alongside challenging the misleading simplicity of the 'listening' imperative, but aims to reframe expert leadership from the New Zealand experience.

While New Zealand's navigation of the Covid-19 pandemic has been widely noted and internationally praised, the lion's share of attention has gone, not undeservedly, to New Zealand's Prime Minister Jacinda Ardern for 'going hard and going early', her rare capacity to 'be strong [and] be kind' and in 'offering a model response of empathy, clarity and trust in science' (BBC, 2020, n.p.). Recent academic scholarship has acknowledged the importance of expertise in New Zealand's response through the identification of three core practices: (1) following the science, (2) using facts and evidence and (3) listening to advice from relevant expertise (Wilson, 2020). However, expertise (and experts) in this framework are considered as an input into leadership and not as leadership itself. Such an approach would appear to have separated out leadership and science, assigned the former to the realm of politics, and the latter, while important, to essentially a supporting role. It also appears to imply that the relationship between politics and science, and political and expert leaders, is primarily functional – the latter supply 'facts' and probability; the former listen and utilize those. This chapter problematizes such a beguiling simplicity and proposes that the acclaim that New Zealand has earned for 'listening to the wise', underpinned by a framing of 'listening to experts', needs to be reframed to 'leading with experts'.

2.   THE EXPERT IN A COVID-19 WORLD

Science and politics have been variously considered throughout history as rivals, enemies and (critical) friends and are in fact reflective of a boundary that 'has to be constantly redrawn and reiterated' to reflect the dynamism and changing ideology of both (Weingart, 1999, p. 160). A common starting point for such a discussion often lies in Weber's ([1919] 1946) seminal 'Science as a Vocation' and 'Politics as a Vocation' lectures, with the challenge of avoiding 'the dangers of avoiding them too closely or separating them too widely' (Eckstein, 1992, p. 37). Consequently, Weber ([1919] 1946) does affirm the importance and role of science in political life but equally insists on its very limits and constraints vis-à-vis politics. Significantly, he makes a distinction between information/knowledge and meaning making where, while science can offer the former, it does not in itself supply the latter. The corollary is that 'listening', while not by all means straightforward (or commonplace globally across pandemic responses), is insufficient in itself but interdependent with inquiry, interpretation, dialogue and decision-making processes. It is these latter processes which complicate and contest the relationship between science and politics.

As a consequence, while Weber ([1919] 1946) asserts their separateness and complementarity, he also warns of their potential overreach with respect to each (which he terms 'scientism'). Weber did foresee a future world where scientism might become the norm, where scientists present as 'moral teachers, agitators, demagogues and "prophets"', politicians seesaw between being 'too resistant' and 'too susceptible', and science becomes a 'surrogate "ism"' or 'potent weapon of mystification' (Eckstein, 1992, p. 45). It surely is not too much of a stretch to portray the Covid-19 crisis as illustrative of a landscape characterized by scientism with the responses of different countries positioned widely in that landscape. This chapter contends that Covid-19 has played out globally in a landscape characterized by varied degrees of scientism.

Furthermore, a second striking global dimension of the science/political landscape in 2020 is anti-intellectualism or the generalized distrust of experts that is both connected to the rise of populism, as evidenced by Donald Trump in the USA and Brexit in the UK, but also to controversial global science issues such as climate change. Anti-intellectualism points to science uneasily 'structured by ideology and partisanship' (Merkley, 2020, p. 1), a suspicion of intellectual elites from whom 'the expert' is usually sourced, and open conflict between intellectual, political, religious and cultural 'authorities' who appear (and often are) at odds with each other. Anti-intellectualism has been found to demonize experts, dismiss even broad scientific consensus, disseminate misinformation and politicize scientific (and social) development (Merkley, 2020). In empirical research exploring anti-intellectualism directly related to the Covid-19 pandemic, Merkley and Loewen (2020, p. 19) have found the proliferation of pseudoscientific and conspiracy-related misperceptions, what they term 'dampened behavioural change' in terms of strategies such as social distancing and wearing masks, and even reduced information searches for Covid-19-related knowledge. They draw the conclusion that the 2020 world is one where we 'cannot take trust in experts for granted' and indeed can expect to encounter active dis-identification, antagonism and indifference to the expert (Merkley and Loewen, 2020, p. 19).

Not surprisingly dis-identification, antagonism and indifference towards experts have been on full display during the Covid-19 crisis, again not surprisingly in countries which have taken a populist turn but perhaps surprisingly in that much of this 'anti-expert' behaviour has been led and fostered by political leaders. The world has watched the President of the United States prescribe injecting disinfectants and irradiating bodies with light as coronavirus treatments, call his world-renowned and revered public health expert Dr Fauci 'an idiot', 'disaster' and 'democrat' (Forrester, 2020) and be empirically assessed as the 'single biggest reason why many Americans distrust science' and the 'super-spreader of disinformation' for Covid-19 (Applebaum, 2020, n.p.). It has also watched the Prime Minister of the UK, Boris Johnson, 'gag' and block his two scientists, Professor Chris Whitty and Sir Patrick Vallance, from answering questions in the daily briefings on the premise that 'it's very, very important that our medical officers and scientific advisers do not get dragged into what I would think most people recognise is fundamentally a political argument' (Mason and Walker, 2020, para. 6).

However, the opposite stance has also been modelled in places like Sweden and Germany. The former, uniquely in the world, followed a much debated (and derided) 'herd immunity' strategy which has largely led to the avoidance of full-scale lockdowns and, rightly or wrongly, occasioned much attention and debate throughout the world. Sweden appears to be an extreme example of a government and country listening to a scientist (notwithstanding not listening to other scientists with often radically different perspectives). Germany of course is led by an expert leader – Angela Merkel has a PhD in quantum chemistry – allowing her to be 'less a commander in chief and more a scientist in chief' through 'modelling the humble credibility of a scientist at work'

(Miller, 2020, para. 1, 2). Germany thus provides an example where politics and science fuse in leadership.

New Zealand is complex to position in such a landscape. It is simple to assert it is not akin to the US and UK in its suspicion, derision and manipulation of experts, but nor is it Sweden or Germany in its evident respect for and enhanced belief in them. Equally, New Zealand could be considered to have an ambivalence to 'the intellectual' but possibly not to the extent of dedicated anti-intellectualism. Harris (2013) proposes that intellectual perspectives in New Zealand intersect with pragmatism, a tacit conservatism and the infamous tall poppy syndrome (the extrapolation of egalitarianism to a suspicion of those who gain rare profile and success) but coexist with a love of ingenuity, novel and innovative ideas and pride in the global visibility of a New Zealand identity. New Zealand's attitude to science and intellectual endeavour thus has a national idiosyncrasy which it will be argued is pivotal in this inquiry into the role and nature of expert leadership in the New Zealand Covid-19 crisis. Such a landscape complicates the definition, nature and aspiration of expert leadership.

3.   EXPERT LEADERSHIP

Compared to the prolific research on managerial leadership, political leadership and community leadership, there is comparatively very little research on expert leadership, although such a judgement is complicated by its overlapping relationship with technical, professional and vocational (such as medical) literatures in leadership. The most common definition of expert leadership is Goodall's (2012) definition of expert leadership as a function of inherent knowledge, industry experience and leadership capabilities. The above 'triangle' of attributes suggests that expert leaders should be considered as specialists with 'firm-specific experience and core-business knowledge and ability' (p. 12). The 'generalist' versus 'specialist' in leadership is a debate of relevance here which research into expert leadership tends to answer in the specialist's favour (Goodall, 2012). We can see that the primary interest in expert leadership appears to be the figure of the individual leader and their associated traits, behaviours and advantages, not, as in this chapter, in its role, position and contribution in relation to other leadership actors and more distributed or collective configurations.

As mentioned earlier in the chapter, it is likely that the expert in the political sphere is not referred to using a leadership frame at all, with a preference to term them policymakers or advisers. However, the relationship between science, politics, policy making and advice has become increasingly more complex in contemporary times due to a number of intersecting factors including 'the changing positions of science and scientific experts in society and the focus on socially robust knowledge and on the democratization of knowledge' (Spruijt et al., 2014, p. 22). Such factors add up to 'the simultaneous scientification of politics and the politicisation of science' (Weingart, 1999, p. 151) with three paradoxes in play: (1) the democratization of science, the loss of status of scientists but the growing value of expertise; (2) a more competitive context for expertise but real complexities in wielding influence; and (3) a loss of authority for experts but an increased demand for expertise. We can draw two conclusions here; that experts need to engage in legitimization and political behaviours alongside more normative science knowledge processes and that political leaders increasingly seek science knowledge and relationships with experts and expertise for explicitly political ends. Moving to a more explicitly leadership frame thus allows us to contextualize experts within such a changing contemporary context without 'the myth' of neutrality, objectivity and scientific detachment dominating.

One school of leadership thinking that does look at the relation of specialist/ expert leadership to generalist leadership is Ron Heifetz's (1994) adaptive leadership theory. Heifetz positions the traditional expert at the forefront of technical leadership which requires someone to 'actually go to somebody and "get it fixed"' (p. 74) and draw directly on expertise that provides ready-made and known 'right' answers that rely on the authority that expertise confers and the form of problem solving that is associated with such expertise. Contrast this with adaptive leadership which cannot supply such answers and must rely on an organization or system being prepared to learn and adapt through a process held and facilitated by often multiple leadership actors. While an expert can be an adaptive leader, their leadership is not reliant so much on their expertise or expert authority but rather on their ability to help the organization/support and engage with the challenges and possibilities that emerge from such a process. Such an adaptive leader fundamentally understands that 'the responsibility for meeting the problem has to be shared' (p. 75). While challenges and contexts can call for either technical or adaptive leadership, many contexts and challenges call for both alongside the judgement to move between the technical and adaptive in relation to multiple other leadership actors.

It is telling that Heifetz is a doctor himself (both surgeon and psychiatrist) and frequently uses medical contexts to illustrate the interrelationship of technical and adaptive leadership approaches but also the distribution of leadership between those engaged in any endeavour. Heifetz (1994) defines an expert leader's expert knowledge as 'a resource' for leadership but argues for 'a leadership that induces learning' that is 'beyond [their] substantive knowledge' (p. 75). If we extrapolate from a more normative medical context (diagnosing and treating a patient) to this Covid-19 context, then the role of these health expert leaders is to help the country 'learn new ways ... to do the work that only [everyone in that country] can do' (p. 75). That positions the expert leader in relation to other kinds of authorities (health ministers and the prime minister for instance) but also other actors (local government, media, citizens, economists and so on). I propose that it is this relational positioning and overall leadership configuration between experts, authorities and social actors to which New Zealand can attribute much of its success.

4.   ANALYSING EXPERT LEADERSHIP

This section highlights three expert leaders who played distinctive roles, understood themselves in relation to a more relational and collective leadership ethos, and would appear to be core actors in what I am calling here a distributed leadership ethos. Material for this section comes from a wide range of primary and secondary sources. The decision to focus on only three figures, regardless of their evident centrality across the Covid-19 crisis, does reflect a necessary limitation in the scope of this chapter which accordingly can seek to be indicative only of the broader interconnections and interactions that position the expert in a leadership configuration. It is my hope that even this constrained illustration does communicate the necessity of viewing expert leadership in more complex and intersubjective ways than is often presented and goes some way to explaining New Zealand's exemplary pandemic response. It is important too to acknowledge that no one actor is confined to one role and that the expert leader arguably needs all three in their repertoire (and more besides), hence this attribution of one role to one leader is simply an illustrative device to anchor this chapter.

4.1   Ashley Bloomfield

The most high profile of the three experts, Dr. Ashley Bloomfield, has reached celebrity and even cult status, eliciting 'a strange obsession' (Ward, 2020, para. 1) from the New Zealand public, involving his face on merchandise from tea towels to T shirts, at least one original song, flowers and cakes when 'thrown under the bus' by a (now ex) government minister, thousands of nominations for the New Zealander of the Year Award, and even an Ashley Bloomfield Junior (a baby rhino in Botswana).

BOX 4.1   ASHLEY BLOOMFIELD

Becoming the face of normally faceless bureaucracy. The 1 pm event each day during lockdown was the one thing that connected us all, that's how we all understood what was happening each day.

Ashley Bloomfield (Satherley, 2020, n.p.)

Leadership is an invitation to collective action.

Ashley Bloomfield (TVNZ, 2020, n.p.)

That daily stand up became quite a critical interface with the public and I soon realised that it was a way for us to get our information out unedited to every-body. And, of course, at that time we were facing that absolutely fundamental leadership challenge … of having to make huge calls and give advice on very big decisions with very limited and incomplete information.

Ashley Bloomfield (Leading through Crisis Webinar, 2020, n.p.)

All you can do is get up every day, play what's in front of you, work with your team members but remain true to your values. If something hasn't gone right, we'll say how we can go and fix it.

Ashley Bloomfield (Kirwan, 2020, n.p.)

The above quotes show Dr. Bloomfield acutely aware of his leadership, visible on a national stage and repeatedly locating himself in relation to other forms of leadership in relational, distributed and collective leadership ways. In fact, it can be noted that, in reference to leading, he continually uses the 'we' and 'us' plural pronouns instead of the singular 'I'. When talking about himself in leadership terms, he doesn't present as the one with the answers – although the whole of New Zealand was in thrall of his grasp of detail and the extent of his expert knowledge – but as someone who is adapting, learning and always in movement. That is the hallmark of adaptive work. In this chapter I represent him as being *on the stage* quite literally in the daily 1 o'clock lockdown pandemic briefings and news conferences but also positionally as New Zealand's Director General of Health and formal health leader. *On the stage* thus represents formal expert leadership mandated through position and officially in relationship with the government, with designated responsibility for the health offensive against Covid-19 which is key to both adaptive and technical leadership.

4.2   Associate Professor Siouxsie Wiles

Siouxsie Wiles is one of New Zealand's most colourful expert leaders as a rec-ognized microbiologist, infectious disease expert and science communicator. Wiles is instantly recognizable to all New Zealanders through her flaming pink hair, Doc Martins and fascination with glow-in-the-dark bacteria (she heads the Auckland University Bioluminescent Superbugs Lab). She has assumed the role of finding accessible, interesting and diverse ways of explaining science and the complexities of viruses to the public through cartoons, images, podcasts, internet forums and media appearances.

BOX 4.2   SIOUXSIE WILES

I don't look like somebody who is supposed to be leading. Authority and expertise can look like something else, and sometimes it's pink, which is distressing for some people, it seems.

Siouxsie Wiles (Barton, 2020, n.p.)

Some people think scientists are outside this sphere of any kind of influence and it's not true. My approach has been to explain, 'These are my core values'. So when I'm looking at the evidence, this is the way I will interpret it.

Siouxsie Wiles (Smith, 2020, n.p.)

Everything was about collaboration, working together, positive language – rather than fear.

Siouxsie Wiles (Smith, 2020, n.p.)

We need our politicians to avoid cluttering the media landscape with political messages and undermining the life-saving information coming from the government, health professionals, scientists and public health officials.

50 health experts (including Siouxsie Wiles) in an editorial to all election politicians (Small, 2020, n.p.)

The quotes above show Wiles identifying as an alternative and 'counter-cultural' expert leader. Indeed, she has been variously celebrated and trolled in social media for the difference she embodies and enacts. She claims and owns subjective, ideological and political dimensions of expertise and indeed argues that expertise is always interpreted through a filter of values (something Weber would agree with theoretically). The final quote shows her as part of a collective group of 50 health experts in an open letter to New Zealand's politicians during the election, warning such politicians against 'cluttering' the communication coming from experts and scientists. Thus, she could be understood as an activist leader who 'fights' for the influence of expertise in communicative and political domains. This article thus positions her as *in-between*, referring to an expert leader who positions themselves in-between scientists and the public, in the process becoming at various times a translator, defender, adviser, protector, critic and conscience of the government and senior health leaders.

4.3   Professor Michael Baker

Referred to as the 'loudest voice calling for lockdown' (Matthews, 2020, n. p), Michael Baker illustrates the expert who is willing to be 'a lone voice, out on a limb' (Easther, 2020) by voicing an opinion that might be contrary, oppositional, singular and against the grain. Such a voice walks a tightrope between evidence and objectivity and passion and emotion as evidenced by Baker owning to 'weeping' at the announcement of moving into lockdown which he had championed early and unusually. It is important to note that he is in no way an 'outside' figure, being a member of the Covid-19 National Technical Advisory Group, the National Science Media Centre, the author of the world's first elimination strategy (later to be adopted by the Labour led government) and in frequent conversation with appointed officials such as Ashley Bloomfield (who frequently discusses conversations with Michael Baker as part of the 1 o'clock briefing), nor is he always oppositional, being free with his support and praise over decisions and approaches when he feels they merit it.

BOX 4.3   MICHAEL BAKER

That feeling of being a lone voice, out on a limb, that I had it all wrong, was very uncomfortable.

Michael Baker (Easther, 2020, n.p.)

You go from a hierarchy to a networked way of operating.

Michael Baker (Matthews, 2020, n.p.)

This experience has reminded me of the power of good government and good science, when they work together, to make a difference to people's lives. Over three or four critical days when everything was on a knife-edge, I had some of the most exceptional conversations I've ever had....

Michael Baker (Easther, 2020, n.p.)

He has been an extraordinary prominent media commentator, informing the public, criticising and praising the Government's policy response and always being a consistent and fearless advocate for ... the most effective responses to the huge challenge that this pandemic has laid down for us.

(University of Otago, 2020, n.p., in relation to Michael Baker)

The quotes above show Michael Baker holding the difference, distance and complementarity of science to politics. He understands the above to be the 'power' that fuels good decision making in such a crisis. I note that this is not a detached, technical and unemotive place to be and that Baker intrinsically perceives himself in collaborative and networked ways. Adaptive leadership directs attention to courageous ('exceptional') conversations, generative use of conflict and tension ('knife-edge') and the ability to speak truth to power ('out on a limb') which Baker demonstrates here. Michael Baker thus represents the independent expert leader role. Such independence through being a *critical resource* would be considered the normative position of the expert leader. Being a critical resource thus is the expert leader prepared to be a critic, conscience, voice and advocate/challenger of an evidence-based strategy. However, Baker also shows that such a position has considerable adaptive work and requires skills that bridge the two.

4.4 Perceptions of Expert Leaders by Political and Professional Leaders and the Public

All three expert leaders understand and position leadership vis-à-vis other sources of leadership, most notably the government, public and other experts. I would argue that the success of New Zealand's response lies in this palpable sense of relationality through distributed leadership networks; something that New Zealand's relatively small size as a country undoubtedly facilitates. We show some of that relationality in Box 4.4.

BOX 4.4 FROM OTHER POLITICAL AND EXPERT COMMENTATORS

I have been disheartened to see some leaders cast doubt on the developments and associated decision-making over the last 48 hours .... To create confusion and suspicion quite frankly could result in reduced trust from our communities in the very institutions we rely on most to keep us all safe.

Green Co-leader James Shaw (Small, 2020, n.p.)

We came together as a country, in part because we believed in our political and health experts to deliver and they did .... When political will backs science, we save lives.

Dr Jagadish Thaker, Massey University researcher (Roy, 2020, n.p.)

Instead of hosting sole conferences, she chose to share the spotlight with an expert in public health ... they [Prime Minister Jacinda Ardern and Ashley Bloomfield] play like a one, two [Punch and Judy]. It's not just Ardern dictating everyone, it's her working with a medical expert to try to put a strategy together.

Professor James Liu (Deguara, 2020, n.p.)

The first quote shows an incident (among many) where a senior government figure 'protected' New Zealand's expert leaders and their work, which again is an adaptive leadership practice where those leading do at times need to be buffered and protected in their work. The one time this didn't happen, when the then Minister of Health David Clark visibly apportioned blame and fault for a problem onto Ashley Bloomfield, had whole segments of the country in quite vocal anger. The second and third are from university academics attesting to the importance of the relationship between politics and science at the level of principles ('when political will backs science, we save lives') and at both a symbolic and embodied level ('play like a one, two').

5.   CONCLUSION

This chapter, then, constructs expert leadership in three different ways, each with their own relational and political dynamics, but each positioned in relation to both political and public leadership. If we can call that a leadership configuration then such a configuration problematizes research on expert leadership which, as shown in the review of literature, overemphasizes the technical and rational knowledge of the expert and underplays the relational, adaptive and communicative ways they must work. This has led to a hesitation to truly embrace the expert as central to leadership activity and frames. For those beyond New Zealand, what can be learnt from the New Zealand Covid-19 response in terms of leadership is the importance of recognizing expertise, expert knowledge and expert leaders firstly through a leadership frame; secondly through relational, distributed and collaborative leadership ways; and finally as leadership actors/agents who are a vital part of the pandemic leadership configuration and the larger leadership response. New Zealand can claim to be world leading in its leadership practices that prioritize such an expansive understanding of leadership expertise.

REFERENCES

Applebaum, A. (2020). 'Trump is a super-spreader of disinformation', *The Atlantic*, 3 October, accessed at https://www.theatlantic.com/ideas/archive/2020/10/trump-super-spreader-disinformation/616604/.
Barton, M. (2020), 'New doco shows Siouxsie Wiles bursting into tears of relief watching COVID-19 alert level four announcement', *Newshub*, 7 September.
BBC (2020), 'Coronavirus: How New Zealand relied on science and empathy', *BBC News*, 20 April.
Deguara, B. (2020), 'Coronavirus: The importance of Jacinda Ardern sharing the spotlight during Covid-19 pandemic', *Stuff*, 30 April.
Easther, E. (2020), 'My story: Professor Michael Baker; "I wept when PM announced that NZ was going into lockdown"', *NZ Herald*, 14 April.

Eckstein, H. (1992), *Regarding Politics: Essays on Political Theory, Stability, and Change*, Berkeley: University of California Press.

Forrester, G. (2020), 'A look at the war of words between US President Donald Trump and Dr Anthony Fauci', *Stuff*, 10 October.

Goodall, A. (2012), 'A theory of expert leadership', *IZA Discussion Paper*, **6566**.

Harris, M. (2013), 'Is New Zealand really anti-intellectual?', *The Aotearoa Project*, 27 March, accessed at https://theaotearoaproject.wordpress.com/2013/03/27/is-new-zealand-really-anti-intellectual/.

Heifetz, R. (1994), *Leadership Without Easy Answers*, Cambridge, MA: Harvard University Press.

Kirwan, J. (2020), 'Covid 19 coronavirus: Ashley Bloomfield opens up on how he handles the stress of managing a pandemic', *NZ Herald*, 7 October.

Mason, R. and P. Walker (2020), 'Johnson blocks top scientists from talking about Cummings', *The Guardian*, 28 May, accessed at https://www.theguardian.com/politics/2020/may/28/johnson-blocks-top-scientists-from-talking-about-cummings.

Matthews, P. (2020), 'Man for this moment – epidemiologist Michael Baker', *Stuff*, 4 April.

Merkley, E. (2020), 'Anti-intellectualism, populism, and motivated resistance to expert consensus', *Public Opinion Quarterly*, **84** (1), 24–48.

Merkley, E. and P. Loewen (2020), 'A matter of trust: Anti-intellectualism and public reaction to the COVID-19 pandemic'. Working Paper, OSF.

Miller, S. (2020), 'The secret to Germany's Covid-19 success: Angela Merkel is a scientist', *The Atlantic*, 20 April 20.

Queen (1975), 'The Prophet's song', available https://genius.com/Queen-the-prophets-song-lyrics.

Roy, E.A. (2020), 'New Zealand beat Covid-19 by trusting leaders and following advice-study', *The Guardian*, 23 July.

Satherley, J. (2020), 'Dr Ashley Bloomfield reveals his own anxiety battle during Covid-19', *1 News*, 23 September 2020, accessed at https://www.tvnz.co.nz/one-news/new-zealand/ashley-bloomfield-reveals-battle-anxiety-self-doubt-during-covid-19-peak.

Small, Z. (2020), '50 New Zealand health experts urge political leaders to "resist temptation to scaremonger" over COVID-19', *Newshub*, 13 August.

Smith, N. (2020), '"A team of five million": How New Zealand beat coronavirus', *Direct Relief*, 3 August, accessed at https://www.directrelief.org/2020/08/a-team-of-5-million-how-new-zealand-beat-coronavirus/.

Spruijt, P., A. Knol, E. Vasileiadou, J. Devilee, E. Lebret and A. Petersen (2014), 'Roles of scientists as policy advisors on complex issues: A literature review', *Environmental Science and Policy*, **40**, 16–25.

Te Herenga Waka, Wellington University (2020), 'Leading through crisis (featuring Dr Ashley Bloomfield)' [Webinar]. *YouTube*, September 17, accessed at https://www.youtube.com/watch?v=7xofzeD7tlI.

TVNZ (2020), 'Dr Ashley Bloomfield responds humbly to news of petition for him to be New Zealander of the Year', 12 April.

University of Otago (2020), 'Otago experts deemed "critic and conscience" of society' [media release], *New Zealand Doctor*, 31 July, accessed at https://www.nzdoctor.co.nz/article/undoctored/otago-experts-deemed-critic-and-conscience-society.

Ward, T. (2020), 'All the weird and wonderful creative tributes to Dr Ashley Bloomfield', *The Spinoff*, 22 May, accessed at https://thespinoff.co.nz/money/22-05-2020/all-the-weird-and-wonderful-creative-tributes-to-dr-ashley-bloomfield/.

Weber, M. ([1919] 1946), *From Max Weber*, translated by H.H. Gerth and C. Wright
   Mills (eds), New York: Free Press.
Weingart, P. (1999), 'Scientific expertise and political accountability: Paradoxes of
   science in politics', *Science and Public Policy*, **26** (3), 151–61.
Wilson, S. (2020), 'Pandemic leadership: Lessons from New Zealand's approach to
   Covid-19', *Leadership*, **16** (3), 279–93.

PART II

Functional and micro-level management
perspectives on Covid-19

5. From brain drain to brain gain: the impact of Covid-19 on talent management in New Zealand

Dana L. Ott and Snejina Michailova

1. INTRODUCTION

Since the global 'war for talent' was declared more than 20 years ago (Chambers et al., 1998), countries and companies have faced growing talent shortages and intensifying competition for talent. Before Covid-19, reports anticipated a talent crunch equating to US$8.5 trillion (Korn Ferry Institute, 2018) and estimated that globally 45 per cent of companies were unable to find the needed talent to drive their competitive advantages (ManpowerGroup, 2018). This has helped fuel practitioner interest and significant investment by companies in talent management (TM). TM involves carefully designed practices to systematically manage people as indispensable human capital that provides a high-value corporate asset to achieve/sustain competitive advantages (Michailova and Ott, 2019; Tarique and Schuler, 2010).

Business executives worldwide continue to be concerned about impending talent shortages and New Zealand (NZ) executives see the imminent talent gap as a significant threat to their business outlooks, stating that 'we are running out of the talent we need in NZ' (PwC, 2019, p. 20). Unlike those in many other countries, NZ executives need to compete for offshore talent due to local talent shortages. Historically, NZ has suffered from high brain drain levels where domestically educated and skilled citizens leave the country to emigrate to destinations worldwide. As NZ currently has the most powerful passport globally (Douglas, 2020b), this trend may continue. Predictions suggest that by 2030 there will be severe worries about the shortage of workers available in NZ (NZ Herald, 2020). However, the current crisis caused by the global Covid-19 pandemic has curtailed overseas travel and caused countries to close their borders and urge their citizens to return home.

For more than 20 years, the NZ government has been trying to attract its citizens back (Greive, 2020). The pandemic has achieved that: within only weeks,

NZ started experiencing a brain gain as talented citizens embarked on repatriating. The scale is substantial as 600 000 to 1 million New Zealanders live overseas (Leahy, 2020). Many are still returning. Also, many highly skilled New Zealanders, who would typically leave the country, are either deciding to stay or are unable to emigrate due to other countries' border closures/restrictions. Furthermore, given the country's response to the Covid-19 pandemic, talented citizens of other countries are also attempting to immigrate to NZ. All this has changed NZ's persistent brain drain into valuable brain gain.

2.   TM IN NEW ZEALAND

TM focuses on key positions within organizations and on managing the flow of talent into them through the use of talent pools (Collings and Mellahi, 2009); it supports workforce differentiation and recommends that organizations disproportionately invest resources into their high-performing and high-potential talents as they are expected to bring greater returns for the organization. This approach focuses on pivotal positions, high potential and high performance.

TM practices include attracting, developing and retaining valued employees (Stahl et al., 2012). Talent attraction supplies the organization with the necessary skills to meet its strategic objectives (Collings and Mellahi, 2009). It is crucial when talent is in short supply or if developing existing talent's skills is resource intensive (Meyers et al., 2013). Talent pipelines help expose high-potentials to differentiated/targeted development to prepare them to move into different roles when necessary (Valverde et al., 2013). Retaining talent addresses talent's needs to improve their organizational commitment and job satisfaction (Michailova and Ott, 2019).

TM at the country level (macro TM) focuses on what countries do to attract talent, develop their workforce and retain talent within their national borders. This includes programmes and activities designed and initiated to enhance both the quality and quantity of talent (Khilji and Schuler, 2017). For example, government policies can influence diaspora and cross-border talent flows by lowering immigration barriers and developing foreigner-friendly systems. Governments can also focus on retaining domestic talent to achieve brain gain, attracting back their qualified citizens who have emigrated and upskilling and growing future talent (Michailova and Ott, 2019). These talent-enhancing activities facilitate productivity, innovation and competitiveness among domestic firms and multinationals to benefit their countries' citizens, organizations, and societies (Khilji and Schuler, 2017).

The Global Talent Competitiveness Index (GTCI), launched in 2013, evaluates and ranks 132 countries across four input pillars (enable, attract, grow and retain) and two output pillars (technical/vocational skills and global knowledge skills) based on 70 indicators (INSEAD, 2020). Similarly, the

IMD World Talent Ranking (WTR) assesses 63 countries on three factors (investment and development, appeal and readiness) by studying 32 criteria to determine the extent to which the countries can attract, develop and retain highly skilled individuals (IMD, 2019). A country's talent competitiveness includes policies and practices that facilitate the attraction, development and empowerment of a country's human capital, contributing to productivity and prosperity (INSEAD, 2020). It indicates the quality of a country's talent pool and, as such, signifies which countries can anticipate experiencing long-term prosperity.

Small advanced economies, like NZ, rank consistently high in these talent competitiveness rankings. Switzerland tops both the GTCI (INSEAD, 2020) and WTR (IMD, 2019), followed by six and seven small advanced economies, respectively. The GTCI (INSEAD, 2020) notes that their high rankings result from talent growth and management being important priorities facilitated by open socioeconomic policies. The WTR (IMD, 2019) attributes these countries' success to aligning talent demand with domestic talent supply. The latter is made available through continuous investments into the workforce's educational development and opportunities beyond academic development. Small advanced economies tend to have higher GDP per capita, employment rates and wages, and lower income inequality but are also more dependent on internationalization and more vulnerable to external developments in global markets (Michailova and Ott, 2019).

In the 2020 GTCI, NZ ranks 16th overall. The country is fifth in attracting talent, ranks well in providing a conducive environment for enabling talent (the regulatory landscape of NZ ranks second best and both the market and business and labour landscapes are in the top 25), but needs to improve in retaining talent and developing vocational and technical skills. On the WTR (IMD, 2019), NZ ranks 17th overall mainly due to its ability to attract international students and highly skilled immigrants, its low pollution levels and growth of its labour force. It performs poorly within the readiness factor, particularly concerning the availability of skilled labour and its low percentage of science graduates.

Approximately 97 per cent of NZ firms are small or micro firms with between five and 19 workers or fewer than five employees, respectively (Ministry of Business, Innovation & Employment, 2017). As a result, there are not many organizations with formalized career progression into high-level positions for NZ's domestic talent (Hutchison and Boxall, 2014), which has historically caused NZ talent to seek opportunities abroad (Gilbert and Boxall, 2009). Particularly noticeable is the loss of Kiwi talent to Australia (BMI Research, 2017). NZ's brain drain has been happening since the 1980s and is often referred to as the 'Kiwi exodus'; it became severe in 2012 when the country experienced a negative net migration of nearly 40 000 New Zealanders

(Stats NZ, 2016). There is also a positive correlation between increases in earned qualification levels and the number of young, domestically trained graduates who emigrate from NZ (Ministry of Education, 2016). Although more recent data (pre Covid-19) showed a decrease in the Kiwi exodus trend, the country still loses domestically developed talent to other countries.

NZ utilizes selective immigration practices to attract talent in the highest demand to counter brain drain, leading to its immigrant population being among the highest skilled within the OECD (2017). Since many talented foreigners immigrate to NZ, the country is likely experiencing a 'brain exchange' rather than an actual 'brain drain' (Glass and Choy, 2001). While this can be beneficial, it also seems to have resulted in 'talent waste' due to the underutilization of talent's skills in many cases, partially resulting from prejudices, perceived threats to the career advancement of potential employers and low levels of cultural intelligence (Carr et al., 2005).

Another contributing factor to the waste of talent is the so-called talent mismatch – in NZ, there has been a widening gap between the skills demanded by local companies and those possessed by the workforce (HRD, 2018). The country also experiences skills and field-of-study mismatches where many of the skills developed among NZ's workforce are not used productively or the skills NZ organizations need are not being developed (OECD, 2017). This results in talented employees being overqualified for their jobs or employed outside their study/qualification field. This causes talent to experience significant wage penalties and NZ to have below-average productivity ratings (Nolan et al., 2018).

NZ also suffers from Kiwi repatriates' general dissatisfaction. Repatriation is a known issue for organizations worldwide; many repatriates leave their companies within the first year of their return (KPMG, 2017). The lack of opportunities available upon repatriation to NZ has become an acute problem. NZ companies have acknowledged the 'dilemma' of losing talent while repatriates find the experience 'rather unsatisfying' (Tahir, 2011, p. 17). Due to more opportunities being available elsewhere, many repatriates return to the country where they originally expatriated (Carr et al., 2005).

3.   THE INFLUENCE OF THE COVID-19 CRISIS ON NEW ZEALAND TM

A crisis is 'a low-probability, high-impact event across countries and regions that threatens the viability of the organisation and is characterised by ambiguity of cause, effect, and means of resolution' (Pearson and Clair, 1998, p. 66). Examples of crises include the Great Depression in 1929, the oil shock in 1973, the Asian financial crisis in 1997 and the 2008 global economic crisis. And, of course, the 2020 Covid-19 pandemic. A global crisis strikes organizations by surprise and exerts threats to existing structures, processes and practices; however, it also provides opportunities (Michailova and Ott, 2020).

3.1   What Has Changed/Is Changing as a Consequence of Covid-19?

NZ closed its borders at 11.59pm on 19 March 2020 to anyone who was not a citizen or permanent resident. As a result, the number of people crossing the NZ border for the 2020 June quarter was 78 400 compared to the 2019 June quarter that saw 3.14 million crossings (Stats NZ, 2020). Of the 21 100 arrivals to NZ, the majority were citizens; of those, half were returning from short-term international travel and more than 7000 were returning after living overseas for more than one year (Stats NZ, 2020). These individuals can be considered Kiwi repatriates; however, it still remains to be seen how many will stay in NZ long term or more than one year to be classified as migrants. Overall, and different from the past, there has been a net migration gain of NZ citizens over the last year ending in June 2020.

The return of thousands of New Zealanders is being referred to as a 'once-in-a-lifetime talent shock' and returnees are said to be 'bringing a burst of international experience, capital and entrepreneurship to a country that has regularly lamented its stocks of all three' (Greive, 2020, para. 7). Additionally, more than 29 000 non-citizens and non-residents had applied for special consideration to be allowed to enter the country as of 4 August 2020 (Leahy, 2020). The requirements for receiving such exemptions have been intentionally set high to only allow those with special high-level skills to enter NZ. Some see considerable opportunity, potential and benefits for the economy due to the skills and experience flowing into the country. Others are less optimistic; with the expectation of an oncoming recession they argue that increased unemployment is likely (Kirkness, 2020). Furthermore, skills mismatches are also likely if the skills of those entering do not match those that are needed (Greive, 2020).

Given there is little precedence to rely on to determine what will result from these changes to the NZ TM terrain, we have sought two practitioners' informed views. Both of them work in executive positions and have deep insights into the TM arena. Executive 1 works with companies and management teams; Executive 2 works with companies sourcing talent from outside NZ, with expatriates and repatriates. We reproduce their views in the boxes below and note that the views are theirs and not necessarily their companies'. We began by inquiring about what has changed and/or is changing within the NZ expatriate and repatriate community as a consequence of Covid-19.

BOX 5.1   EXECUTIVE 1

Traditionally many NZ organizations have been reliant on sourcing over-seas talent to fill specific gaps. In 2019 NZ CEOs had indicated that their expected headcount growth over the next three years was substantially be-hind that of the country's closest trading partners. Just 2 per cent of NZ CEOs expected greater than 5 per cent growth compared to 36 per cent globally. NZ organizations were at risk of falling behind in the 'war for talent'; they were less prepared in terms of talent depth and pipeline.

With the unexpected Covid-19 crunch on internationally sourced tal-ent now having an effect, the talent risk has leapt upon NZ CEOs' list of key risks to become the second greatest perceived threat to organizational growth, only behind cyber risk.

Covid-19 and the consequential closing of NZ's borders have had a sig-nificant impact on the ability of NZ businesses that require 'boots on the ground' to continue operations. Access to critical talent is hamstringing or-ganizations' abilities to deliver on projects and keep going. This is particu-larly the case where required skills are held by very few globally, but border restrictions make it near impossible for those individuals to get here.

BOX 5.2   EXECUTIVE 2

It is now extremely difficult to get expatriate talent across the border. Conversely, repatriate talent can flow into NZ easily and we have seen the most significant influx of returning Kiwis since March 2020. Unfortunately, there is not necessarily a skills match between returning Kiwis and busi-nesses who can't source talent locally. Professional services, central/local government and some sectors such as construction are not facing a signifi-cant downturn in business, so the demand for expatriate talent to meet skill shortages is still there; skill shortages are evident and will only worsen.

Expatriates face high levels of anxiety/stress around the inability to fly, which means in-person visits with family back home can't take place, and there are worries about family illness and being unable to support them. Social dislocation due to remote working and lockdowns has also been harder for expatriates without deep connections to the NZ community.

The next 12 months will be crucial. The NZ government and businesses have a significant opportunity to leverage off our relatively Covid-19-free status to attract international talent on our own terms. We can only har-ness this opportunity if we can provide trustworthy and effective policies and processes to get safely to NZ the people who will fuel our economic recovery.

3.2   From a Global to a Domestic War for Talent?

It is easy to imagine that under the conditions of the Covid-19 crisis the global war for talent became a local one almost overnight, but is that the case? Some recent evidence from a CEO Outlook pulse-check by KPMG (2020) seems to indicate that as the supply of international talent (particularly those with specific and rare skill sets) into NZ continues to be cut off, demand in the domestic market will experience tension and significant challenges in sourcing necessary talent. This concern for access to international talent was also on the minds of the executives we queried.

BOX 5.3   EXECUTIVE 1

To bring talent into the country under existing border restrictions, many organizations are seeking to obtain entry exemptions in the 'critical worker' category. Around 36 000 exemption requests have been submitted to Immigration NZ to date [September 2020], with only around 7000 of those approved to travel. Under the humanitarian exemption category alone there is reportedly an 80 per cent decline rate. Requests for individuals whose skills cannot be readily obtained in NZ are also likely to be declined due to the assessment's subjective nature.

Accordingly, recruitment teams must be more creative in terms of where they are sourcing and finding talent. With the offshore market closing, this means the competition for local talent intensifies as NZ employers now have the opportunity to tap into the returning talent pool, and benefit from repatriates who have international experience and more specialized expertise.

However, the tale of talent access has two sides. For NZ businesses that do not have the same need for in-person personnel, the talent pool has potentially widened significantly. In sourcing talent, NZ businesses may now set their sights offshore to global talent pools that are largely agnostic as to their employer's location. This is possible in the recent climate due to the broader acceptance of remote work and technological enhancements which facilitate and support engagement with team members, irrespective of location.

With remote work becoming accessible and acceptable, the geographic constraints which usually operate in an employment relationship no longer apply. Increasingly, we are seeing individuals operating from a completely different country and time zone to their employers.

The quotes above draw a complex picture and we will be seeing different forces coming into play in the TM terrain long into the future. As Executive 2 points out to us, some of their clients have been able to hire locally for positions that have historically been held by an expatriate. Besides, few external talents or expatriates left NZ when Covid-19 hit. The only exceptions they have seen are those related to selected tourism-related infrastructure projects that were cancelled (e.g., Auckland Airport extension). Therefore, while New Zealanders are returning home, it cannot be assumed that many jobs have been left vacant by fleeing expatriates for them to fill. This will lead to an interesting playground: there are, and will be, push–pull forces to localize while waiting for the borders to eventually open. Many organizations would be wise to focus on developing their internal talent pipelines in the interim, and wait until the opportunity is available to fill remaining positions.

3.3 Will Demands for High Pay when Coming Back to New Zealand Take a Back Seat (or No Seat)?

Not surprisingly, we have also started seeing changes in how both expatriates and companies perceive remuneration and its importance. It seems as though, at least in the short term, expatriates' negotiation power has been reduced, and companies are in a position to gain talent by negotiating differently than they did before the crisis (e.g., focusing on safety and lifestyle vs attractive pay packages). Of all the push and pull factors that have been encouraging New Zealanders to return, the strongest has been the positive perception of how the country has handled the pandemic. This has resulted in a widely shared view that, unlike in many other countries, it is possible to work and live normally in NZ (Greive, 2020). This has changed the monetary or career-oriented priorities of many talented individuals to a focus on lifestyle, security and safety.

BOX 5.4   EXECUTIVE 2

One of our clients, who has previously recruited professionals offshore, partly because their salary offering was not attractive to New Zealanders, has found New Zealanders are now more willing to consider their roles as they offer job security.

I know it is often an issue for returning Kiwis to experience remuneration challenges. Kiwis' motivation to return to NZ right now is either emotional or family driven, or because they have lost jobs overseas. So, they have to be flexible on remuneration.

The above reflections do not imply that NZ organizations can expect everyone to feel this way or always expect lifestyle to be a sufficient factor when specific skills are needed. Given NZ's remote location, external talent will need stronger pull factors than in the past to move away from family and friends as uncertainties around travel and border access persist.

BOX 5.5   EXECUTIVE 1

NZ businesses are now potentially competing against global businesses for the same people. And in this space, NZ market expectations for remuneration packages may not cut it on the global stage. This represents a potentially high additional cost to acquiring and maintaining talent, particularly if the attraction of the NZ lifestyle is no longer sufficient to offset lower remuneration.

As a consequence of fundamental changes in expectations around how talent engages with employers, the latter need to face the reality of remote working arrangements and be creative in ensuring ongoing connection and culture.

4.   LESSONS LEARNED FROM THE NEW ZEALAND STORY

'If any one country knows how to bounce back, it is us'.
NZ Prime Minister Jacinda Arden (Ranosa, 2020)

NZ, like many other countries, is still in a war for talent. Attracting, developing and retaining talented employees remains on the radar of companies and macro TM continues to matter to nations and governments. But several lessons can be learned from the NZ story. Here we focus on two that can be useful to other countries and companies as they continue to deal with the Covid-19 crisis.

The first key lesson is the recognition that what has been so effective in getting NZ to where it is during the Covid-19 pandemic is its culture. From the beginning, the country has been a 'team of 5 million' and have reminded each other how important it is to '*kia kaha*' (be strong). Many companies will now also benefit from this sense of nationwide unity and use this opportunity to future-proof by refocusing on developing their culture (Douglas, 2020a). Although ensuring a cohesive and robust organizational culture may have taken a back seat in recent years, its importance has intensified and organizations will need to refocus on it.

Part of that culture includes an increased level of trust. NZ demonstrated its trust in the country's leadership during the most severe Covid-19 crisis when it followed directives and stamped out the virus (Albeck-Ripka, 2020). Equally, employees demonstrated their trustworthiness to their organizations. In a recent survey of New Zealanders' remote working experiences, many respondents noted that they had proven their trustworthiness during the Covid-19 lockdown and are now asking their organizations to trust them more in return (O'Kane et al., 2020). In some cases, this trust will need to include greater autonomy by providing talent more control over how they do their jobs and more decision-making discretion and power. This is closely related to what Jindal and Boxall (Chapter 8 in this volume) discuss regarding job craft-ing or aligning employees' work with their needs to strengthen identity and meaning and ascertain better fit. As they conclude, trust is key in determining whether employees craft their jobs.

Another aspect of the culture of any organization and, very much related to increased trust, is the need to focus on providing flexibility. In many cases this flexibility relates to a new and continued acceptance of remote working as a norm or, at the very least, as an option for most. Before Covid-19, approxi-mately half of NZ employees reported having at least flexible work hours and, as the level of flexibility increased, so did their levels of satisfaction with their jobs and work–life balance (Stats NZ, 2019). More recent reports (Emmett et al., 2020) found that remote work results in greater engagement and well-being for employees than when there is little flexibility to work from home. While not everyone wants to work remotely, offering the flexibility to do so is critical.

The second lesson that the Covid-19 pandemic is continuing to teach NZ, which will be useful for other countries, is the importance of the interface between the macro- and meso-level TM. Essentially, there must be cooper-ation and intensive communication between the government and businesses – both in general, but particularly in crisis times.

Before the Covid-19 crisis, Michailova and Ott (2019, p. 52) argued that 'in order to fully appreciate and understand the level of complexity associated with managing talent in the current global business environment, a macro-level view of TM is necessary'. Macro factors include those that cannot be con-trolled by or are external to organizations, but which nonetheless influence their strategic decision making and other aspects – and, right now, Covid-19 is a significant one. Working together to ensure businesses' needs are met and the right supply of talent is available must be a priority for governments. As NZ continues to determine what policies will be most effective for its recovery, the government must gain insights from local organizations and ensure critical talent pathways to enter the country safely become available. And when the country has attracted the needed talent, it should do everything possible to develop and retain it. After all, it is likely that the next big crisis is just around the corner.

REFERENCES

Albeck-Ripka, L. (2020), 'New Zealand stamps out the virus. For a second time', *The New York Times*, 7 October, accessed 9 November 2020 at https://www.nytimes.com/2020/10/07/world/australia/new-zealand-coronavirus.html

BMI Research (2017), *New Zealand Country Risk Report – Q3 2017*, London: Business Monitor International, accessed 2 August 2017 at https://search.proquest.com/docview/1911884175

Carr, S.C., K. Inkson and K. Thorn (2005), 'From global careers to talent flow: Reinterpreting "brain drain"', *Journal of World Business*, **40** (4), 386–98.

Chambers, E.G., M. Foulon, H. Handfield-Jones, S.M. Hankin and E.G. Michaels III (1998), 'The war for talent', *The McKinsey Quarterly*, **3**, 44–57.

Collings, D.G. and K. Mellahi (2009), 'Strategic talent management: A review and research agenda', *Human Resource Management Review*, **19** (4), 304–13.

Douglas, E. (2020a), 'Culture is the key to surviving COVID cuts', *Human Resource Director New Zealand*, 25 August, accessed 27 August 2020 at https://www.hcamag.com/nz/news/general/culture-is-key-to-surviving-covid-cuts/231676

Douglas, E. (2020b), 'New Zealand has the world's most powerful passport', *Human Resource Director New Zealand*, 6 October, accessed 8 October 2020 at https://www.hcamag.com/nz/specialisation/learning-development/new-zealand-has-the-worlds-most-powerful-passport/235320

Emmett, J., G. Schrah, M. Schrimper and A. Wood (2020), 'COVID-19 and the employee experience: How leaders can seize the moment', accessed 9 November 2020 at https://www.mckinsey.com/business-functions/organization/our-insights/covid-19-and-the-employee-experience-how-leaders-can-seize-the-moment

Gilbert, J. and P. Boxall (2009), 'The management of managers: Challenges in a small economy', *Journal of European Industrial Training*, **33** (4), 323–40.

Glass, H. and W.K. Cho (2001), *Brain Drain or Brain Exchange?*, New Zealand Treasury Working Paper 01/22, Wellington: The Treasury.

Greive, D. (2020), 'The "staggering" potential of New Zealand's returning diaspora', *NZ Herald*, accessed 19 October 2020 at www.nzherald.co.nz.

INSEAD (2020), Global talent competitiveness index 2020: Global talent in the age of artificial intelligence. Fontainebleau, France: INSEAD.

HRD (2018), 'This is why New Zealand has a "talent mismatch"', *Human Resource Director New Zealand*, 26 September, accessed 18 October 2018 at https://www.hcamag.com/nz/news/general/this-is-why-new-zealand-has-a-talent-mismatch/153406

Hutchison, A. and P. Boxall (2014), 'The critical challenges facing New Zealand's chief executives: Implications for management skills', *Asia Pacific Journal of Human Resources*, **52** (1), 23–41.

IMD (2019), *IMD World Talent Ranking 2019*, accessed 25 August 2020 at https://www.imd.org/research-knowledge/reports/imd-world-talent-ranking-2019/

Khilji, S.E. and R. Schuler (2017), 'Talent management in the global context', in D. Collings, K. Mellahi and W. Cascio (eds), *Oxford Handbook of Talent Management*, Oxford: Oxford Press, pp. 399–419.

Kirkness, L. (2020), 'The brain gain: How returning Kiwis will boost the economy', *NZ Herald*, accessed 21 August 2020 at www.nzherald.co.nz

Korn Ferry Institute (2018), *Future of Work: The Global Talent Crunch*, accessed 8 October 2020 at https://www.kornferry.com/challenges/future-of-work

KPMG (2017), 'HR transformation: Which lens are you using?', accessed 11 November 2017 at https://home.kpmg.com/nz

KPMG (2020), 'Talent risk one of the biggest threats to growth', accessed 15 September 2020 at https://home.kpmg.com/nz

Leahy, B. (2020), 'Twins' letters to Prime Minister Jacinda Ardern: Please let our dad in the country', *NZ Herald*, accessed 21 August 2020 at www.nzherald.co.nz

ManpowerGroup (2018), 'Solving the talent shortage: Build, buy, borrow and bridge', accessed 27 November 2018 at https://go.manpowergroup.com/talent-shortage-2018

Meyers, M.C., M. van Woerkom and N. Dries (2013), 'Talent – innate or acquired? Theoretical considerations and their implications for talent management', *Human Resource Management Review*, **23**, 305–21.

Michailova, S. and D.L. Ott (2019), *Talent Management in Small Advanced Economies*, Bingley, UK: Emerald. doi:10.1108/978-1-78973-449-220191001

Michailova, S. and D.L. Ott (2020), Why the time is ripe to think about talent management, *Human Resources Director New Zealand*, 30 May, accessed 10 June 2020 at https://www.hcamag.com/nz/specialisation/employee-engagement/why-the-time-is -ripe-to-think-about-talent-management/223781

Ministry of Business, Innovation & Employment (2017), 'Small businesses in New Zealand: How do they compare with larger firms?', accessed 6 August 2017 at https://www.mbie.govt.nz/assets/30e852cf56/small-business-factsheet-2017.pdf

Ministry of Education (2016), *Young, Domestic Graduate Outcomes – Destinations*, accessed 10 November 2017 at www.educationcounts.govt.nz/publications

Nolan, P., H. Fraser and P. Conway (2018), 'Moving on from New Zealand's productivity paradox', *Policy Quarterly*, **14** (3), 3–9.

NZ Herald (2020), 'Paul Spoonley book: How New Zealand families have changed', accessed 14 October 2020 at www.nzherald.co.nz

O'Kane, P., S. Walton and D. Ruwhiu (2020), *Remote Working During COVID19. New Zealand National Survey: Initial Report July 2020*, Dunedin, New Zealand: Department of Management, University of Otago.

OECD (2017). *OECD Economic Surveys: New Zealand 2017*, accessed 21 November 2018 at http://dx.doi.org/10.1787/eco_surveys-nzl-2017-en

Pearson, C.M. and J.A. Clair (1998), 'Reframing crisis management', *Academy of Management Review*, **23**, 59–76.

PwC (2019), *Storm Clouds and Silver Linings: What's the Outlook for New Zealand CEOs?*, accessed 11 June 2020 at www.pwc.co.nz/ceosurvey

Ranosa, R. (2020), 'Jacinda Ardern: "2020 has been frankly terrible"', *Human Resource Director New Zealand*, 27 August, accessed 27 August 2020 at https://www.hcamag .com/nz/news/general/jacinda-ardern-2020-has-been-frankly-terrible/231859

Stahl, G.K., I. Björkman, E. Farndale, S.S. Morris, J. Paauwe, P. Stiles, J. Trevor and P.M. Wright (2012), 'Six principles of effective global talent management', *MIT Sloan Management Review*, **53** (2), 24–32.

Stats NZ (2016), 'Kiwi exodus to Australia bungees back', accessed 11 August 2017 at http://archive.stats.govt.nz/browse_for_stats/population/Migration/international -travel-and-migration-articles/kiwi-exodus-australia.aspx

Stats NZ (2019), 'Survey of working life: 2018', accessed 9 November 2020 at https:// www.stats.govt.nz/reports/survey-of-working-life-2018

Stats NZ (2020), 'International travel and migration patterns shift due to COVID-19 pandemic', accessed 21 August 2020 at https://www.stats.govt.nz/news/international -travel-and-migration-patterns-shift-due-to-covid-19-pandemic

Tahir, R. (2011), 'The forgotten employees? Dealing with the repatriation dilemma in New Zealand companies', *New Zealand Journal of Human Resource Management*, **11** (1), 17–27.

Tarique, I. and R.S. Schuler (2010), 'Global talent management: Literature review, integrative framework, and suggestions for further research', *Journal of World Business*, **45** (2), 122–33.

Valverde, M., H. Scullion and G. Ryan (2013), 'Talent management in Spanish medium-sized organisations', *International Journal of Human Resource Management*, **24** (9), 1832–52.

6. Exporting from a remote, open economy during Covid-19: challenges and opportunities for SMEs

Antje Fiedler, Benjamin Fath, Noemi Sinkovics and Rudolf R. Sinkovics

1. INTRODUCTION

This chapter investigates the challenges and opportunities exporting small and medium-sized enterprises (SMEs) encountered during the Covid-19 pandemic in New Zealand (NZ) – a small, open and remote economy. Given the home market's limited size, most exporting SMEs start to engage in some form of internationalization early in their business lifecycle, when slack resources are few (cf. Coviello and Munro, 1997). In the case of NZ SMEs, this tends to take the form of exporting, which is further complicated by what New Zealanders and Australians call the 'tyranny of distance' that manifests as large geographic distance to markets. While committed to free trade, NZ is physically remote from all major trading partners except its neighbour, Australia, a 'mere' 4000 km away. Thus, distance significantly pervades the country's trade history. In general, much of international trade is regional (Rugman and Verbeke, 2004) as businesses tend to initially leverage the advantages of their home region including existing integration, shorter transportation and familiarity with customer preferences. However, remoteness and insularity limit such opportunities for NZ. Therefore, focusing on NZ exporting SMEs provides a unique context from which to derive lessons on how distance can be overcome when traditional means of bridging distance such as colocation, even if temporary, are severely limited.

We draw on data we collected during 30 virtual meetings and webinars offered by two main support organizations for NZ small exporters between 30 March and 1 August 2020, and responses to these. Recordings and our own notes provided snapshots of crisis management and underpinning practitioner and policy debates with respect to engagement with far-off markets during the Covid-19 crisis.

2.   KEY CHARACTERISTICS OF THE NZ EXPORT SETTING PRE-COVID-19

SMEs face a number of export barriers shaped by individual, firm-level and contextual factors. Owner–managers' personal characteristics may influence how critical barriers are assessed. For example, an owner–manager's lack of vision, fear of failure or losing control can represent a significant obstacle (Hutchinson et al., 2009). Further, more entrepreneurially oriented owner–managers are not only more likely to achieve a higher export performance; they are also more likely to use the Internet and other information and communication technologies (ICT) to enable their international operations (cf. Mostafa et al., 2005; Sinkovics et al., 2013). At firm level, resource scarcity (Hennart et al., 2019) and limited market knowledge (Fletcher and Harris, 2012; Shaw and Darroch, 2004) can significantly obstruct SMEs' internationalization. Contextual factors shaping barriers to internationalization include weak financial resources or weak government support at home (Kahiya, 2013), and high uncertainty in the host country such as volatile competitive dynamics (Suarez-Ortega, 2003) or political instability (Kaynak et al., 1987).

However, the remoteness of NZ from the rest of the world, and the government's efforts to promote trade and international expansion, create a unique environment that in turn shapes the opportunities and barriers to internationalization. Kahiya (2020) identifies several ways in which this specific context produced distinctive SME behaviours that contrasted with expectations from other contexts. This small, open, developed economy of about 5 million inhabitants strives to provide a business-friendly environment by freeing up internal markets, privatizing and supporting trade liberalization (Ministry of Foreign Affairs and Trade, 2020). To grow, SMEs must internationalize early, given the small size of the domestic market. Remoteness from major markets has been a significant driver of increasing governmental innovation and export support policies (de Serres et al., 2014) to help SMEs internationalize (Battisti et al., 2014; Simmons, 2004). Yet, despite such efforts, labour productivity and the global connectedness of manufacturing and services have stayed behind those of other OECD members, resulting in a discrepancy between the policy progressiveness of the country and business performance. This NZ 'productivity paradox' appears to be partially due to the penalty of distance from major markets (OECD, 2013).

Whereas this penalty is reduced for highly standardized goods due to lower transportation costs, it increases in the context of high-value-added exports. This is because both goods and services in this category often demand local market knowledge, integration into global value chains and advanced customization and customer service (McCann, 2009). Since distance to markets hinders business models based on close customer relations, collaborative value creation and idea exchanges, policymakers are seeking to achieve a better understanding of how distance affects the innovation–exporting relationship (Fiedler et al., 2021).

New Zealand Trade and Enterprise (NZTE), the NZ government's international business development agency, plays an important role in government export promotion. About half of its 600 staff are located in about 40 international locations. NZTE also consolidates complementary capabilities from other government agencies, the private sector and New Zealanders living overseas, through the Kiwi Expats Association (KEA) network – a backronym named for a popular, mischievous native parrot – now Kea New Zealand. Support focuses on 700 exporters, large and small, with 11 000 smaller exporting companies receiving fewer comprehensive services. 'Focus 700' companies mainly represent manufacturing, food and beverages (F&B) and technology, and this portfolio grew by 3.6 per cent above NZ's export benchmark in 2018/19 (NZTE, 2019).

NZ's export profile has stayed focused on primary products, headed by F&B – especially dairy – and logs. More elaborately transformed products have lagged behind OECD standards. However, there is a noteworthy transition that occurred pre-Covid-19. Since the early 2000s, many exporters have reoriented towards emerging Asia, especially China (trade almost tripled over 2006–16) but also increasingly Southeast Asia. Thus the composition of export markets, if not exports, has changed considerably, as Figure 6.1 shows for merchandise.

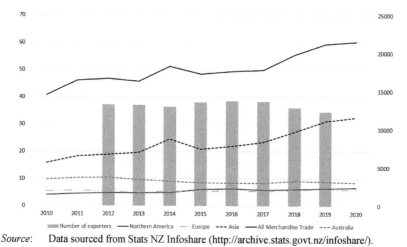

Source: Data sourced from Stats NZ Infoshare (http://archive.stats.govt.nz/infoshare/).

Figure 6.1   *New Zealand merchandise trade (in billion NZD) by region and number of exporting firms*

Table 6.1   *Ranking of ten most common perceived barriers to growing internationally*

	Potential exporters		Exporters	
	Interested in exploring new markets	Actively exploring new markets	Actively exploring new markets	Initiatives underway
Limited experience in expanding beyond New Zealand	1	1	6	6
Limited knowledge about specific markets	2	2	7	5
Limited access to finance for expansion beyond New Zealand	3	3	9	8
Limited access to distribution networks	5	4	5	10
Exchange rate volatility	4	7	1	1
Exchange rate level	7	10	2	2
Distance from markets	6	6	4	3
Language and cultural differences	10	5	10	7
Low demand or increased competition in overseas markets	8	9	3	4
Overseas government regulations or tariffs	9	8	8	9

Note: 1 = most important; 10 = least important barrier.
Source: Business Operations Survey. Data sourced from: Sanderson (2016).

This transition leads to many NZ SMEs engaging more with both geographically and psychically distant, non-traditional export markets. Psychic distance, a multidimensional construct, includes culture, language, religion, education and political systems (Dow and Karunaratna, 2006). However, although the increasing government support to facilitate trade with Asia has opened up opportunities to grow exports, many SMEs are distinctly challenged by their lack of language capabilities or experiential market knowledge (Fiedler et al., 2021).

Further, as Table 6.1 shows, potential exporters and active exporters perceive export barriers very differently. Potential exporters are held back largely by a general unfamiliarity with export markets, citing as their top three barriers their 'limited experience in expanding beyond NZ', 'limited knowledge about specific markets' and 'limited access to finance for expansion beyond New Zealand'. In contrast, active exporters aspiring to expand their export markets further rank such reasons much lower (around fifth to ninth out of ten) and worry more about in-market demand, exchange rates and distance to markets (Sanderson, 2016).

This observation implies that, in the NZ context, a lack of aspiration to export is less of a barrier than an adequate understanding of the implications of distance. This explains the increasing importance of trade shows as a significant stimulus for exporting and as a means to reduce some of the distance-based barriers to internationalization (Gerschewski et al., 2020; Kahiya, 2020).

3.   EXPORT CHALLENGES AND OPPORTUNITIES DURING A PANDEMIC

To derive insights into the challenges and opportunities SME exporters have faced during the Covid-19-induced crisis, we draw on observational data from 30 virtual exporter meetings and webinars between 30 March and 1 August 2020. The meetings were organized by two NZ export support organizations to help exporters reshape export strategies. Specifically, one author attended six such meetings targeting exporters from key sectors, between 11 May and 22 July. Industry sectors included health and beauty, creative services, manufacturing and high tech, F&B and ICT. The author took notes. We also draw on data from 24 publicly available export recovery webinars delivered by an NZTE channel partner between 27 March and 1 August 2020. Webinars and meetings both mainly targeted exporters outside Focus 700. Speakers included managers of large businesses, owner-managers of SMEs and industry experts, among them private business consultants with expertise in exporting and government officials in trade service roles. The export recovery webinar series was supported by Kea New Zealand and the Ministry of Foreign Affairs and Trade.

3.1   Triaging Challenges: Cash Flow Management, Inventory Management and Country Diversification

The main theme of early webinars and virtual meetings was how to ensure business survival. Cash flow and risk management were the most frequently discussed topics. Export market dynamics changed rapidly, and experts advised exporting SMEs to strengthen their cash position to ensure a positive future flow. These webinars frequently drew on examples of SMEs and larger businesses, which operate in, or depend on, the tourism and entertainment sector. The international business of these firms plummeted by more than 90 per cent within weeks. One owner–manager explained: 'before the pandemic, we planned to win, now we plan not to lose' – a radical shift, from focusing on growth to risk management. Exporters were advised to envisage multiple scenarios, plan for contingencies and understand shifting realities in their main markets. Cash flow management received much less attention in later meetings. Among strategies to keep a positive cash flow were actively managing payment risk in international markets; renegotiating payment terms with international partners; agreeing short-term expenses relief with local banks and property owners, including payment holidays and rent reduction; and seeking financial help from shareholders. Some less hard-hit business partners extended payment terms for SMEs, or discounted their services. Meanwhile, businesses were also encouraged to scrutinize the sustainability of their business model and ask what reconfigurations might be necessary going forward.

Another theme commonly shared early on was inventory and supply chain management. Notably, supply chains were not broken but severely disrupted, as airfreight collapsed by more than 90 per cent. In general, various industries suffered delays getting products into channels. However, exporters were informed that international markets recognized the difficulty, creating opportunities to renegotiate pricing and supply terms. Communication with key business partners was critical to navigating disrupted supply chains. As the challenges of Covid-19 were widely understood globally, business partners frequently offered concessions such as accepting delayed delivery.

Expert speakers also recommended that exporters consider country diversification to reduce risk. In particular, they should consider entering new markets that seemed less affected by the pandemic. During earlier webinars, greater optimism still prevailed about North America, specifically for ecommerce opportunities. Experts, however, warned that the US is a sophisticated market, often requiring a dual-channel strategy; and that Covid-19 conditions demanded innovative solutions like click and collect delivery models and packaging innovation, such as switching to single or multiple packs. Later, the optimism shifted to Asian markets, particularly China and Japan, which showed signs of a better economic recovery. Overall, initial meetings and webinars encouraged exporters to entertain new, less impacted export markets and thus reduce risk by diversifying their export markets.

3.2   Creating New Opportunities and Building Online Capacity

The impact of Covid-19 fell unevenly across industries, and across different countries. Some owner–managers in F&B reported their industry being relatively unscathed; while sectors like tourism and international education suffered severely from the lockdown. However, adjusting to the 'new normal' typically required reshaping business models, even for the more lightly affected, and during meetings SME owner–managers from various industries described adapting their businesses model to create new opportunities.

First, we record adaptations on the employee side. Owner–managers explained how changing their communication methods with employees enabled working from home. Further, continual communication gave vital certainty, assurance and transparency and maintained engagement. For instance, an owner–manager explained how daily meetings via Microsoft Teams, which offers workplace chat and videoconferencing, set clear goals and expectations, helped to share information about international market updates and even facilitated some social activities, such as virtual Friday drinks and quiz nights. Continuity with, and support from, existing employees were in turn often critical to owner–managers in export industries that needed to reconfigure their business model. Noteworthy examples included shifts from entertainment to furniture and from tourism to residential aged care in their international markets. Participants highlighted that some employees had crucial skills, like design, that could be leveraged to create new products and carry out innovations allowing the firm to stay better connected to their customers or business partners overseas.

Second, we noted adaptations on the customer side. More frequent communication was needed to maintain customer relationships in overseas markets, while some owner–managers described concentrating on retaining high-risk customers to reduce churn such as offering 'service breaks' (voluntary suspensions) or improved services. For example, an owner–manager explained that some of their international customers were severely affected by the pandemic. When these customers cancelled their subscription for the service offering, he quickly decided to offer free-of-charge suspensions of their contracts hoping to maintain these customers in the longer term.

Later into the lockdown, the dominant theme became the shift toward online channels and virtual communication to reach consumers in distant markets. Lockdowns in different markets lifted online sales everywhere and during very early meetings, exporters had already been advised to either develop or strengthen their online sales channels and digital channels and presence in overseas markets. At that early stage, discussions centred on raising awareness and an appreciation of urgency around embracing online channels for the international strategy among exporters reliant on bricks-and-mortar sales through distribution partners. Engaging with online channels seemed to yield business continuity as well as valuable end-customer data on evolving needs as the crisis unfolded. An associated point was often mentioned: digital platforms were an important line of communication with existing in-market partners for updates on market developments and trends across export sectors like F&B, high-tech manufacturing and ICT.

The advice on developing a digital strategy grew more nuanced over time. It included how to reshape elements of the business model to fit a post-Covid-19 market environment. Further, the need to supply digital content for both consumers and business partners in distant markets and to run live streaming or other live events to reach international customers was discussed. For example, an owner–manager explained how their business-to-business SME pivoted its service model. They developed an app that helped business customers connect and communicate better with their clients during lockdown restrictions in India by enabling them to share digital content. Meanwhile, as traditional trade shows migrated online, exporters had to nimbly put more relevant content online themselves to attract potential partners. Face-to-face product demonstration moved to Zoom, and exporters shared advice on how to do this effectively. For instance, a winemaker described the feat of online wine tastings in one of their key overseas markets, and a creative company recounted posting educational videos to teach international partners about their innovative products. Overall, the main theme was the necessity to advance the digitalization of firms' business models on multiple fronts such as channels, key activities and customer relationships.

3.3   Falling Back on Strength

As virtual meetings continued, two themes emerged more strongly: collaboration, including with NZ government partners, and the relevance of NZ's Covid-19 story for distant consumers. First, whereas collaboration had been a constant theme, the importance of collaborating specifically with government agencies like NZTE came increasingly to the fore. Many speakers highlighted the value of in-market support by government agencies, especially when in-person visits ceased due to restrictions. NZTE supported its members by mobilizing their staff in the respective host countries. These representatives undertook client visits on behalf of the NZ SMEs to help maintain business relationships. Further, Kea NZ members residing in export markets were also mobilized and helped by sharing in-market information and research. These expats were contactable via Kea NZ.

Second, later meetings stressed the value of NZ's own Covid-19 success story and its impact on the country's brand and by extension on customers' trust in NZ's products. Experienced exporters and industry experts reported that Covid-19 has strengthened the national brand in international markets. Accolades for the government's pandemic management and long periods of near-zero community transmission have strengthened existing consumer trust in certain sectors such as F&B. One owner–manager shared that their Chinese consumers refer to NZ as 'Earth's last paradise'. Further, the pandemic-driven increase in the use of digital technologies on both the business and consumer side have enabled NZ SMEs to share video content online that features both their own and NZ's stories, thus further leveraging NZ's reputation to build and maintain trust.

4. LESSONS FOR ENGAGING WITH DISTANT MARKETS FROM THE PERIPHERY

Overcoming the various facets of distance (cf. Cano-Kollmann et al., 2016; Törnroos et al., 2017) in global trade is critical for exporting SMEs, in particular for those operating from remote locations. Sinkovics et al. (2019) demonstrate that in adverse political environments firms can improve their chances of survival by taking distinct, digital technology-enabled strategic action to improve connectivity with their business partners. In contrast to Sinkovics et al.'s (2019) study, in our context the restrictions to movement within and across country borders did not stem from political disturbance and an ensuing negative country image. The pandemic and the resulting lockdowns and social-distancing policies created an unprecedented drive toward digital interaction. Whereas pre-Covid digitalization and digital transformation efforts in SMEs were slowed by the preoccupation of owner–managers with operational issues at the detriment of strategic planning (Eller et al., 2020), the pandemic-imposed restrictions made digitalization and digital transformation an operational issue. As a result, the ability of NZ businesses to adopt digital technologies and digital transformation of parts of their business model became a matter of survival. Furthermore, some experts suggested that Asian markets, including China, might recover from Covid-19 faster than other markets, including the US. Future research could investigate whether the pandemic may have triggered shifts in the export market orientation of NZ businesses.

Following the evolution of export markets became even more difficult as, in the absence of colocation, the distance to market interacted with pandemic-destabilized market dynamics. Our study demonstrates that the uncertainties of Covid-19 have unsettled even seasoned exporters, despite continued high demand for many NZ export products. This has forced these exporters to go back to basics and become better market learners and experiment. Exporting SMEs have been encouraged to test their assumptions through multiple mechanisms, including seeking knowledge from network partners and engaging with overseas consumers through new digitally enabled means. Uncertainty coupled with distance has meant most businesses struggled to fully exploit their experiential market knowledge and existing networks.

International business scholars have long recognized that international networks are key to overcoming barriers to internationalization (Vahlne and Johanson, 2017). However, amidst Covid-19, building new network relationships from afar is challenging. Owner–managers must creatively leverage their existing networks and build relationships with accessible potential network partners. For market learning, some NZ exporting SMEs are exploiting government-supplied international networks more, particularly NZTE, reaching out to New Zealanders abroad through Kea NZ, or learning about export markets from migrants in NZ. Such entrepreneurial network strategies can help distant exporters adapt quickly to different and unpredictably changing markets in a world where frequent market visits are hard or impossible.

This yields clear implications for owner–managers of exporting SMEs and policy makers. Owner–managers are advised to keep their entrepreneurial spirit even in times of relative stability and not allow operational issues to distract from strategizing and experimentation. The strength of weak ties is even more important in crises. Investing in networks through business associations and other relevant memberships (cf. Kurt et al., 2020) can hedge against business failures in times when building new relationships is difficult or not possible. Whereas some SMEs were able to leverage the latent capabilities of their workforce to engage with new channels, not all SMEs have employees with the necessary skills. To this end, government support is needed to equip SMEs with the necessary skills and capabilities to successfully navigate digital channels in key markets, enabling them to maintain existing, and build new, relationships with distant customers and network partners.

REFERENCES

Battisti, M., T. Jurado and M. Perry (2014), 'Understanding small-firm reactions to free trade agreements: Qualitative evidence from New Zealand', *Journal of Small Business and Enterprise Development*, **21** (2), 327–44. doi: 10.1108/JSBED-10-2013-0151

Cano-Kollmann, M., J. Cantwell, T.J. Hannigan, R. Mudambi and J. Song (2016), 'Knowledge connectivity: An agenda for innovation research in international business', *Journal of International Business Studies*, **47** (3), 255–62. doi: 10.1057/jibs.2016.8

Coviello, N. and H. Munro (1997), 'Network relationships and the internationalization process of small software firms', *International Business Review*, **6** (4), 361–86. doi: 10.1016/S0969-5931(97)00010-3

de Serres, A., N. Yashiro and H. Boulhol (2014), 'An international perspective on the New Zealand productivity paradox', *New Zealand Productivity Commission Working Paper 2014*, **1**.

Dow, D. and A. Karunaratna (2006), 'Developing a multidimensional instrument to measure psychic distance stimuli', *Journal of International Business Studies*, **37** (5), 578–602. doi: 10.1057/palgrave.jibs.8400221

Eller, R., P. Alford, A. Kallmünzer and M. Peters (2020), 'Antecedents, consequences, and challenges of small and medium-sized enterprise digitalization', *Journal of Business Research*, **112**, 119–27. doi: 10.1016/j.jbusres.2020.03.004

Fiedler, A., B. Fath and D.H. Whittaker (2021), 'The dominant narrative of the New Zealand–China free trade agreement: Peripheral evidence, presumptive tilt and business realities', *New Political Economy*, **26** (3), 328–43. doi: 10.1080/13563467.2020.1755243

Fletcher, M. and S. Harris (2012), 'Knowledge acquisition for the internationalization of the smaller firm: Content and sources', *International Business Review*, **21** (4), 631–47.

Gerschewski, S., N. Evers, A.T. Nguyen and F.J. Froese (2020), 'Trade shows and SME internationalisation: Networking for performance', *Management International Review*, **60** (4), 573–95. doi: 10.1007/s11575-020-00421-y

Hennart, J.-F., A. Majocchi and E. Forlani (2019), 'The myth of the stay-at-home family firm: How family-managed SMEs can overcome their internationalization limitations', *Journal of International Business Studies*, **50** (5), 758–82. doi: 10.1057/s41267-017-0091-y

Hutchinson, K., E. Fleck and L. Lloyd-Reason (2009), 'An investigation into the initial barriers to internationalization: Evidence from small UK retailers', *Journal of Small Business and Enterprise Development*, **16** (4), 544–68.

Kahiya, E.T. (2013), 'Export barriers and path to internationalization: A comparison of conventional enterprises and international new ventures', *Journal of International Entrepreneurship*, **11** (1), 3–29. doi: 10.1007/s10843-013-0102-4

Kahiya, E.T. (2020), 'Context in international business: Entrepreneurial internationalization from a distant small open economy', *International Business Review*, **29** (1). doi: 10.1016/j.ibusrev.2019.101621

Kaynak, E., P.N. Ghauri and T. Olofsson-Bredenlow (1987), 'Export behavior of small Swedish firms', *Journal of Small Business Management*, **25** (2), 26–32.

Kurt, Y., N. Sinkovics, R.R. Sinkovics and M. Yamin (2020), 'The role of spirituality in Islamic business networks: The case of internationalizing Turkish SMEs', *Journal of World Business*, **55** (1), 101034. doi:10.1016/j.jwb.2019.101034

McCann, P. (2009), 'Economic geography, globalisation and New Zealand's productivity paradox', *New Zealand Economic Paper*, **43** (3), 279–314. doi: 10.1080/00779950903308794

Ministry of Foreign Affairs and Trade (2020), 'NZ trade policy – Why does New Zealand advocate free trade?', accessed 11 May 2020 at https://www.mfat.govt.nz/en/trade/nz-trade-policy

Mostafa, R.H., C. Wheeler and M.V. Jones (2005), 'Entrepreneurial orientation, commitment to the internet and export performance in small and medium sized exporting firms', *Journal of International Entrepreneurship*, **3** (4), 291–302.

New Zealand Trade & Enterprise (2019), *Annual Report 2018/2019*, Wellington, NZ: New Zealand Trade & Enterprise.

OECD (2013), *OECD Economic Surveys: New Zealand 2013*, Paris: OECD.

Rugman, A.M. and A. Verbeke (2004), 'A perspective on regional and global strategies of multinational enterprises', *Journal of International Business Studies*, **35** (1), 3–18. doi: 10.1057/palgrave.jibs.8400073

Sanderson, L. (2016), *Barriers to Generating International Income: Evidence from the Business Operations Survey*, Working Paper, Wellington, NZ: New Zealand Treasury.

Shaw, V. and J. Darroch (2004), 'Barriers to internationalisation: A study of entrepreneurial new ventures in New Zealand', *Journal of International Entrepreneurship*, **2** (4), 327–43. doi: 10.1007/s10843-004-0146-6

Simmons, G. (2004), 'The impact of scale and remoteness on New Zealand's industrial structure and firm performance', in J. Poot (ed.), *On the Edge of the Global Economy*, Cheltenham, UK and Northampton, MA, USA: Edward Elgar Publishing, pp. 123–43.

Sinkovics, N., R.R. Sinkovics and R.-J.B. Jean (2013), 'The internet as an alternative path to internationalization?', *International Marketing Review*, **30** (2), 130–55. doi: 10.1108/02651331311314556

Sinkovics, N., U.S. Choksy, R.R. Sinkovics and R. Mudambi (2019), 'Knowledge connectivity in an adverse context – Global value chains and Pakistani offshore service providers', *Management International Review*, **59** (1), 131–70. doi: 10.1007/s11575-018-0372-0

Suarez-Ortega, S. (2003), 'Export barriers: Insights from small and medium-sized firms', *International Small Business Journal*, **21** (4), 403–19. doi: 10.1177/02662426030214002

Törnroos, J.-Å., A. Halinen and C.J. Medlin (2017), 'Dimensions of space in business network research', *Industrial Marketing Management*, **61**, 10–19. doi: 10.1016/j.indmarman.2016.06.008

Vahlne, J.-E. and J. Johanson (2017), 'From internationalization to evolution: The Uppsala model at 40 years', *Journal of International Business Studies*, **48** (9), 1087–102. doi: 10.1057/s41267-017-0107-7

7. The lighter side of lockdown: laughter, psychological well-being and coping through crisis

Barbara Plester

Lockdown is a state of isolation where people are restricted as a measure to minimize risks or harm to people. It can constitute a 'stay-at-home' order such as much of the world has been subject to throughout 2020. This chapter argues that New Zealand workers invoked humour during lockdown to reconstruct their challenging situation as amusing by recognizing light-hearted elements. Sharing humorous stories of lockdown experiences offered these New Zealand workers the opportunity to reframe the impact of crisis in a light-hearted manner that relieved pressure caused by the crisis. Using humour to make light of a crisis situation is a coping strategy that enhances individual well-being, and sharing humour with coworkers fosters collegiality and is a supportive mechanism (Holmes, 2006). One person sharing an amusing story encourages colleagues to share similar anecdotes and achieve comparable well-being outcomes. Humour shared with colleagues improves coworker solidarity and has psychological benefits for all (Hay, 2000).

This chapter focuses on individual and group-level workplace behaviours, arguing that in crisis conditions humour can be a beneficial and appropriate mechanism for coping and enhancing individual psychological well-being (PWB). At the group level, humour is a valuable psychosocial phenomenon that is a conduit for sharing difficult times with colleagues and friends in a non-threatening manner. Using five short narratives from New Zealand workers, humour is positioned as a coping mechanism that alleviates pressures of working from home while coping with competing demands for resources, time and family needs.

1. PSYCHOLOGICAL WELL-BEING

PWB is the lens for examining coping mechanisms related to humour and is defined as the *absence* of mental disorders (such as anxiety and depression) and the *presence* of positive attributes such as: self-acceptance, positive personal relationships, autonomy, environmental mastery, purpose in life and personal growth (Ryff and Keyes, 1995). Eudaimonic well-being is an element of well-being that extends the definition of well-being 'beyond feeling good to include functioning well' (der Kinderen and Khapova, 2020, p. 1). PWB is particularly salient to key workplace functions and performance and is linked to success and health (Robertson and Cooper, 2011).

Crisis episodes are integral to our development and every crisis is both a development opportunity as well as a danger to PWB, as it can create mental disorder (Robinson and Smith, 2009). Suffering through a crisis carries the risk of mental deterioration but crisis experiences can be transformed into generative or positive outcomes (McAdams 2006; Robinson and Smith, 2009). In their four-phase process of crisis episodes, Robinson and Smith (2009) identify the feeling of being 'locked in' as the first phase of a transformation process that involves working through isolation and despair and reconstructing the self to reach an enlightening place of warmth, hope and well-being. Their findings were identified through autobiographical life stories from participants who had been through crises. A similar narrative approach is adopted in this chapter through analysing five New Zealand humorous crisis narratives.

2.   HUMOUR AS A RESPONSE TO CRISIS

Humour is multifaceted and includes cognitive, social, emotional and behavioural aspects (McCreaddie and Payne, 2014). Humour has many effects but in a crisis situation it can neutralize highly emotional events which assists PWB and social interaction (Ridanpää, 2019). It is well established in psychological literature that humour is a coping mechanism and can relieve stress, and Freud ([1905] 1991) found that humour offers relief and release from everyday tensions. Laughter is both psychological and physiological and the expulsion of air through the diaphragm can feel physically liberating while simultaneously offering psychological relief. Building on Freud's early work, psychologists have further established that a good sense of humour has positive effects that bolster self-esteem while lowering depression and anxiety levels (Lefcourt and Martin, [1986] 2012; Martin, 2007). While there are maladaptive elements of humour that are self-defeating and belaboured, these tend to focus on other people rather than the self and thus are not as strongly related to personal well-being (Kuiper et al., 2004). Maintaining a humorous perspective about life's experiences and throughout crisis helps to create stability that leads to resilience and PWB (Cann and Collette, 2014; Plester, 2009b)

Psychologist Rod Martin has spent his research career focusing on the relationship between humour, self-concept, well-being and coping with stress. He established that higher levels of humour foster a more positive self-concept and better levels of self-esteem and that this transfers to times when a person experiences extreme stress and negative life events (Martin et al., 1993). As well as reducing stress, humour enhances positive life experiences and alleviates anxiety and existential threat which can improve PWB. The narrative research approach used in this chapter helps to draw out significant aspects of emotional anxiety as well as coping mechanisms used by research participants.

3.   METHODOLOGICAL NOTES

We 'inhabit a narrative universe' where stories 'emerge', 'interact', 'compete' and 'sustain meaning' (Gabriel, 2018, p. 64). The plot of a story allows people to understand the significance and deeper meaning in events and we can experience emotions in stories that 'mould human experience and drive human action' (Gabriel, 2018, p. 65). Narrative methodology is increasingly common in management research and narratives are especially useful when individuals examine their work identity, have to reinvent themselves and significantly change their work process (Gabriel, 2018) – as was the case for the participants in this study.

It is accepted that narratives are ambiguous and display contradictions and dilemmas which make analysing them highly challenging. Gabriel (2018) claims that researchers must recognize that their values and experiences become embedded in narrative research, but that previous experience and sensitivity are also useful in the analysis process. According to Gabriel, the rewards, discoveries and illuminations revealed through analysing stories justifies the challenges of collecting, interpreting and analysing data in this way.

The data used in this chapter is elicited from a series of narratives that were spontaneously shared by work (university) colleagues during Zoom meetings held during lockdown conditions. In a snowball sampling technique (see Sharma, 2017) other participants were suggested and identified as having lockdown stories and the cache of narratives grew to include university colleagues and participants from other industries. The stories selected for inclusion in this chapter are representative of the wider collection of narratives but those selected clearly demonstrate key themes found in the analysis (see Table 7.1).

4.   NARRATIVES FROM A CRISIS

The following stories were shared with lightness, laughter and humour, but prior experiences in this field of research (see Gabriel, 2018) focused the researcher on some implicit underlying themes (see Table 7.1). This study considers new forms of work and new workspaces as an important contextual element for the sharing of fun and humour at, and about, work.

4.1   Snowing Feathers

Frankie's light-hearted story of feathers, children, pets and 'getting the giggles' opens the section in detailing the personal aspects of her life that are newly impacting her work meetings, creating novel issues that she frames as highly amusing:

> Preparing for my important Zoom meeting my small son arrives swathed in his bedding to talk to me in the doorway of my home office. As he talks, he removes the cover from his feather duvet and – surprise! The feather duvet inner has burst inside the cover and it is basically snowing (feathers) inside. I frantically clean up the mess all over the room and then turn to my Zoom meeting. As if the cloud of feathers wasn't enough my small dog interrupts my meeting persistently and the whole situation has me choking back 'church giggles' the whole way through my meeting. (Frankie)

Frankie highlights the humour in her own situation as she struggles to present a professional work image from her home office while dealing with the aftermath of a feather inundation and the incessant barking of her small dog. Seeing the funny side has her erupting into 'giggles' which relieves the pressure of managing home, family and work in extraordinary conditions. Sharing her story makes her colleagues smile in recognition while also expressing the difficulties created by her new work set-up. Giggling at the situation is positive and reframes her situation in a way that offers her relief and a coping mechanism beneficial to her PWB, and this relief is shared with colleagues.

4.2   Head-Banging Baby

Ciara shared this story with her academic department, and it illustrates the issues and tensions caused by trying to work effectively at home with a crawling baby demanding her attention. Her story has both humour and pathos as she describes her tiny daughter banging her head against the glass of her home office in a bid to get her attention. Ciara herself frames this as 'funny and cute' but also as 'scary'. She feels organizational pressure to 'get on with her job' regardless of her baby's needs, but her story shows that this is not easily done. In sharing this tension, she makes the story light and amusing for her colleagues who respond to the wry humour, but they can also perceive the very real pressure in this situation where work and home have become intrinsically blended.

> For me, it's the convenient silence on this, masked by a 'We got this team!' rhetoric and an underlying narrative that 'children are no excuse, get on with it!' A lot will slide for me over the forthcoming months – research and writing being two, as they require the headspace and focused thinking that my makeshift office does not allow.

I have set up for work in a small sunroom with glass doors. My crawling baby can see me working and having Zoom meetings, so when she wants my attention she crawls over, and head bangs the glass doors. It's cute and funny but also scary. (Ciara)

4.3   Invisible Students and Paper Planes

Adam shares a detailed, diary-like account of a working week in his home with him, his wife and their three children. He lightly recalls his son's questioning 'Where are the students?' as he competes for his dad's attention and seeks help in making 'a paper plane'. Although written in a light-hearted tone that recognizes the gentle humour, Adam also identifies his own anxiety and the importance of having a 'place' to work that mitigates competing demands for his attention. He wryly acknowledges the soothing qualities of drinking wine in a self-deprecating comment and concludes by minimizing his struggles as 'petty'.

I started to experience anxiety as my 8-year-old son came to show me his paper plane Monday morning. I wanted to give him my attention. Instead I told him: 'I'm teaching, and I have 129 students'. 'But where are they?' he asks.

So, he came back to show me another 'better plane' 10 minutes later. 'Oh, how interesting! How about you make those paper planes right here beside me while I work?' You can guess how productive I was.

By Wednesday, I hung signs on my little office door: 'RECORDING IN PROGRESS – PLEASE COME BACK IN 20 MINUTES'. Twenty minutes went by fast. On Thursday I dressed up in my collar shirt and work shoes to signal 'I'm working' to my 4 other wonderful family members. They didn't think that was strange.

By Friday morning, I announced to my family: 'I am working and unavailable until 5pm!' But so did my wife! We worked it out.

I'm amazed how much 'place' matters to routines. My family bliss was easier with campus, the local library and the Solar Café as my workplaces. I have struggled to separate these places under lockdown. The cues at home trigger happy times playing with kids, meals and rest – why would I want that to change? I felt anxiety as I switch between militantly scheduling time for myself and then, remembering Jacinda's [Ardern: NZ Prime Minister] words, being kind and flexible acknowledging the changes we've been able to make. Wine helps.

All 5 of us at home are adjusting. So, it's others in my household that have to come to grips with 'working-Dad'. I see how equity in this rapidly imposed online learning environment is significant. Equity for students who are sharing accommodation, sharing devices, have children at home really is a concern. It's not that these things can't be managed. My concern is the insidious stress of these situations that people don't get. I have the luxury of a little office space. Some don't have that. My thoughts go out to those families around the world who are losing elders. My problems are petty. (Adam)

4.4   Piles of Laundry and Dirty Dishes

Sandra makes light of the piles of laundry and dirty dishes that she feels compelled to hide whenever she has a Zoom meeting. She also wryly notes that this new mode of working has her making regular trips to the fridge for chocolate and she jokingly compares herself to a hibernating bear. She makes light of some very real tensions, the interface of work and home that is her new workspace, the increase in comfort eating during a stressful time and her envy of other colleagues' homes.

> When my University suspended all classroom teaching. This was a critical shift and one fraught with challenges for both students and lecturers, as we navigated unfamiliar 'online' terrain to recreate a reassuring sense of continuity and community in a time of social distancing. Zoom became the new classroom and we got to see a more personal side of our colleagues. Yes, I admit it I have had 'house envy' on more than one occasion. I resorted to using Zoom backgrounds from around the world to camouflage the many piles of laundry and dirty dishes that could be seen around my dining table! This became my new office and from where I would take short trips to procrastinate in front of the fridge. I know lockdown was meant to 'flatten the curve', well I on the other hand fattened everywhere like a brown bear going into hibernation. I kept telling myself I was not spending any money and a piece of chocolate here and there or between every meal was well deserved. (Sandra)

4.5   Shhhhh

In this final narrative, Luke shares a story at his own expense, that he found both amusing but also embarrassing. Again, it highlights the workplace–homelife tension when his small child interrupts his Zoom meeting. Although Luke found this funny and laughed in the retelling, he also felt concerned that he may have inadvertently upset or offended the applicant (in the story). Additionally, he was a bit embarrassed that he had made a mistake in a Zoom meeting attended by many colleagues and applicants and also felt uncomfortable that he had hushed his son's normal curiosity. His position of responsibility in this situation was compromised by his working from home and trying to manage his small son. His gesture in trying to keep his son from disrupting the meeting was misinterpreted and he worries that he caused accidental offence or distress to the person who was speaking:

> My international Zoom presentation is in full swing and the applicants are making their pitches to try and get funding for their exciting, innovative projects. A young Pasifika man is fervently describing his proposal and justifying his need for the funding. I'm listening intently when my four-year old son enters the room, but he is not visible on the computer screen as he starts to ask me questions. Without thinking I raise my finger to my lips and gently hiss 'shhhhh'. The young applicant looks

alarmed but immediately complies and stops talking. He thinks the 'shhhhh' is for him! Embarrassed, I try to explain ... (Luke)

5.   NARRATIVE ANALYSIS AND THEMES

Each of the five stories above was either verbally retold or written as a short email narrative by the participants to share with colleagues and friends. A narrative is a sequence of events connected in a meaningful way that creates an interaction between reader and the text (Herman and Vervaeck, 2019). When people use narratives or share experiences through stories, they incorporate patterns and perceptions that explain their experiences and allow readers to hear their voice and construct meaningful perceptions of events (Cortazzi, 2014). Narrative analysis is useful in ambiguous situations to help deal with tensions and confusions and narratives can establish connections between exceptional events and the ordinary (Bruner 1986, in Czarniawska, 1997). Boudens (2005) argues that work-related emotion is best accessed through narrative analysis as narratives are ubiquitous (Czarniawska, 2000), they teach and offer opportunities for interpretations that develop new knowledge.

Thematic analysis (Braun and Clark, 2014) elicited a range of themes that caused these participants amusement but also stress and anxiety. Retelling their stories seemed to be cathartic for participants and prompted further stories from their colleagues as these workers elucidated their lockdown experiences framed as humour. The following typology (Table 7.1) presents six key themes, the narrative(s) from which they were derived and an interpretation of the emotional impact that the experience caused the narrator. The third column also indicates key studies linked to the identified theme.

Table 7.1   Typology of themes

Theme	Narrative	Impact on PWB
Children visible in the workplace	1, 2, 3 & 5	Tension, embarrassment, amusement, fear, unhappiness, guilt (Johnson et al., 2018)
Professional identity versus home identity	1, 2, 3, 4 & 5	Tension, anxiety, negotiation (Ibarra, 1999)
Domestic life on show	1, 4 & 5	Embarrassment, envy, concealment (Ibarra, 1999)
Divided attention – work/ family	1, 2, 3, 4 & 5	Tension, confusion, anxiety, guilt, ambiguity (Clark, 2000)
Eating/drinking as coping in crisis	3 & 4	Guilt, coping, comfort, long-term effects (Páez et al., 2013)
Dislocation effects	1, 2, 3, 4 & 5	Boundaries porous, work/home blended, anxiety, coping with ambiguity (Robertson and Cooper, 2011)

6.   DISCUSSION

These narratives take place in extreme and unusual circumstances in which all of the participants experienced lockdown conditions and having to work from home using electronic communication platforms such as email, Skype and Zoom. The themes that emerge are similar in all five narratives. There is the tension of home and work being entwined, and facets of home life leak into the workplace in different ways including a feathered disaster, interrupting pet, children clamouring for parental attention, the detritus of domestic life visible in work videos and comfort eating and drinking as a coping mechanism. Having one's children and domestic arrangements visible and on show may compromise professional identity, causing embarrassment and upset which may hamper efforts to perform professionally. Professional identity is defined as self-concept based on beliefs, values, attributes, motives and experiences (Ibarra, 1999). The participants use humour to navigate a new professional identity that incorporates elements of their family identity previously unseen in their work identity – such as their parenthood or pet ownership. They concep-tualize themselves anew through sharing problematic stories in a light-hearted way as they reflect on their repurposed identity in the crisis situation. Their stories use self-deprecating and self-enhancing humour which helps to put their difficulties into perspective, allows them to cope with difficult circum-stances and is psychologically healthy (Martin et al., 2003). This creates solidarity and cohesion (Holmes and Marra, 2002) with their colleagues who are experiencing similar effects.

Denying attention to one's children is stressful and impacts upon PWB significantly. PWB is obviously strained in all of these narratives and therefore these workers have invoked humour as a way of dealing with the stress and distress of these newly difficult circumstances. This is considered to be an adaptive form of humour use (Ruch, 1998) that positively influences PWB.

It is notable that each of these narratives was shared, not just with the researcher, but with colleagues, friends and family. Each event was slightly dramatized and crafted into a narrative to enhance the retelling. The story is told through humour, a wry, gentle type of humour that lightly mocks the self and makes light of the tensions, ambiguity and embarrassment caused in the scenarios. Luke openly admits his embarrassment at seemingly telling someone giving a presentation to 'shhhhh', yet it makes an amusing story as people laugh at the surprise and incongruity in this situation. Incongruity is a key component of much humour especially when something unexpected occurs (McGhee, 1979; Wilson, 1979).

Each participant has made light of their situation, using their experience to laugh at themselves. In doing so they achieve several things. Firstly, they enhance their own PWB by turning angst, anxiety and embarrassment into a funny story. This gives relief from the pressure of the situation. Secondly, they share the story with others, willingly laughing at their own mistakes, anxieties and difficulties. In sharing this it further mitigates the stress and anxiety and allows others to laugh along. Laughter is mostly a shared phenomenon so retelling their stories invites the good feeling of shared laughter. Although shared laughter is an everyday, mundane component of work conversations, it serves an important purpose as it displays 'mutual co-orientation' and affiliation that is important to collegial interaction (Glenn, 1991, p. 139). Sharing their stories through humour encourages others to share in a similar way, generating further shared laughter and camaraderie that helps cope with the difficulties of their situation. This offers wider benefits and helps build PWB for workgroups.

Finally, it is important to note the style of humour used here – it is mild and self-deprecating, whereby the person relating the story makes themselves the target of the joke and the narrators present themselves as slightly foolish, instigating laughter at their own behaviour, mistake or misfortune. This works well especially with work colleagues. This would not be as favourable should someone else take over the story and tell it on their behalf, loudly laughing *at* the protagonist. The key here is that these narrators make themselves the subject, decide how much to reveal and carry it off in a wry, amused tone, adding some of their own reflections and insights. The humour is not derogatory or mocking because sardonic humour, although prevalent in workplaces, does not ease stress and tension during crisis but is confronting and risky (see Billig, 2005; Plester, 2015, 2016). The amusing commentary used in these narratives portrays the vagaries of what has been an extraordinary, novel and challenging time but does so in a gentle, wry and reflective manner. Humour enacted this way remains within appropriate workplace boundaries as it does not denigrate, mock or harm others (see Plester, 2009a, 2016). Sharing it is collegial and inclusive and generates goodwill and further sharing. Although some humour has a dark side that can be harmful (Plester, 2015, 2016) such humour would be a step too far in such trying times. Therefore, the light, self-deprecatory versions portrayed here play a positive role in enhancing PWB for the narrator and others, and constitute a useful coping strategy for the continuing crisis situation. Keeping the humour about everyday domestic foibles means that humour can be safely enjoyed while riskier, more confronting jokes about death, misery and global pandemic responses are *not* voiced in these work situations.

In analysing dark humour after the 9/11 tragedy, Gournelos and Green (2011) note that political and crisis humour is never 'innocent' and can be a highly complex, political and social device that causes 'fallout' (see also Lockyer and Pickering, 2009). For some crises, joking about them will always be considered 'too soon'. Humour that parodies or satirizes painful crises can be experienced as both 'attractive and repulsive' (Gournelos and Green, 2011, p. xix) which creates, rather than alleviates, tension. Our participants have recognized these dynamics and kept their humour 'light', non-political and focused upon their own domestic situation, thus avoiding the chance of strong critique and fallout.

6.1   New Zealand-Specific Learnings

There are some specifically New Zealand features apparent in the analysed narratives. New Zealanders have a humour style that is often self-deprecating and generates laughter at their own expense. New Zealanders value informality in workplace discourse (Vine et al., 2009) and work colleagues recognize familiar humour frames that they understand, appreciate and frequently agree with (Hay, 2001). New Zealand workers particularly support self-deprecating, humble humour and sharing personal humorous stories generates collegial support, approval and recognition. Therefore, the PWB experienced by the narrator is recognized and shared by their 'Kiwi' work colleagues, enhancing PWB for the wider group as well as the individual storyteller. The New Zealand government has been internationally applauded for ardently endorsing *kindness* during this pandemic and these stories exemplify and invoke this ethos in their warmth, gentleness and concern for family, colleagues and the self.

6.2   Global Relevance

Humour is universal, ubiquitous and is a common element of workplace interactions that enhances workgroup cohesiveness while reducing stress (Romero and Cruthirds, 2006). Successful humour generates positive workplace outcomes and is a driver of happiness and PWB through creating positive affect (Robert and Wilbanks, 2012). Using humour in crisis situations is a positive coping strategy that can help individual workers and groups of colleagues. However, workplace humour needs to avoid hard-hitting political satire and parody that is better left to professional comedians. These gently amusing New Zealand lockdown stories model a coping strategy that can be emulated and encouraged globally. Such gentle humour may be a necessary panacea for this current time.

ACKNOWLEDGEMENTS

This project has ethical approval: University of Auckland Human Participants Ethics Committee: Ref. 024713 (2020). Pseudonyms have been used for all participants to preserve confidentiality.

REFERENCES

Billig, M. (2005), *Laughter and Ridicule. Towards a Social Critique of Humour*. London: Sage.

Boudens, C.J. (2005), 'The story of work: A narrative analysis of workplace emotion', *Organization Studies*, **26** (9), 1285–306.

Braun, V. and V. Clarke (2014), 'What can "thematic analysis" offer health and wellbeing researchers?', *International Journal of Qualitative Studies on Health and Well-Being*, **9**.

Cann, A. and C. Collette (2014), 'Sense of humor, stable affect, and psychological well-being', *Europe's Journal of Psychology*, **10** (3), 464–79.

Clark, S.C. (2000). 'Work/family border theory: A new theory of work/family balance', *Human Relations*, **53** (6), 747–70.

Cortazzi, M. (2014), *Narrative Analysis*, London: Routledge.

Czarniawska, B. (2000), 'The uses of narrative in organization research, GRI Report, 2000:5', http://hdl.handle.net/2077/2997

Czarniawska, B. (1997), *A Narrative Approach to Organization Studies*, Thousand Oaks, CA: Sage Publications.

der Kinderen, S. and S.N. Khapova (2020), 'Positive psychological well-being at work: The role of eudaimonia', in S. Dhiman (ed.), *The Palgrave Handbook of Workplace Well-being*, London: Palgrave, pp. 1–28.

Freud, S. ([1905] 1991), *Jokes and Their Relation to the Unconscious* (A. Richards, Trans.), London: Penguin.

Gabriel, Y. (2018), 'Stories and narratives', in C. Cassell, A.L. Cunliffe and G. Grandy (eds), *The SAGE Handbook of Qualitative Business and Management Research Methods: Volume 2*, London: Sage, pp. 63–81.

Glenn, P.J. (1991), 'Current speaker initiation of two-party shared laughter', *Research on Language & Social Interaction*, **25** (1–4), 139–62.

Gournelos, T. and V. Greene (eds) (2011), *A Decade of Dark Humor: How Comedy, Irony, and Satire Shaped Post-9/11 America*, Jackson: University Press of Mississippi.

Hay, J. (2000), 'Functions of humor in the conversations of men and women', *Journal of Pragmatics*, **32** (6), 709–42.

Hay, J. (2001), 'The pragmatics of humor support', *Humor*, **14** (1), 55–82.

Herman, L. and B. Vervaeck (2019), *Handbook of Narrative Analysis*, Lincoln: University of Nebraska Press.

Holmes, J. (2006), 'Sharing a laugh: Pragmatic aspects of humor and gender in the workplace', *Journal of Pragmatics*, **38** (1), 26–50.

Holmes, J. and M. Marra (2002), 'Humour as a discursive boundary marker in social interaction', in A. Duszak (ed.), *Us and Others: Social Identities across Languages, Discourses and Cultures*, Pragmatics and Beyond New Series, Amsterdam: John Benjamins Publishing, pp. 377–400.

Ibarra, H. (1999), 'Provisional selves: Experimenting with image and identity in professional adaptation', *Administrative Science Quarterly*, **44** (4), 764–91. https://doi.org/10.2307/2667055

Johnson S., I. Robertson and C.L. Cooper (2018), *Well-being: Productivity and Happiness at Work* (2nd ed.), Cham: Palgrave Macmillan, https://doi.org/10.1007/978-3-319-62548-5_1

Kuiper, N.A., M. Grimshaw, C. Leite and G. Kirsh (2004), 'Humor is not always the best medicine: Specific components of sense of humor and psychological well-being', *Humor: International Journal of Humor Research*, **17** (1–20), 135–68.

Lefcourt, H.M. and R.A. Martin ([1986] 2012), *Humor and Life Stress: Antidote to Adversity*, Springer Science & Business Media, New York: Springer, https://books.google.co.nz/books?hl=en&lr=&id=8s0hBAAAQBAJ&oi=fnd&pg=PA1&dq=Lefcourt,+H.M.+and+R.A.+Martin+(2012),+Humor+and+life+stress:+Antidote+to+adversity,+Spring-er+Science+%26+Business+Media.+(Original+work+published+1986)&ots=bWa-YFbLw8&sig=kYLimK5pUCGCROTQnLqwSVQdyUM&redir_esc=y#v=onepage&q&f=false

Lockyer, S. and M. Pickering (eds), (2005), *Beyond a Joke: The Limits of Humour*, New York: Palgrave Macmillan.

McAdams, D.P. (2006), 'The role of narrative in personality psychology today', *Narrative Inquiry*, **16** (1), 11–18.

McCreaddie, M. and S. Payne (2014), 'Humour in health-care interactions: A risk worth taking', *Health Expectations*, **17** (3), 332–44.

McGhee, P.E. (1979), *Humor, its Origin and Development*, San Francisco: W.H. Freeman.

Martin, R.A. (2007), *The Psychology of Humor: An Integrative Approach*, Burlington, MA: Elsevier.

Martin, R.A., N.A. Kuiper, L.J. Olinger and K.A. Dance (1993), 'Humor, coping with stress, self-concept, and psychological well-being', *Humor*, **6**, 89.

Martin, R.A., P. Puhlik-Doris, G. Larsen, J. Gray and K. Weir (2003), 'Individual differences in uses of humor and their relation to psychological well-being: Development of the Humor Styles Questionnaire', *Journal of Research in Personality*, **37** (1), 48–75.

Páez, D., F. Martínez-Sánchez, A. Mendiburo, M. Bobowik and V. Sevillano (2013), 'Affect regulation strategies and perceived emotional adjustment for negative and positive affect: A study on anger, sadness and joy', *The Journal of Positive Psychology*, **8** (3), 249–62.

Plester, B.A. (2009a), 'Crossing the line: Boundaries of workplace humour and fun', *Employee Relations*, **31** (6), 584–99.

Plester, B.A. (2009b), 'Healthy humour: Using humour to cope at work', *Kotuitui: New Zealand Journal of Social Sciences Online*, **4** (1), 89–102.

Plester, B.A. (2015), 'Take it like a man! Performing hegemonic masculinity through organizational humour', *Ephemera*, **15** (3), 537–59.

Plester, B.A. (2016), *The Complexity of Workplace Humour: Laughter, Jokers and the Dark Side*, Dordrecht: Springer.

Ridanpää, J. (2019), 'Crisis events and the inter-scalar politics of humor', *GeoJournal*, **84** (4), 901–15.

Robert, C. and J.E. Wilbanks (2012), 'The wheel model of humor: Humor events and affect in organizations', *Human Relations*, **65** (9), 1071–99.

Robertson, I. and C. Cooper (2011), *Well-being: Productivity and Happiness at Work*, Hampshire: Palgrave Macmillan.

Robinson, O. and J. Smith (2009), *Metaphors and Metamorphoses: Narratives of Identity During Times of Crisis*, Huddersfield: University of Huddersfield.

Romero, E.J. and K.W. Cruthirds (2006), 'The use of humor in the workplace', *Academy of Management Perspectives*, **20** (2), 58–70.

Ruch, W. (1998), *The Sense of Humor: Explorations of a Personality Characteristic*, Berlin/New York: Mouton de Gruyter.

Ryff C.D. and C.L. Keyes (1995), 'The structure of psychological well-being revisited', *Journal of Personality and Social Psychology*, **69** (4), 719.

Sharma, G. (2017), 'Pros and cons of different sampling techniques', *International Journal of Applied Research*, **3** (7), 749–52.

Vine, B., S. Kell, M. Marra and J. Holmes (2009), 'Boundary-marking humor', N.R. Norrick and D. Chiaro (eds), *Humor in Interaction*, Pragmatics & Beyond New Series, Amsterdam: John Benjamins Publishing, pp. 125–40.

Wilson, C.P. (1979), *Jokes. Form, Content, Use and Function*, London: Academic Press.

# 8.	Job crafting in New Zealand during Covid-19: some key examples and their implications

Deepika Jindal and Peter Boxall

## 1.	INTRODUCTION

Job crafting, an important area in contemporary organizational behaviour, refers to how employees shape their jobs so that they are more aligned with their needs and abilities (Wrzesniewski and Dutton, 2001). Although personal motives and characteristics can trigger job-crafting behaviours, so can organizational change. Walk and Handy (2018, p. 352) comment that 'employees facing organizational change may experience a need to regain control over the job and make meaning of their (changing) work, which is a major motivational factor for job crafting'. The Covid-19 pandemic has had a range of effects on organizations, destroying some while creating opportunities for others. In those that survived, it induced a range of changes in strategies and operational practices, requiring the employees who were retained to make various changes in the way they conducted their jobs. Although these changes can be viewed as temporary adjustments to deal with the situation created by the pandemic and the accompanying lockdowns, some of them have triggered job-crafting behaviours. This chapter will draw on primary research to understand how New Zealand employees crafted their jobs following the arrival of Covid-19. The typical workplace culture of New Zealand, often viewed as friendly, relaxed and egalitarian, may have made job-crafting more likely. However, the findings from this New Zealand study suggest some lessons of wider relevance.

## 2.	THEORETICAL FRAMEWORK

Individuals have a propensity to seek meaningful work that is satisfying for them and leads to favourable outcomes (Wrzesniewski, 2003). Unlike management strategies of job design or redesign, employees play an active role in job crafting, with or without the knowledge of their managers (Demerouti and Bakker, 2014; Wrzesniewski and Dutton, 2001).

Job crafting depends on the motivation to craft a job and the opportunities present in the environment to do so and there are three motivating factors that lead to job crafting (Wrzesniewski and Dutton, 2001). The first factor is the desire to have control over one's work. Even in jobs that offer little work autonomy, employees who are strong in this motivation may work hard to create opportunities for crafting. The second motivation stems from an employee's drive to build a positive self-image and the third is associated with the need for connecting with others. Perceived opportunities for job crafting refer to the discretion individuals have in conducting their work (Wrzesniewski and Dutton, 2001).

2.1   Types of Job Crafting

Job crafting encompasses the task-related (number, type or scope), cognitive (one's perceptions), and relational (quantity and quality of interactions) changes that people make in their job to experience enhanced identity and meaning, and achieve a better person–job fit (Wrzesniewski and Dutton, 2001). According to Berg et al. (2013), task crafting can be promoted by adding more tasks that have to be done, focusing more time and effort on those aspects of the job that are thought to be more meaningful and redesigning tasks to derive a better meaning. Cognitive crafting can be initiated by changing one's perception of the purpose of the job and focusing on those aspects of the job that are more meaningful (Berg et al., 2013). Relational crafting can be achieved through building new relationships, changing the purpose of relationships and adapting current relationships. These three types of job crafting are not mutually exclusive and can be adopted in isolation or in combination (Wrzesniewski et al., 2013).

2.2   Antecedents of Job Crafting

Wrzesniewski and Dutton (2001) suggest that predictors such as work autonomy and job demands can initiate job-crafting behaviours. There is also evidence of a need for positive self-image (Niessen et al., 2016), task interdependence (Leana et al., 2009), and task complexity (Ghitulescu, 2007) as antecedents of job crafting. Although 'little is known regarding the predictive value of personality traits for job crafting' (Roczniewska and Bakker, 2016, p. 1028), there is evidence that job crafting is related to individual characteristics such as proactive personality (Bakker et al., 2012), 'approach temperament' (Bipp and Demerouti, 2015) and promotion focus (Brenninkmeijer and Hekkert-Koning, 2015). In a study conducted on Fort Hare University's administrative employees in South Africa, Bell and Njoli (2016) found that all the big-five personality factors of conscientiousness, extraversion, agreeableness, openness to experience and neuroticism predicted job-crafting behaviours in some way.

2.3   Outcomes of Job Crafting

Job crafting has been related to many positive outcomes, such as task performance (Leana et al., 2009), increases in job resources (Tims et al., 2013), person–job fit (Chen et al., 2014), work engagement (Karatepe and Eslamlou, 2017) and job satisfaction (de Beer et al., 2016).

2.4   Role of Autonomy

Hackman and Oldham (1975) define work autonomy as 'the degree to which the job provides substantial freedom, independence, and discretion to the individual in scheduling the work and in determining the procedures to be used in carrying it out' (p. 162). Wrzesniewski and Dutton (2001) argue that 'autonomy in the job leads to perceived opportunities for job crafting and encourages employees to alter the task and relational boundaries of their jobs' (p. 184). They argue that individuals like to have control over their environment and even if the opportunity to do so is low, they may still try to shape their work.

2.5   Role of the Organization

Job crafting varies in its value for an organization. Berg et al. (2007) give the example of a marketing employee who may focus more on new ideas and may ignore the implementation of existing strategy, thus leading to personal satisfaction, but at the cost of organizational performance. Encouraging employees to discuss how they would like to craft their jobs can be a win–win for the employees and the organization. This encouragement may make employees feel more trusted. Hence, they are more likely to craft their jobs in a way that is in the best interests of the organization (Berg et al., 2007). Emphasizing the role of organizations in job crafting, Berg et al. (2013) introduce the concept of 'landscapes' to explain that a job should enable an employee to visualize end goals and, at the same time, provide a view of the interrelatedness of the job with others, so that an employee is able to view constraints as well as foresee opportunities. Lyons (2008) argues that, at the same time, employees should perceive a supportive environment in which they can craft their jobs since, at times, managers may perceive job crafting as a challenge to their power and authority.

Table 8.1   *Industry- and occupation-wise breakdown of the participants*

Industry	No. of participants	Occupation	No. of participants
Banking	1	Communication	1
Financial Advisory	1	Marketing & Sales	5
Food	1	Data Science	1
Health	1	HRM	4
Marketing & PR	1	Operations	2
Media	2	Project Management	1
Professional Services	1	Investment Research	1
Property	1		
Public sector	1		
Software	1		
Telecommunications	4		
TOTAL	15		15

3.   METHOD

3.1   Study Participants

In order to understand the job-crafting experiences of the New Zealand work-force during Covid-19, we interviewed 15 full-time employees across various industries and occupations (Table 8.1). There were six female and nine male participants drawn from eight large, three medium-sized and four small organizations, based on the number of employees. Table 8.2 details the job level and age of the participants. Nine participants had at least one person reporting to them. The average total work experience of participants was 10.53 years and their average tenure in their current job was 2.83 years.

The participants in the study were recruited through an email that was sent out to the wider network of the authors. Semi-structured interviews of 30 to 45 minutes with the participants were recorded (over Zoom) and transcribed by the first author, in the period between August to October 2020. We asked open-ended questions relating to their work experiences during the lockdown that commenced in March 2020. The questions covered issues relating to: their degree of freedom to perform in their role; their degree of independence from, or reliance on, others; the changes they made in how they worked during the period, including changes they made in how they interacted with stakeholders; the capabilities they developed to cope in the 'new normal'; the kind of support they received from their organization; and how the changes that occurred affected their attitudes toward the job and the organization.

Table 8.2   *Job level and age of the participants*

Job level	No. of participants	Age	No. of participants
Senior	5	18–27	5
Middle	7	28–37	5
Junior	3	38–47	5
TOTAL	15		15

3.2   Data Analysis

We analysed the interviews using the six phases of thematic analysis outlined by Braun and Clarke (2006). Phase 1 involved getting immersed in the data by reading the transcripts several times and noting ideas for themes. In Phase 2, we produced the initial codes based on the three types of job-crafting behaviours (task, relational and cognitive). Phase 3 involved searching for themes within the codified data. Viewing the data through the lens of the job-crafting literature, we identified themes in a theoretical or deductive way, since we were coding for specific research questions. In Phase 4, we reviewed the themes and subsequently refined them. This was followed by defining and naming the themes in Phase 5. Lastly, we wrote up the thematic analysis as part of our sixth phase.

4.   RESULTS

The analysis provided interesting themes related to how New Zealand employees crafted their jobs during the Covid-19 pandemic and the ensuing countrywide lockdown.

4.1   Task Crafting

4.1.1   Nature of the role

The propensity of participants to change the boundaries of their tasks greatly depended on the nature of their job. One commented that there was a 'lack of a need for change' as their role remained the same. This was more evident in project management, data analysis and research roles. In many cases where participants stopped doing certain tasks, it was due to a management directive and change of focus. For HRM and marketing roles, in-person events stopped due to restrictions and social-distancing requirements; work had to be redesigned to fit the new normal. As a participant observed, 'things that were not a priority before lockdown like e-learning and things like nice-to-have, became priorities, because [they] had impact on more people'.

Several participants simply adapted to the new ways of working and reverted to the old ways once the lockdown ended. One remarked that they 'gradually revert[ed] back to pre-lockdown operating ways'. During the lockdown, participants who were working in HRM roles often found themselves working more fully in the learning and development and employee-engagement spaces, as that was management's focus. However, they shifted back to other areas once that phase passed. Others stayed with some of the changes they had made, such as continuing with online meetings and online delivery of training. The frequency of meetings increased during the lockdown and reduced once everyone came out of it.

Not everyone shifted to working from home. One of the participants, who is in an operations role, was given permission to be on site during the lockdown, giving them the perfect opportunity to increase their task boundaries:

> I have this hunger of learning new stuff. So, I take on more activities, and because most of the people were working from home, and I was allowed to go in, a lot of people were relying on me to do certain parts of their roles. Therefore, I got an essence of working in other people's roles to understand what they do on a day-to-day basis.

4.1.2   Task interdependence

Participants whose roles were quite independent did not make many changes in the way they were working. Dependence on others for timely execution of tasks was a source of frustration for some of the participants. Although people were generally tolerant toward others who were juggling different responsibilities while working from home, especially those who had young children, this did lead to delays and the blurring of time boundaries.

4.1.3   Supportive environment

The lockdown led to 'compulsory flexibility' for employees in terms of where they worked and how they worked. However, many organizations created or formalized their flexible work practices after the restrictions were lifted. This was driven by increased levels of satisfaction reported by the participants as well as the cost savings available if organizations could reduce their office space or renegotiate their property leases. Therefore, a hybrid model of working emerged or grew in significance. One participant noted that 'so far what we have got from employees is that people were happy with the mixed approach and they want to do some work from home and then want to come sometimes to [the] office'.

Many participants expressed the desire to have greater flexibility in where they worked but recognized that it needed to be balanced with organizational needs. For example, participants in the telecommunications, software and media industries had greater choice in where they worked but those in health and banking had less choice. A participant summed it up by suggesting that 'there is a personal preference [in] how people want to work but that needs to also fit what the team requires, and the customers' need of the team'.

More than half of the participants highlighted the high levels of autonomy that they were given by their manager because they were trusted to use it wisely. This was evident from statements such as: 'they showed faith in me' and 'our leadership team and my manager completely trust me to do my role'. The data suggest that this was more evident in senior jobs. On the other hand, some participants felt that they had no control over their work, leading them to put little effort into redesigning their tasks. As one participant put it: 'I am not valued in the organization, so I don't put ideas anymore'. Organizational culture played a part and although most of the participants felt that their working environment was conducive, there were others who felt quite unsupported.

4.2   Relational Crafting

Directly due to the lockdown, participants reported an increase in the frequency of meetings conducted online and a concomitant decrease in meetings involving an in-person presence. All of the participants indicated that the pandemic and the lockdown changed the quantity and the quality of their interactions with internal and external stakeholders. This was influenced by their own personal characteristics as well as their need for social interactions, the readiness of customers to cope with technology and the need for work–life integration.

4.2.1   Personal characteristics/need for social connection
The lockdown led to a need for interactions with colleagues through virtual platforms such as Zoom, Microsoft Teams and Skype. Most people experienced a sense of camaraderie and closeness through these meetings. Many participants shared that it gave them a glimpse into their colleagues' personal lives, with the occasional appearance of children, partners or pets on the screens. There were quite a few remarks, such as 'lockdown was a real bonding experience' and there was value in 'getting to know each other on a deeper level outside of work', indicating the positive effects on the quality of relationships.

The more extroverted participants were particularly proactive in building relationships with others through organizing virtual catch-ups. 'I think I was missing people' was a frequent comment from such individuals. On the other hand, the more introverted participants were grateful to be away from the office environment and from being constantly disturbed in open-plan offices. We heard comments such as: 'I don't feel like I need to have too much contact with people, and I have quite a stable personality as well' and 'I think lock-down was pretty uniquely suited to my kind of person'. Some even actively avoided interacting with others and the lockdown provided them with a perfect opportunity to do so. One participant remarked that 'being isolated from colleagues is good because being close to them may bring more work'. Too much interaction could be counterproductive, as indicated by a participant's remark that 'you ended up having so many meetings in a day that your day is filled with meetings and you are then not able to focus on what you need to do'.

Apart from personal characteristics, the need for social connection also depended on the type of role being performed. For example, roles in sales, marketing, HRM and operations that involved lot of interaction with stake-holders, both internally and externally, had an increased expectation of greater virtual contact. Participants in senior jobs felt a stronger need to connect as compared to participants in middle- or junior-level jobs. The number of virtual interactions was accentuated in such cases.

4.2.2   Readiness of customers with technology

As with colleagues, participants in customer-facing roles found themselves turning to virtual media. Although our participants said that they were them-selves technology savvy, they found challenges with their external stakehold-ers such as suppliers and customers, who either did not have sophisticated systems or were not so confident with technology. Hence, more time was spent in adapting current relationships to the new needs. Participants felt that they may not transition totally to virtual interactions in the future as they may not be as effective. One participant unpacked it further by highlighting that 'If the relationship is established, I think it's okay via Zoom. But, if you are trying to build new contacts or your relationships, the online platform is not as good'.

4.2.3   Work–life integration

Lockdown provided an opportunity for our participants to create a more inte-grated approach to their work and personal life. Many shared that they were better able to meet their personal needs. Individual examples emerged, such as 'I was spending more time with my son; every time I had a break from the computer, I would go play with him'; 'I was spending more time recognizing my emotions and the emotions of others and how I could work towards being in the most positive space that I could possibly be in'; and 'I did find myself going for lunchtime walks or runs, which I wouldn't do in the office'. With a hybrid model of work location emerging in many organizations, most partic-ipants feel they have been able to build a better work–life balance.

But not everyone was pleased with the new ways of working, as evidenced by statements such as, 'The biggest change was that you didn't feel the start and end of the day because you are at home' and 'Through lockdown I started to associate the apartment with my workplace and that association has continued'. This led to increased feelings of isolation for some and affected their motivation.

4.3 Cognitive Crafting

Lockdown changed people's perceptions of their role as well as of their organization. This impacted their job attitudes and their willingness to stay with the organization.

4.3.1 Personal motivations

Lockdown was an eye-opening experience for participants, helping them to better understand their own motivations. Some commented that 'It was meaningful for me because I got to know what I am capable of doing' and 'It was a learning experience in terms of time management and learning in a new environment'. One talked of being 'in control of your job and do[ing] it so well that it doesn't control you' and another said that 'I perform at my best when I have a sense of freedom and when I am empowered to take my own decisions'.

4.3.2 Attitude toward the organization

Almost all participants reported that their organizations implemented a variety of interventions related to mental well-being during this period. As one participant observed, 'When I think of the two and a half months of lockdown, it really determines how much an employer values their employees. And a lot of people know what type of organization they want to work for when they go forward as well'. Another one said that 'In challenging times, you get to know people, and get to know how organizations take care of employees'. This helped to enhance job satisfaction and organizational commitment. We heard sentiments such as, 'I think I feel very positive about this organization right now'. A strong alignment between one's work values and organizational values was another factor leading to positive work attitudes. On the other hand, participants who did not feel supported said that it made them better understand about good places to work. They talked of going for another job opportunity the moment one opened up.

We also observed that participants in essential businesses in food, health and telecommunications expressed a strong sense of pride in their organization's purpose. This increased their sense of job satisfaction and organizational commitment. As one participant remarked:

> I think Covid-19 made me realize the impact that our organization can have in terms of business support. My pride towards the organization increased because I knew

that what we were doing was having an impact on people and more so than I had realized beforehand.

Such participants can be described as cognitively crafting their job in terms of the meaning it brings them.

5.   DISCUSSION AND CONCLUSION

The external shock of Covid-19 brought restrictions on customary ways of working in New Zealand. It led to adjustment responses by employees, including some crisis-imposed changes as coping mechanisms and some job-crafting behaviours. Online communication methods brought in, or escalated, to cope with teamworking during Covid-19 produced mixed responses. Once the restrictions lifted, some employees reverted to pre-Covid working behaviours while others committed to lasting changes by way of crafting their jobs. Some participants preferred working from home, others did not. This was influenced by personality, personal situation and/or the nature of job. Working from home meant that not everyone respected each other's time boundaries, which led to some working longer hours. The nature of the work (particularly in terms of the opportunity for location autonomy, that is, the extent to which people can work remotely), task and social interdependence, along with individual circumstances at home and differences in individual personality, affected the degree and type of job-crafting behaviours. The extent of change in work practices varied from low to high.

Participants who saw their organizations as doing meaningful work for society in the crisis experienced feelings of pride and belonging and engaged in cognitive crafting. On the other hand, there were participants who reported a low level of connection with an organization that did not provide a sufficiently supportive environment. A key variable in the extent to which job crafting occurred was the level of trust between employers and employees. The highest degree of crafting took place in the relational space, with participants experiencing an enhanced sense of bonding with their colleagues, although their interactions with customers may have suffered. A key reason for a low level of changes in task crafting was that technology helped in keeping work tasks going and, hence, there was a low need to change task boundaries.

The context of New Zealand, as a small island nation with a strong sense of community that people enjoy, may have contributed to an increase in job crafting, especially the relational aspects. The culture of New Zealand is perceived as being friendly, relaxed and supportive. Generally, the New Zealand organizations in our sample offered a lot of employee support and people liked to interact with each other. Friday afternoon drinks were a norm in most organizations, and lockdown showed that people kept the same spirit (so-to-speak) alive, enjoying online drinks and catch-ups.

However, these New Zealand-specific experiences and insights do have a broader relevance. Autonomy and trust are universal constructs and transcend occupation, industry and national boundaries. With many parts of the world moving to new ways of working due to the benefits that may be gained from employees working from home, such as lower rental or lease costs for businesses and the saving of commuting time, enabling employees to craft their jobs can make work more meaningful and lead to higher levels of job satisfaction and organizational commitment.

Wrzesniewski and Dutton (2001) argue that managers must accept that job crafting happens all the time, with or without their knowledge. Hence, supporting employees in crafting their jobs will ensure that the end results are not counterproductive for the organization. Managers can influence job-crafting behaviours through enactment of HRM policies, such as collaborative forms of work redesign (Wrzesniewski and Dutton, 2001). As reported by the participants, many organizations adopted or reinforced a flexible, hybrid model of working location, enabling a mix of at-home or in-office locations to suit the individual or to be negotiated with their team. In the current changing environment in terms of technology, globalization and diversity, it makes sense to ensure that any top-down job-design processes are complemented with bottom-up job-crafting approaches (Demerouti and Bakker, 2014). The current pandemic has helped to highlight the value of employees as active participants in shaping their job boundaries, which can lead to win–win outcomes for the individuals and organizations. With more employees working from home, a job description that has flexibility built into it is more likely to lead to job-crafting behaviours compared to job descriptions that are over-prescribed (Berg et al., 2008).

REFERENCES

Bakker, A.B., M. Tims and D. Derks (2012), 'Proactive personality and job performance: The role of job crafting and work engagement', *Human Relations*, **65** (10), 1359–78. doi: 10.1177/0018726712453471

Bell, C. and N. Njoli (2016), 'The role of big five factors on predicting job crafting propensities amongst administrative employees in a South African tertiary institution', *SA Journal of Human Resource Management*, **14** (1). http://dx.doi.org/10.4102/sajhrm.v14i1.702

Berg, J.M., J.E. Dutton and A. Wrzesniewski (2007), 'What is job crafting and why does it matter?', accessed 15 March 2016, at http://positiveorgs.bus.umich.edu/wp-content/uploads/What-is-Job-Crafting-and-Why-Does-it-Matter1.pdf

Berg, J.M., J.E. Dutton, A. Wrzesniewski and W.E. Baker (2008), 'Job crafting exercise', accessed 10 February 2016 at https://positiveorgs.bus.umich.edu/wp-content/uploads/Job-Crafting-Exercise-Teaching-Note-Aug-101.pdf

Berg, J.M., J.E. Dutton and A. Wrzesniewski (2013), 'Job crafting and meaningful work', in B.J. Dik, Z.S. Byrne and M.F. Steger (eds), *Purpose and Meaning in the Workplace*, Washington, DC: American Psychological Association, pp. 81–104.

Bipp, T. and E. Demerouti (2015), 'Which employees craft their jobs and how? Basic dimensions of personality and employees' job crafting behaviour', *Journal of Occupational and Organizational Psychology*, **88** (4), 631–55. doi:10.1111/joop .12089

Braun, V. and V. Clarke (2006), 'Using thematic analysis in psychology', *Qualitative Research in Psychology*, **3** (2), 77–101.

Brenninkmeijer, V. and M. Hekkert-Koning (2015), 'To craft or not to craft: The relationships between regulatory focus, job crafting and work outcomes', *Career Development International*, **20** (2), 147–62. http://dx.doi.org/10.1108/CDI-12-2014 -0162

Chen, C.Y., C.H. Yen and F.C. Tsai (2014), 'Job crafting and job engagement: The mediating role of person–job fit', *International Journal of Hospitality Management*, **37**, 21–28. http://dx.doi.org/10.1016/j.ijhm.2013.10.006

de Beer, L.T., M. Tims and A.B. Bakker (2016), 'Job crafting and its impact on work engagement and job satisfaction in mining and manufacturing', *South African Journal of Economic and Management Sciences*, **19** (3), 400–412. http://dx.doi.org/ 10.17159/2222-3436/2016/v19n3a7

Demerouti, E. and A.B. Bakker (2014), 'Job crafting', in M.C. Peeters, J. de Jonge and T.W. Taris (eds), *An Introduction to Contemporary Work Psychology*, Chichester, UK: Wiley-Blackwell, pp. 414–33.

Ghitulescu, B.E. (2007), 'Shaping tasks and relationships at work: Examining the antecedents and consequences of employee job crafting' (Doctoral dissertation), University of Pittsburgh, accessed 20 September 2020 at http://d-scholarship.pitt .edu/10312/

Hackman, J.R. and G.R. Oldham (1975), 'Development of the job diagnostic survey', *Journal of Applied Psychology*, **60** (2), 159–70. http://dx.doi.org/10.1037/h0076546

Karatepe, O.M. and A. Eslamlou (2017), 'Outcomes of job crafting among flight attendants', *Journal of Air Transport Management*, **62**, 34–43. http://dx.doi.org/10 .1016/j.jairtraman.2017.02.005

Leana, C., E. Appelbaum and I. Shevchuk (2009), 'Work process and quality of care in early childhood education: The role of job crafting', *Academy of Management Journal*, **52** (6), 1169–192. http://www.jstor.org/stable/40390365

Lyons, P. (2008), 'The crafting of jobs and individual differences', *Journal of Business and Psychology*, **23** (1–2), 25–36. doi:10.1007/s10869-008-9080-2

Niessen, C., D. Weseler and P. Kostova (2016), 'When and why do individuals craft their jobs? The role of individual motivation and work characteristics for job crafting', *Human Relations*, **69** (6), 1287–313. doi:10.1177/0018726715610642

Roczniewska, M. and A.B. Bakker (2016), 'Who seeks job resources, and who avoids job demands? The link between dark personality traits and job crafting', *The Journal of Psychology*, **150** (8), 1026–45. doi: 10.1080/00223980.2016.1235537

Tims, M., A.B. Bakker and D. Derks (2013), 'The impact of job crafting on job demands, job resources, and well-being', *Journal of Occupational Health Psychology*, **18** (2), 230–40. doi:10.1037/a0032141

Walk, M. and F. Handy (2018), 'Job crafting as reaction to organizational change', *The Journal of Applied Behavioral Science*, **54** (3), 349–70. doi:10.1177/ 0021886318777227

Wrzesniewski, A. (2003), 'Finding positive meaning in work', in K.S. Cameron and J. Dutton (eds), *Positive Organizational Scholarship. Foundations of a New Discipline*, San Francisco, CA: Berrett-Koehler, pp. 296–308.
Wrzesniewski, A. and J.E. Dutton (2001), 'Crafting a job: Revisioning employees as active crafters of their work', *Academy of Management Review*, **26** (2), 179–201. http://www.jstor.org/stable/259118
Wrzesniewski, A., N. LoBuglio, J.E. Dutton and J.M. Berg (2013), 'Job crafting and cultivating positive meaning and identity in work', in A.B. Bakker (ed.), *Advances in Positive Organizational Psychology*, Bingley, UK: Emerald Group Publishing, pp. 281–302.

9. Covid-19 governance challenges: the board's role in Covid-19 crisis management

Maureen Benson-Rea, Ljiljana Eraković and Susan Watson

1. INTRODUCTION

The board of any organization is responsible for decisions about its direction and strategic management. It is the board that champions the organizational purpose and values, envisions its future, provides direction and protects the organization's assets. The board acts as the representative of the organization in the world either itself or in partnership with management interacting with other organization stakeholders. The board sits at the nexus of the organization's participants (Cikaliuk et al., 2020).

In stable times, the board's central governance (fiduciary) responsibility is to act in the best interests of the company and, in doing so, ensure the effective and efficient use of assets and resources, set financial parameters and monitor and assess the effectiveness of strategy implementation. The Covid-19 pandemic, however, prompts the existential question for organizations of: 'What is the role of the board in a global crisis situation?'

To answer that question, this chapter presents an exploratory study with two aims. First, we attempt to position our research within the current literature on boards and crisis management. Second, based on a carefully selected (purposeful) sample of informants (Patton, 2006), we aim to uncover the major practical and strategic challenges (internal and external) that board members (individually and collectively) faced in the first six months of the Covid-19 crisis.

The Covid-19 pandemic has directly affected all organizations and their functioning. It has threatened their existence, tested their coping mechanisms (Weick, 1993) and challenged their members' individual and collective capabilities. In all cases, whether organizations have had to significantly downsize or completely reshuffle their operations, it has led to some sort of organizational crisis. Management and boards have been at the forefront of organizational efforts to manage the crisis. The study we report on aims at analysing board members' lived experiences in responding to the crisis. We do this by implementing an interpretive (qualitative) research approach. In particular, the chapter reports on our investigation of how the actual responses unfolded, which strategies and processes were used, and the role of internal and external stakeholders. By exploring the perceptions of board members, chairs and CEOs from different types of organizations, we provide a preliminary overview of major themes specifically addressing board behaviour in the crisis. These key themes can clarify whether existing research findings on boards and crises can be extended to the context of a major, exogenous and unpredictable crisis and what areas should be examined in future research.

2.   THE BOARD AND ITS ROLE DURING CRISES

In the existing literature on the board's roles, responsibilities and behaviours during an organizational crisis, we found scarce research on board behaviour in situations of sudden crisis (James and Wooten, 2005). Corporate governance scholars and commentators seem to agree, however, that active corporate governance is more important in turbulent times than in stable situations (see for example, Birshan et al., 2020; Chatterjee and Harrison, 2001; McKinsey & Company, 2011).

Three major aspects of boards and crises have been examined in studies published in the last two decades. The first relates to the context or type of crisis. The literature has predominantly focused on boards' (re)actions in the wake of the 2008 global financial crisis (GFC) (see McNulty et al., 2013; Sun et al., 2011) or how boards deal with internal organizational crises caused by various external and internal factors, such as hostile takeovers (see Tomasic and Akinbami, 2016), corporate collapses (see Deakin and Konzelmann, 2004) and 'predictable and preventable surprises' (Thamotheram and Le Floc'h, 2012), such as BP's Gulf of Mexico oil spill (see Lin-Hi and Blumberg, 2011) and the Pike River mining disaster in New Zealand (see Pavlovich and Watson, 2015). Intriguingly, we could not find any studies published in management and governance journals about governance and board responses to major sudden crises caused by extreme events such as the September 11 2001 terrorist attack in the USA or the 11 March 2011 Fukushima disaster in Japan. Both these events were unexpected crises of significant magnitude with overwhelming consequences for individuals, businesses and societies, which required prompt organizational responses (Comfort and Kapucu, 2006). Research in organizational governance and boards has seemingly missed the opportunity to provide some insights and lessons from these situations. The Covid-19 pandemic, ironically, provides an excellent opportunity to fill this gap in governance research and to investigate in action how boards and executive teams responded to this threat to the survival and existence of their businesses and organizations.

The second aspect of boards and crises refers to the content of the board's work. Studies on boards and crises pay more attention to the board's active role in strategy formation and strategic decision making rather than what is traditionally perceived to be the board's role of reviewing and approving strategy (Golden and Zajac, 2001). For example, Weitzner and Peridis (2011) focused on ethical aspects of a company's long-term strategy and the board's consideration of all-important stakeholders, suggesting that such an orientation could prevent future financial crises. Keenan (2007) and Worthington et al. (2009) addressed the board's responsibilities for and involvement in strategic scenario planning and risk assessment exercises and argued that these should include internal and external disruptions and shocks to which organizations might be exposed. When organizational survival is under threat, the board is supposed to help management to make strategic decisions and may be likely to initiate changes (Dowell et al., 2011). Interestingly, although numerous studies and analyses point to the importance of active board engagement in strategy interventions during a crisis and board involvement in strategy (re)development after a crisis, the McKinsey & Company (2011) survey conducted three years after the 2008 GFC highlighted the lack of real progress in this area of board work.

The third characteristic of boards and crises concerns various behavioural aspects of board work in that context. The behavioural approach emphasizes the importance of the board's internal dynamics (McNulty et al., 2013; Mellahi, 2005) and relationships with other groups within and outside the organization (Alpaslan et al., 2009). Observing boards in crises, behavioural studies complement the literature on boards' structural characteristics, claiming that features of board composition (demography and cognition) are more important in uncertain and turbulent than in stable environmental and organizational situations (Dowell et al., 2011). This claim has been established on evidence from several studies investigating relationships between cognitive and structural aspects of the board as a group (George and Chattopadhyay, 2008).

Scholars have argued that the board's effective response to and handling of a crisis depends on directors' individual and collective understanding of the organization's situation. This understanding is informed by their previous experience, knowledge, ability to collect and process information, leadership skills, information network and board culture. Such characteristics influence directors' interpretations of the problem, and recognition and formulation of potential solutions (Merendino and Sarens, 2020). The assumption is that the board's cognitive and demographic heterogeneity is likely to promote more innovative and creative responses to crisis. McNulty et al.'s (2013) examination of board decision making (with a focus on financial risk) during the 2008 GFC demonstrated important links between board process and financial risk taking. Their findings confirmed that board heterogeneity and cognitive conflict reduce extreme financial risk and contribute to sound risk management (McNulty et al., 2013). Merendino and Sarens (2020) further developed this line of thought by analysing cognitive processes of boards and directors during a crisis. They identified three major cognitive constraints (individual, collective and hybrid) that prevent directors and boards from being actively involved in crisis resolution. To build on previous studies of how boards behave in a crisis, we explored the lived experience of a group of New Zealand organizations as they responded to the first six months of the Covid-19 pandemic.

3.   THE NEW ZEALAND EXPERIENCE

To explore ideas about the board's roles and behaviour in crisis, we conducted a pilot study looking at major challenges experienced by New Zealand boards. We interviewed six participants, representing various organizations, who were purposefully selected to secure knowledgeable individuals and multiple perspectives. The sample of participants included six board members and CEOs (some covered both) of for-profit and not-for-profit organizations from different sectors of the economy. All participants have governance or executive positions in medium-sized New Zealand organizations. Three participants had several directorships (as independent, nonexecutive directors) and two were CEOs. We conducted in-depth semi-structured interviews six months after the global crisis hit (the country and business lockdown).

Before we proceed with our findings, it is useful to briefly introduce the New Zealand corporate governance regime and practice. New Zealand's corporate governance is regulated by a combination of legal acts, codes and principles. The key act is the Companies Act 1993, according to which: 'Directors must act in good faith and in what the director believes to be the best interests of the company' (s 131). What a director believes is subjective, as recently confirmed by the New Zealand Supreme Court in Debut Homes, Madsen-Ries v Cooper, [2020] NZSC 100. Although the reaffirmation of the subjectivity of the duty of good faith and the stated reluctance of the Court to use hindsight judgment might imply that a form of business judgment test now exists in New Zealand, the Court makes it clear qualifications and exceptions exist including where there is no evidence of actual consideration of the interests of the company, or where there is evidence of irrationality. Directors also owe the company a duty of care, which is assessed objectively (Companies Act 1993, s 137). Directors must exercise the care, diligence and skill that a reasonable director would exercise in the same circumstances taking into account the nature of the company and the decision, and the position of the director and the nature of the responsibilities undertaken by him or her. Decisions are made contextually and the Covid-19 crisis changes the environment in which companies and their boards operate.

New Zealand boards are one-tier boards with separate CEO and chair roles for companies listed on the New Zealand Stock Exchange (NZX). Corporate boards are small (with an average size between six and seven members), populated by a majority of independent directors (73 per cent) and 77 per cent are headed by independent chairs (Chapman Tripp, 2019).

Given the limited literature on board responses and actions in the situation of a sudden and unpredictable crisis, this New Zealand exploratory study provides preliminary but valuable insights into this subject. Our thematic data analysis revealed several intertwined characteristics of board responses during the early stages of the crisis which we organize around three overarching themes; namely, the board as a communications hub, the board as a strategic change agent and the board as an organizational guardian.

3.1   The Board as a Communications Hub

In New Zealand the crisis began on 23 March 2020 when the Prime Minister announced that in two days the whole country would enter a month-long lockdown. This meant that almost all businesses except supermarkets and pharmacies would be closed. Organizations had two days to prepare for the unknown.

Our study participants emphasized prompt reactions from their boards and management teams. Boards got together quickly and continued with regular, at least weekly Zoom meetings throughout the first three months of the crisis. Weekly board meetings included management as well. CEOs and chairs would often communicate daily. All meetings were action/decision oriented; while there were a number of crucial decisions to be made, there was a lack of information, and what little information there was would change frequently. Therefore, the board members had to be flexible in their availability and agile with their decisions.

In some of the organizations, the boards formed special subcommittees, which included directors with financial and IT expertise. In others, the whole board, as one of the interviewees put it, 'became the crisis committee'. One board chair explained: 'It was really important in every board that there were no board members who were left behind. Everyone had to be totally up to play with what was going on, and understand the consequences of it.' Another board chair reiterated: 'I'm a great believer in separation between governance and management. But I felt that this was one of those situations where if board members had to get in and muck in it would've been the time to do it.'

As with standard (as opposed to sudden and unpredictable) crisis plans, the organizations had clear procedures around communications. The management teams prepared reports and communicated with internal and external stakeholders, and the CEOs kept their boards updated with everything that was going on. An important aspect of board–management communication was sharing information and experience from other boards and organizations where directors had appointments. However, there were a lot of situations where neither boards nor management had information or did not know how to respond to some issues. As some of our interviewees emphasized, the Covid-19 crisis is a situation when no-one is in control and boards had to be transparent about this – they needed to be open and honest about what they did not know.

The board chairs managed communication with shareholders, with many admitting that this type of communication was intensive. One chair explained:

> I ran an AGM for a publicly listed company last week, and I spent half the meeting talking about our Covid-19 response. Normally you'd talk about the year that's been, but shareholders want to know how well you're doing, how you're responding, what are the kind of things you're doing. So I think the level of communication with shareholders increased.

3.2   The Board as a Strategic Change Agent and the Crisis as a Strategic Opportunity

At the beginning of the crisis, the boards focused on survival. In some cases, entire business operations closed for more than a month. In others, organizations started working remotely (from home). For a small number of companies (and industries) which were deemed to be essential services, the business operations were not directly impacted. The board meetings at the time were a combination of reviewing cash positions, discussing possible cashflow scenarios, well-being of staff, wage subsidies and other urgent operational issues. Boards and management, depending on underlying resources, were engaged in various scenario planning exercises producing three to four different revenue options and outcomes.

About four months into the crisis, the organizations were in recovery or resetting mode. Boards, together with management teams, began to engage in discussions about the future of their businesses. The board of a company operating in the health sector acted very quickly (after the first few weeks of the lockdown) and decided to implement a radical strategic change to its operational model. This was a business strategy the company was considering just two months before the crisis struck. According to the chair, Covid-19 was 'a catalyst that [we] needed to do something differently'. Instead of offering its services directly to clients in clinics, the company would now deliver its services through online solutions. The chair (who has IT health expertise) and the

CEO (with expertise in business growth and development) gained important support from the rest of the board and the majority shareholder to undertake such a radical and cash-demanding move in the middle of the crisis.

Similarly, the board of the nonprofit organization decided to pursue an aggressive fundraising campaign in April 2020. The board of this children's charity recognized the importance of its activities for a wider community in the Covid-19 situation and used this story to get the message to its donors. In the first three weeks of the lockdown, the organization provided grocery vouchers to more than 2000 families. The chair explained:

> Our projects are for kids, but we could leverage what we do for the kids to help their families as well. And, we were also helping local businesses. We decided to get out there and ask our donors to help. Once we got that decision, our [management] team was 100 per cent behind us.

The fundraising campaign was very successful not only in terms of the amount of donations collected, but also in terms of the number of individuals and businesses who joined the charity in working collaboratively to support the cause. Responses therefore were driven by the Covid-19 context in which companies found themselves, with instances of that context accelerating or even driving organizational change.

3.3   The Board as an Organizational Guardian

The care for the survival of the organization, its people and those dependent on the organizational services and operations, continuously occupied much of the boards' attention. All chair-participants emphasized that the well-being of employees was a regular item on boards' weekly meeting agendas.

The survival of the organization and financial issues, as mentioned earlier, were the boards' focus of attention in the early stages. There were a lot of discussions around cost-cutting strategies. Interestingly, however, a number of boards decided that this 'traditional approach' in dealing with a crisis was not going to be correct this time. One of the chairs remembered a discussion around their board table:

> It was all about 'look at costs' and 'cut costs', and the majority of our costs are people. I said, 'from my perspective, [our employees] are probably the most important people right now in what's going on. And, how are they feeling? They'll be feeling very vulnerable.' I explained that people were working from home. They had kids, husbands and wives working as well, they had no rooms for their desks and so they were working out of children's bedrooms .... So, the last thing I want to do is cut jobs, especially when we're asking the wage subsidy.

In those organizations where job losses were inevitable, board members and CEOs unanimously admitted that was the most difficult decision they made.

All research participants emphasized the importance and work of their management teams. Management teams needed a lot of support from their boards. The support was not only demonstrated in their advice, proactivity and prompt decisions but was shown in board members' understanding of the emotional and moral burden that management teams had on their shoulders.

How New Zealand as a country responded to the Covid-19 pandemic had an important impact on board behaviour in this crisis. A chair and director of multiple corporate entities explained:

> The New Zealand public generally were kept pretty well up to date with what was going on, and there was a high degree of trust around government response. And, that helped the corporate sector. So that all kind of rubbed off, and so if you said 'well this is what we're doing and these are the restrictions', it's kind of like totally understand. Whereas, if the public thought 'well I don't like the responses generally to this', then that would've been a lot harder sell. So I think that the whole wider society context made a real difference to corporate New Zealand as well.

In summary, a priority for all of our participants was to take what we have termed a 'humane approach', which involved the need to check in on colleagues and employees to 'pay attention to everybody's anxiety' because, as one participant put it: 'Employees need to know that you [the board] care' and, a key joint role of boards and senior management is 'listening and understanding your community'. The approach also reflects international trends in corporate governance around stakeholder capitalism where it is increasingly considered that the role of the board in acting in the best interest of the company is to consider the interests of all stakeholders, and growing recognition that appropriately taking account of the interests of stakeholders benefits the company itself.

4.   DISCUSSION AND CONCLUSIONS

On the board's role, our pilot study findings indicate that the situation of the global, unpredictable crisis requires a 'new' type of board or board behaviour. Traditionally, as many research studies have demonstrated (Golden and Zajac, 2001), during a crisis the board is expected to continue monitoring management actions and intervene only if necessary. The Covid-19 crisis, however, has shown that for a business or organization to survive, every single effort or action matters. This unprecedented crisis required boards to step-up and step in (especially in the early stages). New Zealand's experience through the first six months of the Covid-19 pandemic, of which we illustrate the workings of only several boards, reveals three important strengths of boards in managing the crisis: (1) the importance of innovative and creative thinking, (2) active and participative engagement and (3) willingness to take risky decisions.

4.1   Innovative and Creative Thinkers

Sudden crises, such as the Covid-19 pandemic, present boards and management teams with novel problems that require 'innovative' solutions. Boards are challenged to move away from their usual monitoring mode and act as a strategic group. Our pilot study has shown that the crisis brought to the forefront the importance of having diverse and integrative thinkers on the board. That is, people with different knowledge, skills and experiences who, as a group, can handle complex problems and shape creative solutions. Or, as one of our interviewees said, 'Responding to crises isn't about second guessing exactly what's going to happen. But it's about having good capability around the board table and within management teams'.

4.2   Active Engagement

The board members we interviewed took actions immediately. They stepped up as organizational leaders. With little time to analyse and reflect, major decisions had to be taken around employees, relationships with the bank, customers and other key stakeholders. A major feature of the New Zealand response, reflected in the actions of our board participants, was the national consensus that the country was doing the right thing and that the role of the government, in communication and actions, was central to the country's success in facing the crisis. We would argue that this is a key feature of New Zealand's small and somewhat geographically remote society. The New Zealand boards, with their prompt and active engagement with all stakeholders, nonetheless, have demonstrated that governance is not (only) about monitoring and setting policies. It is about the attachment to the organization's values, active representation of the organization's responses, and actions which benefit the organization and its stakeholders.

4.3   Risk Taking

The courage to take strategic actions and move into unknown contexts and futures in the middle of the crisis was a bold move for many New Zealand organizations. Boards and management believed that the crisis was the right time to pursue new opportunities: form new partnerships, adopt leading-edge technology or develop new products and services. Leadership was challenged in unprecedented ways with the requirements to be careful in decision making set against the requirements that decisions be made quickly, in an unfamiliar context and with genuine uncertainty about the future:

> My major lesson [from this crisis] was, act fast and absolutely invest in a time of crisis. If you can, if you can afford to absolutely invest in your future and if you need to pivot, pivot. Like if you need a different direction, do it. Look after your people, absolutely. Yeah, and just don't be afraid. Don't let that crisis control you ... I had no idea how it was going to end up.

5.   CONCLUDING POINTS

The findings of our pilot study have highlighted that, in contrast to 'traditional' views of crisis management, the internal boundaries of the locus of board and senior management work was blurred. Sudden changes in the organization's context prompted emergent strategy implementation which, to be effective, necessitated management working in partnership with boards. Moreover, the external boundaries of the organization's interactions in meeting the crisis also changed. The social cohesions and humanity, together with the key role of government, appear to have helped to define a national context for board responses to the Covid-19 crisis in New Zealand.

What can international boards learn from the experience of New Zealand boards? The old adage 'Never waste a good crisis' was proven, with a key learning how the crisis accelerated or even triggered major organizational change. In addition, the increasing recognition that taking care of the interests of key stakeholders (employees, customers and community) may not just be the right thing to do, but is also in the interests and to the benefit of the organization itself, may strengthen the international shift away from board decision making being driven by short-term profit maximization. Ultimately a business being good, doing the right thing by employees and other stakeholders, may prove to be good business.

REFERENCES

Alpaslan, C.M., S.E. Green and I.I. Mitroff (2009), 'Corporate governance in the context of crises: Towards a stakeholder theory of crisis management', *Journal of Contingencies and Crisis Management*, **17** (1), 38–49. https://doi.org/10.1111/j.1468-5973.2009.00555.x

Birshan, M., M. Goerg, A. Moore and E.-J. Parekh (2020), *Investors Remind Business Leaders: Governance Matters*, October, accessed at 9 October 2020 at https://www.mckinsey.com/business-functions/strategy-and-corporate-finance/our-insights/investors-remind-business-leaders-governance-matters

Chapman Tripp (2019), *New Zealand Corporate Governance: Trends and Insights: April 2019*, Auckland: Chapman Tripp, accessed at 31 October 2020 at https://chapmantripp.com/media/qdbfq3zi/corporate-governance-trends-insights-2019.pdf

Chatterjee, S. and J.S. Harrison (2001), 'Corporate governance', in M.A. Hitt, R.E. Freeman and J.S. Harrison (eds), *The Blackwell Handbook of Strategic Management*, Oxford: Blackwell, pp. 543–64.

Cikaliuk, M., L. Eraković, B. Jackson, C. Noonan and S. Watson (2020), *Corporate Governance and Leadership: The Board as the Nexus of Leadership-in-Governance*, Cambridge: Cambridge University Press.

Comfort, L.K. and N. Kapucu (2006), 'Inter-organizational coordination in extreme events: The World Trade Center attacks, September 11, 2001', *Natural Hazards*, **39** (2), 309–27. https://doi.org/10.1007/s11069-006-0030-x

Companies Act 1993.

Deakin, S. and S.J. Konzelmann (2004), 'Learning from Enron', *Corporate Governance: An International Review*, **12** (2), 134–42. https://doi.org/10.1111/j.1467-8683.2004 .00352.x

Dowell, G.W., M.B. Shackell and N.V. Stuart (2011), 'Boards, CEOs, and surviving a financial crisis: Evidence from the internet shakeout', *Strategic Management Journal*, **32** (10), 1025–45.

George, E. and P. Chattopadhyay (2008), 'Group composition and decision making', in G.P. Hodgkinson and W.H. Starbuck (eds), *The Oxford Handbook of Organizational Decision Making*, New York: Oxford University Press, pp. 361–82. https://doi.org/ 10.1093/oxfordhb/9780199290468.003.0019

Golden, B.R. and E.J. Zajac (2001), 'When will boards influence strategy? Inclination × power = strategic change', *Strategic Management Journal*, **22** (12), 1087–111.

James, E.H. and L.P. Wooten (2005), 'Leadership as (un)usual: How to display competence in times of crisis', *Organizational Dynamics*, **34** (2), 141–52. https://doi.org/ 10.1016/j.orgdyn.2005.03.005

Keenan Jr., W. (2007), 'Preparing for the worst', *Conference Board Review*, **45** (3), 52–57.

Lin-Hi, N. and I. Blumberg (2011), 'The relationship between corporate governance, global governance, and sustainable profits: Lessons learned from BP', *Corporate Governance: The International Journal of Business in Society*, **11** (5), 571–84. https://doi-org.ezproxy.auckland.ac.nz/10.1108/14720701111176984

Madsen-Ries v Cooper [2020] NZSC 100.

McKinsey & Company (2011), *Governance Since the Economic Crisis*, July, accessed at 3 November 2020 at https://www.mckinsey.com/featured-insights/leadership/ governance-since-the-economic-crisis-mckinsey-global-survey-results

McNulty, T., C. Florackis and P. Ormrod (2013), 'Boards of directors and financial risk during the credit crisis', *Corporate Governance: An International Review*, **21** (1), 58–78. https://doi.org/10.1111/corg.12007

Mellahi, K. (2005), 'The dynamics of boards of directors in failing organizations', *Long Range Planning*, **38** (3), 261–79. https://doi.org/10.1016/j.lrp.2005.04.001

Merendino, A. and G. Sarens (2020), 'Crisis? What crisis? Exploring the cognitive constraints on boards of directors in times of uncertainty', *Journal of Business Research*, **118**, 415–30. https://doi.org/10.1016/j.jbusres.2020.07.005

Patton, M.Q. (2002), *Qualitative Research and Evaluation Methods* (3rd edn), Thousand Oaks, CA: Sage.

Pavlovich, A. and S. Watson (2015), 'Director and shareholder liability at Pike River Coal', *Canterbury Law Review*, **21**, 1–43.

Sun, W., J. Stewart and D. Pollard (eds) (2011), *Corporate Governance and the Global Financial Crisis: International Perspectives*, Cambridge: Cambridge University Press.

Thamotheram, R. and M. Le Floc'h (2012), 'The BP crisis as a "preventable surprise": Lessons for institutional investors', *Rotman International Journal of Pension Management*, **5** (1), 68–76.

Tomasic, R. and F. Akinbami (2016), 'Effective risk management and improved corporate governance', in M. Hollow, F. Akinbami and R. Michie (eds), *Complexity and Crisis in the Financial System*, Cheltenham, UK and Northampton, MA, USA: Edward Elgar Publishing, pp. 214–40. https://doi.org/10.4337/9781783471331.00019

Weick, K.E. (1993). 'The collapse of sensemaking in organizations: The Mann Gulch disaster', *Administrative Science Quarterly*, **38** (4), 628–652. https://doi.org/10.2307/2393339

Weitzner, D. and T. Peridis (2011), 'Corporate governance as part of the strategic process: Rethinking the role of the board', *Journal of Business Ethics*, **102** (S1), 33–42. https://doi.org/10.1007/s10551-011-1195-0

Worthington, W.J., J.D. Collins and M.A. Hitt (2009), 'Beyond risk mitigation: Enhancing corporate innovation with scenario planning', *Business Horizons*, **52** (5), 441–50. https://doi.org/10.1016/j.bushor.2009.04.008

10. Manawa Ora – a conceptual model of Māori resilience

**Rachel Maunganui Wolfgramm,
Carla Houkamau and Tyron Love**

'Ehara taku toa i te toa takitahi, ēngari taku toa he toa takatini'
'My success is not one of a single warrior, but one of many'[1]

1.   INTRODUCTION

In Western psychological literature, the concept of resilience is widely understood to include the capacity to maintain psychological and physical well-being in the face of adversity and is typically conceptualized as a characteristic of an individual (Patterson and Kelleher, 2005; Schoon, 2006). In management literature, the term *career resilience* refers to a person's resistance to career disruption in less-than-optimal environments (Ledesma, 2014; O'Leary, 1998) with emphasis also placed on individual characteristics such as hardiness, self-efficacy, optimism, adaptability, risk-taking, low fear of failure, determination, perseverance and high tolerance for uncertainty and ambiguity (Patterson et al., 2002). For Māori and Indigenous writers and scholars, the notion of resilience is relational, encompassing the individual and collective, and can be defined as 'the means by which Indigenous people make use of individual and community strengths to protect themselves against adverse outcomes' (International Collaborative Indigenous Health Research Partnership/ICIHRP, 2004, p. 1 cited in Penehira et al., 2014, p. 98).

In this chapter, we extend a Māori perspective of resilience. Māori are the Indigenous peoples of New Zealand and the second-largest ethnic group in New Zealand at 16.5 per cent of the population. The majority group commonly referred to as 'Pākehā' or 'New Zealand European' comprised around 74 per cent of the New Zealand population in 2018 (Stats NZ, 2018). Māori were colonized by Pākehā who arrived in numbers from the early 1800s (Orange, 2013). Colonization in New Zealand was violent. It involved physical warfare, mass land confiscations, and the loss of lives for Māori, including loss from imported diseases (Durie, 1998). Against this history we consider the Māori response to the Covid-19 pandemic.

We begin with providing a background or context followed by a review of the Māori resilience literature. We put forward a new model of resilience – *Manawa Ora* – and offer four critical factors central to maintaining Māori community resilience: (1) Pūmahara, (2) Te Ao Māori, (3) Whakapapa, and (4) Rangatiratanga. In very practical ways, we draw insight from Māori demonstrations of community resilience in Aotearoa during the 2020 Covid-19 response. The Covid-19 pandemic placed Māori communities in full view. It not only brought into focus the socioeconomic disparities that already exist but also emphasized: the strong social networks among Māori, how Māori adapted tikanga (Māori values) to respond to the pandemic, the ability to distribute leadership, the safe use of social infrastructure (especially marae as tribal meeting places), and how Māori responded individually and collectively in times of crisis. We finish by setting a foundation for future research.

2.   BACKGROUND

Internationally, in response to the threats associated with Covid-19, governments have enforced lockdowns, controlled borders, managed isolation facilities and quarantines, closed businesses, halted international travel, and enforced physical distancing. When the first case of Covid-19 was reported in Aotearoa New Zealand on 28 February 2020, the central government had already imposed border restrictions and was monitoring the spread of the virus. A state of emergency was declared and at midnight on 25 March the country mostly shut down. At that stage, 47 other countries had reported the existence of Covid-19. On 27 April, restrictions were relaxed in Aotearoa New Zealand starting a period of transition away from government-imposed sanctions on people, communities, and businesses for the most part.

Prime Minister Jacinda Ardern was lauded for her empathetic approach toward the public, for her communicative style in rallying the country's population to adopt strict personal health measures, and for her ability to instil trust in the nation's population (McCarthy, 2020). At the same time US President Donald Trump faced criticism for his 'combative' style (McCarthy, 2020) and his public discourse fuelled conflict across, and within, state lines; even US state governors were launching lawsuits against state mayors over disagreements around ordinances such as the mandatory wearing of facemasks (Romo, 2020). Whilst the political landscape in the US now embraces a new era with President Joe Biden and the first elected female Vice President, Kamala Harris, both harmony and conflict appear to be playing out across countries, states, and communities as ideas emerge on how best to manage and serve the best interests of lives and livelihoods through the ongoing Covid-19 pandemic.

Adversity, and therefore the need to build resilience, are not new for Indigenous communities. Indeed, pandemics are not new to Indigenous peoples and communities. In the 1500s, smallpox 'ushered in the decline of the Aztec, Maya, and Incan civilisations' (Dicorato, 2020, n.p.); two centuries later, colonial weaponizing of smallpox against Native Americans devastated communities in North America (Fenn, 2000). Now, in a world battling Covid-19, the stakes are high for Indigenous communities, on a global scale. In Brazil, legal commentators are already considering whether genocide is playing out as Indigenous people die of Covid-19 at an alarming rate; some predictions suggest the disease 'could infect up to 40% of the Yanomami communities surrounded by illegal mining' (Amparo, 2020, para. 2). Back in the US, the Navajo Nation in Utah, New Mexico, and Arizona is experiencing one of the worst pandemics to hit its communities. American Indians and Alaska Natives are at a higher risk in the US, given greater rates of secondary chronic conditions such as diabetes and high blood pressure (Davis, 2020).

Indigenous communities in Bangladesh have been hit hard during the pandemic. Young garment workers have lost their jobs, forcing them to return to their villages without income. Farming families have failed to sell crops due to the closure of local markets; many face severe food shortages and large numbers have limited access to healthcare and receive little-to-no government relief (Chakma, 2020). In Bolivia, where almost half the people are Indigenous, Covid-19 cases increased drastically at the start of the pandemic. The pandemic posed greater threats to Indigenous groups because of vulnerable elder populations, their communal ways of living, and their limited access to resources (Dicorato, 2020). Such threats required immediate localized responses, and early actions by some tribal leaders have been highly effective in those locations. Early moves by the Alaska Native Tribal Health Consortium and by native community leaders in Alaska have been lauded for low case counts (Davis, 2020).

In Aotearoa New Zealand, it was evident that, whilst the government had created strategies in the national interest, Māori communities and leaders felt the need to respond in a focused and a sustained way. That response centred on whānau (family/extended), hapū (kinship entity/subtribe) and iwi (tribes), highlighting the role and importance of whakapapa (kinship relationships). Tribes went fishing for their people and the take was distributed around the motu (area) to all whānau with whakapapa connections. Te Rōpū Whakakaupapa Urutā (the Māori pandemic group) was set up by Māori health professionals to provide public health advice for whānau, Māori health providers, community groups and iwi. Māori primary health providers and tribal councils (Runanga) throughout Aotearoa were quick to respond to the whānau they serve (Health Quality & Safety Commission, 2020).

We argue that these community initiatives, interventions or actions were (and are) underpinned by deeper level structures worth knowing, and sharing, for the purposes of building community resilience in pandemic times. The questions remaining are: (a) What are these deeper level structures? and (b) What have Māori researchers said about them? We will continue by addressing these in the next section.

3.   RESEARCHING MĀORI AND INDIGENOUS RESILIENCE

Māori and Indigenous research is often motivated by a wider agenda to reclaim, reconstruct, and reformulate research to advance social justice, cultural survival, restoration, self-determination, and healing for Indigenous peoples (Battiste, 2011, 2017; Battiste and Youngblood, 2000; Denzin et al., 2008; Smith, 2013). Smith and colleagues outline different ways in which Indigenous research projects advance a collective philosophy; Mātauranga Māori (Māori knowledge) and Kaupapa Māori (Māori principles and values) align with this agenda and we seek to advance that agenda here. Drawing on the work of others, we propose as a starting position that resilience is, 'the means by which Indigenous people make use of individual and community strengths to protect themselves against adverse outcomes' (ICIHRP, 2004, p. 1 in Penehira et al., 2014, p. 98). Penehira et al. (2014) continue to argue that resilience needs to incorporate acceptance and resistance, reactive and proactive strategies, survival and flourishing, individual and collective resilience, and tensions between state control and self-determination.

Professor Mason Durie (1997) offers a framework of the determinants of Indigenous resilience which incorporates demographic transitions, human capability, cultural affirmation, attitudinal biases, the economy, lifestyle environments, policies of the state, Indigenous mobility, and leadership. In addition, in *Resilient Systems, Resilient Communities* Stewart-Harawira (2018) highlights that Indigenous peoples have displayed remarkable resilience in the face of adversity and have sought, through legal and other means, to regain and retain cultural and traditional rights, including traditional practices, languages, and identities, as well as the right to culturally appropriate forms of economic development. This resilience by Indigenous peoples can be described as grounded in culture, place and in Indigenous forms of spirituality.

Models of Indigenous resilience, therefore, take into account dynamic processes that move beyond response and survival to include proactively working to enhance thriving and well-being, or what some refer to as 'oranga' (Kirmayer et al., 2011; Wolfgramm et al., 2020). Yet operationalizing such models within institutions – which often operate under non-Māori structures and systems designed to hinder Māori well-being – is a major challenge for Māori. This became even more apparent during the Covid-19 pandemic. Leading Māori health expert, Rhys Jones, called for more Māori governance and leadership at all levels of the Aotearoa New Zealand Covid-19 pandemic response: within district health boards as well as across all other sectors (Jones, 2020). He noted that 'Whilst iwi, hapū, whanau, and Māori communities were mobilizing to respond during the pandemic, it needed to be supported and linked to the appropriate information, resources and infrastructure' (Jones, 2020).

The issues raised during Covid-19 confirm that Māori perspectives of resilience, whilst powerful tools locally, need institutional support and a broad suite of resources essential for well-being. Since Māori place significance on whānaungatanga (family relationships), maintaining high-quality social connections with whānau (extended family), and identification with wide tribal networks (Durie, 1997), models have been designed to assist those institutions in supporting local Māori communities. The most cited model of Māori well-being in this space is Mason Durie's (1985), Te Whare Tapa Whā (The House with Four Sides). This includes four elements: (1) te taha wairua (spiritual well-being), (2) te taha whānau (whānau well-being), (3) te taha hinengaro (mental well-being), and (4) te taha tinana (physical well-being).

The Families Commission (Social Policy Evaluation and Research Unit [Superu], 2015) developed the Whānau Rangatiratanga Conceptual Framework (Baker, 2016) to tease out factors that enhance whānau thriving and to operationalize the many dimensions contributing to whānau well-being and resilience; it identifies five dimensions of whānau well-being: (1) kotahitanga – collective unity including as Māori, as whānau and, supporting whānaungatanga, leadership and resilience; (2) wairuatanga – a spiritual embodiment including religion, spiritual well-being, faith and wider community relationships with environment and ancestors, and holistic connectedness; (3) manaakitanga – duties and expectations of care and reciprocity acknowledging other people's mana, or authority/status/power, reciprocal obligations to different whānau and to people outside whakapapa; (4) rangatiratanga – governance, leadership, and the traditional nature of Māori society including governance, leadership, authority and control, and whānau empowerment; and (5) whakapapa – descent, kinship, the essence of whānau, hapū, and iwi. This framework also identifies four capability dimensions: social capability (trust, connectedness), human resource potential (health, education, and quality of life), economic capability (employment, wealth, and housing) and sustainability of Te Ao Māori (language, identity, cultural institutions). There are also a further 20 outcome indicators to assess the well-being of Māori whānau (Baker, 2016).

In a comprehensive study capturing resilience in diverse whānau contexts, Waiti (2014) combines insight from systems theory of family resilience with his own study of whānau resilience. His key contribution is a framework, Whakaoranga Whānau, a whānau resilience framework detailing a resilience platform, protective factors, and coping strategies as well as key factors that facilitate resilience. The platform focuses on four key areas, (1) whānaungatanga (networks and relationships), (2) pākenga (skills and abilities), (3) tikanga (values and beliefs), and (4) tuariki-a-Māori (cultural identity). These resilience factors were all considered essential to the well-being of individuals and whānau. Given that hapū and iwi are also primary social communities for Māori, the iwi vitality outcomes framework developed by Porter and Ratima (2014) adds important considerations to our understanding of Māori resilience: securing identities, te reo Māori (the Māori language) proficiency in iwi knowledge, knowing customary practices, and having access to the natural environment are some essential components.

What follows is our conceptual model of Māori resilience in pandemic times, taking inspiration from the researchers we have introduced above. Our thesis is that broader national and governmental institutional understanding and support of the five elements we put forward will enable enduring forms of community resilience.

4.   DISCUSSION

We use the term, *Manawa Ora*, for our model. In te reo Māori (the Māori language) the word *ora* means to be well, healthy and flourishing. It is common in Aotearoa New Zealand. For instance, it is used in the Māori greeting, kia ora, which means, 'I hope you have continued good health and that you will be well'. Ora is also used in terms such as mauri ora (strong life force), hauora (physical well-being), whānau ora (healthy family), and so on. *Manawa* means heart, and combined with *ora* it references hope. Now to the main elements of *Manawa Ora*. As we stated earlier, these are: (1) pūmahara, (2) te ao Māori, (3) whakapapa, and (4) rangatiratanga; they will be explained briefly, below.

4.1   Pūmahara: Guiding through Learned Resilience

For Māori, *pūmahara* is a generative collective memory code cocreated in social institutions which connects back to the many different ways in which a Māori and Indigenous narrative is crafted. Of course, these social memories also reside within the lived realities of colonization. The Covid-19 crisis activated pūmahara. According to Smith (2013), for Indigenous peoples, remembering is painful but also necessary for holistic healing. In our framework of Māori resilience, we argue that accessing this social memory was critical in activating a response from Māori communities and leaders during the Covid-19 crisis.

When Europeans first arrived in Aotearoa New Zealand, Māori had no immunity against many of the virulent diseases new immigrants brought with them. Significant diseases were introduced by Europeans including venereal infections, measles, influenza, typhoid fever (enteric fever), dysentery, and tuberculosis (Lange, 2018). These new diseases had a disproportionate and significant impact on Māori communities; the cumulative effect of introduced diseases led to death, food shortages, a decreased labour force, and unspeakable pain and suffering (Rice, 2018).

Such is the importance of activating social memory. Building resilience from lived experience is critical. It is no surprise that Māori leaders and communities drew on the pūmahara of their communities to act swiftly in response to the threat of the Covid-19.

4.2   Te ao Māori: Guiding through Philosophical Resilience

Underpinning *te ao Māori* (the Māori world view) are Māori values or tikanga (Durie, 1995; Henare, 1988, 2001, 2014; Mead, 2016; see also Harmsworth, 2005): the priorities and preferences of individuals and groups that reflect what is important to them (Henderson et al., 2006). Unprioritized values create conflict and so clear values in communities and organizations are their real leader. Tikanga or values are the DNA of culture as they determine what happens and why (Henderson et al., 2006). Henare's (2001) koru (spiral) of values best captures the principles guiding tikanga at the heart of te ao Māori. They include, but are not limited to, tikanga te ao marama (wholeness, cosmos), tikanga hau (spiritual basis of reciprocity in relationships), tikanga whānaungatanga (belonging), and tikanga tiakitanga (guardianship of creation and resources).

As with pūmahara, Māori resilience is guided by te ao Māori as a philosophy of practice. Māori keenly demonstrate values, such as those above, through rituals, ceremonies, and daily life. Māori followed strict Covid-19 lockdown level guidelines when they were imposed by government which meant compromising on certain practices. For example, rituals such as hongi (pressing of noses when greeting) and tangihanga (funerals) were most prohibited and Māori had to adapt. But Māori developed new ways of mourning through televised poroporoaki (defined in this context as farewell ceremonies) and utilized user-friendly technologies to ensure whānau around the country, and indeed the world, could come together to mourn the loss of loved ones thereby maintaining deeper values connected to, and driven by, te ao Māori.

4.3   Whakapapa: Building a Layered Resilience

Māori identify themselves through their connections to people as well as the natural environment. *Whakapapa* refers to the layering of relationships and is key to the creation and maintenance of te ao Māori. Whakapapa is an analytical tool employed to facilitate building an appreciation of our relationships in the world and to understanding identity construction (Henry and Wolfgramm, 2016). As a form of genealogical recital, whakapapa is defined as the layering and ordering of people and events across time and space. As a heuristic device, whakapapa is used to articulate relationships of self with others in terrestrial (lands, mountains, waterways), ancestral (lineage), spiritual (guardians/gods of the cosmos), and social spheres (tribes) (Henry and Wolfgramm, 2016).

To support Māori communities Te Rōpū Whakakaupapa Urutā/the Māori pandemic group (comprised of some of the nation's leading Māori medical and health experts including primary care specialists, public health experts, public health physicians, Māori nurses and iwi leaders) was set up to provide public health advice for whānau, Māori health providers, community groups, and iwi. The group created a website and digital platforms to provide expert health advice for whānau, iwi, and health providers (Te Rōpū Whakakaupapa Urutā National Māori Pandemic Group, 2020). Driven by whakapapa connections, various subgroups emerged throughout Aotearoa New Zealand working across different areas, including Māori hospital-based specialists, and GPs working in primary health care, policymakers, and funders serving the Māori community (for example, see Health Quality & Safety Commission, 2020 for examples of the responses from iwi organisations, Māori providers and community groups throughout Aotearoa/New Zealand). Furthermore, social enterprises led by Māori emerged across Aotearoa New Zealand. Te Pataka Inc was established to provide kai (food) and firewood to assist whānau experiencing hardship and Te Puni Kokiri (the Ministry for Māori Development) proactively focused on ensuring Māori remained healthy, strong and resilient.

4.4   Rangatiratanga: Leading through Resilience

According to Durie (1997), Māori aspirations for greater control over their own destinies and resources is variously described as a search for sovereignty, autonomy, independence, self-governance, self-determination, tino rangatiratanga, and mana motuhake. The overall aim is Māori advancement, economic self-sufficiency, social equity, cultural affirmation, and political strength.

This was evidenced in the Covid-19 crisis as Māori leaders and tribal iwi took measures into their own hands to stop the virus from entering and spreading into their communities, particularly in isolated communities. Iwi-led checkpoints (roadblocks) emerged throughout the country. Te Whānau a Apanui chose to close their borders, on 25 March 2020, to all who did not reside in the area. The remote community of Te Araroa also created plans to establish their checkpoint before lockdown as did communities in Hicks Bay, Te Araroa, Ruatoria, and Tokomaru Bay. Iwi in the Far North, Taranaki, Maketu, and Murupura followed. Although these were controversial, many Māori throughout the country supported these roadblocks as a symbol of Māori exercising tino rangatiratanga (see Dutta et al., 2020; Harris and Williams, 2020). Tribal iwi decision makers and police, along with local government decision makers, worked together to place restrictions on travel and to shelter susceptible communities from the dangers of Covid-19. Early actions by tribal leaders in other countries was also evident. Early moves were made by the Alaska Native Tribal Health Consortium and by native community leaders in Alaska and have subsequently been credited for the low case count in their communities and villages (Davis, 2020).

5. CONCLUSION

The Māori response to the Covid-19 pandemic was an exercise in the contemporary expression of Māori resilience and indicative of the strong adaptive capacity of Māori. Māori leaders and communities acted with swiftness and a collectively to ensure the well-being of whānau and communities. In the process, Māori demonstrated strong leadership based on the strength and resilience of whakapapa connections guided by historical learnings and a deep philosophy of resilience grounded in te ao Māori philosophy. In many cases, iwi leaders responded faster and with more decisiveness than government to ensure their people were well informed, and their exposure to Covid-19 was minimized (Hitchcock, 2020).

These current and future challenges motivated us to contribute a conceptual framework that would extend the understanding of key factors underpinning Māori resilience. We derived insights from Māori demonstrations of community leadership and adaptive capacity during the Covid-19 pandemic. The pandemic not only bought into focus the socioeconomic disparities that already exist, but also emphasized strong social networks, and how Māori adapt tikanga to the times; and demonstrated distributive leadership, the value of safe use of social infrastructure (especially marae – tribal meeting places), and how Māori respond individually and collectively in times of crisis. Manawa Ora, the model of Māori resilience which is the heart of this chapter, offers a timely contribution to understanding resilience from a collective perspective. Future research will focus on investigating strategies to enhance resilience and rebuild Māori economies of well-being in a post-Covid-19 environment.

NOTE

1. Māori whakataukī (proverb) attributed to Paterangi of Ngāti Kahungunu (Māori iwi/tribe) cited in Mead and Grove (2007, p. 24).

REFERENCES

Amparo, T. (2020), 'The flawed legal battle to save Brazil's Indigenous from COVID-19', accessed 15 August 2020 at https://www.americasquarterly.org/article/the-flawed-legal-battle-to-save-brazils-indigenous-from-COVID-19/

Baker, K. (2016), *The Whānau Rangatiratanga Frameworks: Approaching whānau well-being from within te ao Māori*, accessed 29 October 2020 at https://thehub.swa.govt.nz/assets/Uploads/Whanau-rangatiratanga-frameworks-summary.pdf

Battiste, M. (2011), *Reclaiming Indigenous Voice and Vision*, Vancouver: UBC Press.

Battiste, M. (2017), *Decolonising Education: Nourishing the Learning Spirit*, Vancouver: UBC Press.

Battiste, M. and Youngblood, J. (2000), *Protecting Indigenous knowledge and Heritage: A Global Challenge*, Vancouver: UBC Press.

Chakma, P. (2020), 'With music, Bangladesh's indigenous youth offer hope amid COVID-19' accessed 15 August 2020 at https://news.trust.org/item/20200812142321-6ovaz/

Davis, H. (2020), 'COVID-19 is disproportionately impacting indigenous Americans' accessed 15 August 2020 at https://www.alaskasnewssource.com/2020/08/12/covid-19-is-disproportionately-impacting-indigenous-americans/

Denzin, N.K., Y.S. Lincoln and L.T. Smith (eds) (2008), *Handbook of Critical and Indigenous Methodologies*, Thousand Oaks, CA: Sage.

Dicorato, A. (2020), 'Opinion: In Bolivia, a model for Indigenous groups grappling with COVID-19', *Undark*, accessed 15 August 2020 at https://undark.org/2020/08/13/bolivia-indigenous-COVID-19/

Durie, M. (1985), 'A Māori perspective of health', *Journal of Social Science and Medicine*, **20** (5), 483–86. doi:10.1016/0277-9536(85)90363-6

Durie, M.H. (1995), 'Mental health patterns for the New Zealand Māori', in I. al Issa (ed.), *Handbook of Culture and Mental Illness: An International Perspective*, Madison, CT: International University Press, pp. 331–45.

Durie, M. (1997), 'Whānau, whānaungatanga, and healthy Māori development', in P. Te Whaiti, P. McCarthy and A. Durie (eds), *Mai i Rangiatea: Māori Well-being and Development*, Auckland: Auckland University Press, pp. 16–19.

Durie, M. (1998), *Te mana, te kāwanatanga: The Politics of Māori Self-determination*, Auckland: Oxford University Press.

Dutta, M.J., C. Elers and P. Jayan (2020), 'Culture-centered processes of community organising in COVID-19 response: Notes from Kerala and Aotearoa New Zealand', *Frontiers in Communication*, **5**, 1–16. doi:10.3389/fcomm.2020.00062

Fenn, E. (2000), 'Biological warfare in eighteenth-century North America: Beyond Jeffery Amherst', *The Journal of American History*, **86** (4), 1552–80. doi:10.2307/2567577

Harmsworth, G.R. (2005), *Report on incorporation of traditional values/tikanga into contemporary Māori business organisations and process*, report prepared for Mana Taiao, Palmerston North, New Zealand: Landcare Research.

Harris, M. and D.V. Williams (2020), 'Community checkpoints are an important and lawful part of NZ's Covid response', *The Spinoff*, 10 May, accessed 27 July 2020 at https://thespinoff.co.nz/society/10-05-2020/community-checkpoints-an-important-and-lawful-part-of-nzs-covid-response/

Henderson, M., D. Thompson and S. Henderson (2006), Leading through Values: Linking Company Culture to Business Strategy, Auckland: HarperCollins.

Health Quality & Safety Commission (2020, November 3), 'Te Rohe o te Wairoa, Hawke's Bay, Ngāti Kahungunu and the response to COVID-19 between February and May 2020'. Retrieved from https://www.hqsc.govt.nz/news-and-events/news/4146/

Henare, M. (1988), *Ngā tikanga me ngā ritenga o te ao Māori: Standards and Foundations of Māori Society*, Wellington: Royal Commission on Social Policy.

Henare, M. (2001), 'Tapu, mana, mauri, hau, wairua. A Māori philosophy of vitalism and cosmos', in J. Grimm (ed.), *Indigenous Traditions and Ecology: The Interbeing of Cosmology and Community*, Cambridge: Harvard University Press, pp. 197–221.

Henare, M. (2014), 'The economy of mana', in D. Cooke, C. Hill, P. Baskett and R. Irwin (eds), *Beyond the Free Market: Rebuilding a Just Society in New Zealand*, Auckland: Dunmore, pp. 65–9.

Henry, E. and R. Wolfgramm (2016), 'Relational leadership–An indigenous Māori perspective', *Leadership*, **14** (2), 203–19.

Hitchcock, J. (2020), 'The effects of the COVID-19 recession will hit Māori hardest', *The Spinoff*, accessed 29 October 2020 at https://thespinoff.co.nz/atea/08-04-2020/the-effects-of-the-COVID-19-recession-will-hit-maori-hardest/

Jones, R. (2020, March 20), Why equity for Māori must be prioritised during the COVID-19 response. Retrieved from https://www.auckland.ac.nz/en/news/2020/03/20/equity-maori-prioritised-covid-19-response.html

Kirmayer, L.J., S. Dandeneau, E. Marshall, M.K. Phillips and K.J. Williamson (2011), 'Rethinking resilience from Indigenous perspectives', *The Canadian Journal of Psychiatry*, **56** (2), 84–91. doi:10.1177/070674371105600203

Lange, R. (2018), 'Te hauora Māori i mua – history of Māori health – Health devastated, 1769 to 1901', *Te Ara - the Encyclopedia of New Zealand*, accessed 11 December 2020 at http://www.TeAra.govt.nz/en/te-hauora-maori-i-mua-history-of-maori-health/page-2

Ledesma, J. (2014), 'Conceptual frameworks and research models on resilience in leadership', *Sage Open*, **4** (3), 2158244014545464.

McCarthy, J. (2020), 'Praised for curbing COVID-19, New Zealand's leader eases country's strict lockdown', *NPR*, 25 April, accessed 14 August 2020 at https://www.npr.org/sections/coronavirus-live-updates/2020/04/25/844720581/praised-for-curbing-COVID-19-new-zealands-leader-eases-country-s-strict-lockdown?t=1588940528046

Mead, H.M. (2016), *Tikanga Māori: Living by Māori Values* (rev. ed.), Wellington: Huia Publishers.

Mead, H.M. and N. Grove (2007), *Ngā Pēpeha a ngā Tipuna: The Sayings of the Ancestors*, Wellington: Victoria University Press.

Orange, C. (2013), *The Story of a Treaty*, Wellington: Bridget Williams Books.

O'Leary, V.E. (1998), 'Strength in the face of adversity: Individual and social thriving', *Journal of Social Issues*, **54** (2), 425–46.

Patterson, J.L. and P. Kelleher (2005), *Resilient School Leaders: Strategies for Turning Adversity into Achievement*, Alexandria, VA: ASCD.

Patterson, J.L., J. Patterson and L. Collins (2002), *Bouncing Back! How your School can Succeed in the Face of Adversity*, Plano, TX: Eye on Education.

Penehira, M., A. Green, L.T. Smith and C. Aspin (2014), 'Māori and indigenous views on R and R: Resistance and resilience', *MAI Journal: A New Zealand Journal of Indigenous Scholarship*, **3** (2), 96–110.

Porter, J. and M. Ratima (2014), 'Ka pīoioi i te tihi o ngā kahikatea: Measuring Ngāi Tai iwi vitality', *MAI Journal: A New Zealand Journal of Indigenous Scholarship*, **3** (3), 268–85. accessed 10 December 2020 at http://www.review.mai.ac.nz

Rice, G. (2018), 'Epidemics – The influenza era, 1890s to 1920s', *Te Ara – the Encyclopedia of New Zealand*, accessed 12 December 2020 at http://www.TeAra.govt.nz/en/epidemics/page-4

Romo, V. (2020), 'Governor drops lawsuit against Atlanta mayor over masks, but fight may not be over', *NPR*, 13 August, accessed 14 August 2020 at https://www.npr.org/sections/coronavirus-live-updates/

Schoon, I. (2006), *Risk and Resilience: Adaptations in Changing Times*, Cambridge, UK: Cambridge University Press.

Smith, L.T. (2013), *Decolonising Methodologies: Research and Indigenous Peoples*, London: Zed Books.

Social Policy Evaluation and Research Unit (2015), *Families and whānau status report 2015*, accessed 29 October 2020 at https://thehub.swa.govt.nz/assets/Uploads/Families-and-Whanau-Research-Summary.pdf

Stats NZ (2018), 2018 Census Ethnic Group Summaries, accessed December 5 2020 at https://www.stats.govt.nz/tools/2018-census-ethnic-group-summaries/m%C4%81ori

Stewart-Harawira, M. (2018), 'Indigenous resilience and pedagogies of resistance: Responding to the crisis of our age', in J. Kinder and M. Stewart-Harawira (eds), *Resilient Systems, Resilient Communities*, Edmonton: University of Alberta, pp. 158–79. https://doi.org/10.7939/R38K75B1W (Original work published 2015)

Te Rōpū Whakakaupapa Urutā National Māori Pandemic Group (2020), retrieved from https://www.uruta.maori.nz/

Waiti, J. (2014), *Whakaoranga whānau: A whānau resilience framework* (Unpublished doctoral thesis), Massey University, Wellington, New Zealand.

Wolfgramm, R., C. Spiller, E. Henry and R. Pouwhare (2020), 'A culturally derived framework of values-driven transformation in Māori economies of well-being (Ngā hono ōhanga oranga)', *AlterNative: An International Journal of Indigenous Peoples*, **16** (1), 18–28.

PART III

Moving forward and sector perspectives on Covid-19

11. Focusing on sustainable value creation amidst and beyond the Covid-19 crisis through the use of Integrated Thinking

Ruth Dimes and Charl de Villiers

1. INTRODUCTION

In this chapter, we discuss how the adoption of Integrated Reporting and its underpinning management philosophy of Integrated Thinking prior to the Covid-19 crisis helped to improve internal decision making and communication for a New Zealand company in the energy sector, enabling a focus on longer term strategic sustainability goals amidst the considerable disruption caused by Covid-19.

Integrated Reporting and Integrated Thinking are recent developments in corporate reporting, attracting significant interest since the global financial crisis (GFC) of 2007/08 emphasized the shortcomings of traditional profit-based corporate reporting (Rowbottom and Locke, 2016). Although Integrated Reporting and Integrated Thinking have been adopted as a reaction to crisis situations (de Villiers and Maroun, 2018), there is little evidence to date of their usefulness during a crisis. One of the few prior examples of using Integrated Thinking in a crisis (a military conflict) found that a focus on information sharing and collaboration gave the company significant agility when dealing with unforeseen changes (Al-Htaybat and von Alberti-Alhtaybat, 2018). Our findings support this, giving early evidence of the potential for Integrated Thinking to help organizations to navigate other crisis situations.

Integrated Reporting requires an organization to report on its use of six 'capitals' (financial, natural, intellectual, social, human and manufactured) to create sustainable value into the future. Integrated Reporting's combination of financial and non-financial reporting has developed from earlier corporate reporting movements such as the 'triple bottom line' (Elkington, 1998) and combines standalone Corporate Social Responsibility (CSR) and sustainability reports and traditional financial reports into a single concise forward-looking document (de Villiers et al., 2014). Integrated Reporting is unique, however, in its dual aim to change external reporting through Integrated Reporting and to simultaneously change internal decision making through Integrated Thinking (Simnett and Huggins, 2015). Integrated Thinking is the process by which internal decisions are made with reference to the same six capitals, and is associated with improved internal communication, the breakdown of organizational silos and improved stakeholder relationships (Knauer and Serafeim, 2014).

EnergyCo,[1] the case study company which is the focus of this chapter, is a listed company in the New Zealand energy sector. The company has a long history of sustainable business, with a focus on renewable energy and a commitment to energy sustainability by 2025. In 2017, EnergyCo adopted Integrated Reporting, but this was poorly understood internally. In 2018, the organization focused on embedding Integrated Thinking first, and saw more success. A series of semi-structured interviews were conducted with senior managers during 2018 and 2019 to understand how EnergyCo had used management control systems to embed Integrated Thinking into the organization (Dimes and de Villiers, 2020). As these initial interviews were conducted well in advance of the Covid-19 pandemic, during a time of economic success and stability for EnergyCo, they did not consider the role Integrated Thinking might play when managing an organization during a crisis. Indeed, during one of the pre-Covid-19 interviews, one of the participants had even highlighted that many of the recent initiatives that EnergyCo had engaged in had never been tested in a 'burning platform' situation: 'There has never been a contextual scenario that's meant ... "You are bloody well going to do this ... and there will be consequences if you don't." We are just not in that territory'.

The subsequent development of the Covid-19 crisis in early 2020 therefore handed us a unique opportunity to conduct follow-up interviews for participants to reflect on their recent experiences during the crisis. We conducted these interviews on Zoom during the first New Zealand lockdown period, and focused our questions on how individuals and the company as a whole were reacting to the crisis.

Our findings from this uniquely timed case study of EnergyCo illustrate how consistent alignment with clearly communicated long-term strategic goals, embedded into both formal strategic planning processes and the organizational culture, helped to focus decisions on long-term goals rather than short-term financial concerns. The transition to online working was relatively seamless, supported by well-functioning cross-functional teams and prompt and honest communication. EnergyCo focused on financial support for their suppliers and customers, understanding their contribution to long-term sustainable value creation rather than chasing them for payment. The company also continued to focus on supporting employees and maintaining a collaborative culture to encourage information sharing.

2.   BACKGROUND

Integrated Reporting is a type of organizational reporting which has gained increasing interest from both practitioners and academics since the GFC of 2007/08. Integrated Reporting requires organizations to explain in a single concise document how they use six types of capital (financial, natural, intellectual, social, human and manufactured) to create sustainable value into the future (de Villiers et al., 2020; International Integrated Reporting Council [IIRC], 2013). The focus on these six capitals recognizes the importance of considering the many intangible non-financial resources that play a significant part in long-term value creation (Schorger and Sewchurran, 2015).

Integrated Reporting is not just focused on external reporting, however. Integrated Reporting is unique in its dual aim to streamline and simplify external reporting and to simultaneously change internal decision making processes through the adoption of Integrated Thinking (IIRC, 2013). Integrated Reporting therefore also recognizes the importance of combining financial and non-financial information for internal decision making, aligning with other popular management accounting developments such as the balanced scorecard (Esch et al., 2019; Kaplan and Norton, 1996). Integrated Reporting's unique focus on combining internal decision making and external reporting means that it has the potential to be one of the most disruptive developments in corporate reporting (Simnett and Huggins, 2015).

So what exactly is Integrated Thinking? Integrated Thinking is the process of considering the six capitals of Integrated Reporting in everyday decision making, and is associated with improved internal communication, the breakdown of a 'silo' mentality and increased employee confidence in their stakeholder engagement strategy (Knauer and Serafeim, 2014). Integrated Thinking can be considered a form of management, as the 'attribute or capacity for senior management to constructively face the tensions between corporate efficiency and a model that considers broader societal health and well-being' (Oliver et al., 2016). Although an exact definition remains elusive, Integrated Thinking is considered to be part of the 'virtuous' cycle of Integrated Reporting adoption, with the majority of practitioners considering it valuable in improving organizational communication and efficiency (Black Sun, 2014).

3.   THE CASE OF ENERGYCO

3.1   Case Study Background

EnergyCo is a renewable energy producer and retailer which was formed by the privatization of a New Zealand government-owned energy authority.

Under the influence of a new CEO, EnergyCo underwent a major rebranding in 2015, committing to energy sustainability by 2025. EnergyCo adopted Integrated Thinking and Integrated Reporting in 2017, with the aim of embedding a commitment to sustainability across the organization. It became clear, however, that the external reporting and metrics for 2017 had not been well understood internally, resulting in a decision to focus more on Integrated Thinking for 2018:

> The 2017 report ... was driven by reporting frameworks, GRI in particular ... it was kind of obvious that it had been done as a reporting exercise and yes [the executive team] had seen it and read it, but they hadn't really engaged with it ... that was the important first step ... to get them to take ownership of it.

EnergyCo developed a sustainable vision underpinned by strategic pillars aligning closely to the six capitals model and focused on embedding Integrated Thinking by developing a culture of trust and collaboration, focusing on the development of individuals and teams. The Covid-19 pandemic in 2020 came after EnergyCo's second full year of this integrated approach, causing major disruption to its ways of working and to its customer and supplier operations.

3.2   Embedding Integrated Thinking

EnergyCo encouraged the internal adoption of Integrated Thinking by clearly communicating the corporate vision to its employees and by deliberately incorporating the six capitals into the strategic planning process. Developing a culture of trust and collaboration was key to the success of this. Many of these changes were achieved through social rather than technical management controls,[2] reinforcing the importance of an investment in people and organizational culture. The examples below illustrate the effectiveness of this approach when challenged by Covid-19.

3.2.1   Clear communication of organizational vision and goals
EnergyCo's clear and consistent messaging around corporate values was evident during the Covid-19 pandemic. Interviewees confirmed that following the first New Zealand lockdown, their conversations with suppliers and customers were focused on honest conversations around business continuity and the preservation of relationships rather than on financial penalties. Employees understood the organizational vision and the need to remain focused on customers and suppliers as relationships that were critical to the long-term survival of EnergyCo:

> And right out of the blocks [the CEO] was clear to say ... 'We will look after our supply base; we will not have suppliers going bust because of us' .... There have

been some scenarios where we've just paid retainers to say 'you're not doing any work for us at the moment ... we'll continue to pay you to keep you afloat'. And we've also triggered a regime of increased frequency of payment runs ... just to help ensure cash fly, fly, fly.

EnergyCo's organizational vision is communicated using a simple diagram and mission statement. These portray a sustainable energy production and consumption story for their broad stakeholder base which includes customers, partners, employees and the natural environment. The vision and mission statement are used both to communicate information to external stakeholders and to guide employees towards desired organizational outcomes (Gond et al., 2012). Sustainability is widely understood as every employee's responsibility, from the main board downwards:

> Sustainability is fundamental to the way we are operating the business. It is not going to be added on to [power] generation, because that is where the environmental team sits, it is not going to be in customer because it is just related to an opportunity to promote our brand in a particular way, it is actually the whole thing.

EnergyCo's corporate vision is supported by five 'pillars' which underpin the mission of the company and determine its strategic priorities. These five pillars map closely to the six Integrated Reporting capitals (financial, natural, intellectual, social, human and manufactured). Instead of using Integrated Reporting's six capitals, EnergyCo chose to use their own five pillars, feeling that they were more representative of the company and would be better understood by employees. The iconography associated with EnergyCo's five pillars is very distinctive and is evident not only on external documents such as their integrated reports, but also on external communications such as their website, and on internal documents, office lobbies and walls. The vision diagram in particular is well recognized: 'This diagram ... is on the wall in every office' and the diagram is well understood and repeatedly referenced in internal presentations: 'This is always the second slide that is presented ... we just reorient ourselves to that constantly ... it is emphasized by management fairly repetitively which is good'.

The CEO set the tone for business operations very quickly during Covid-19, and employees clearly regarded the CEO as instrumental to the clear and continuing communication of the overall mission of EnergyCo: 'Our CEO is incredibly strong about this bigger nuanced view of our place in the system and of the role and opportunity that we have as a business to be successful by the rest of the system being successful'.

Prior to Covid-19, the CEO had led a focus on the development of people as the key competitive advantage for the company. A series of internal workshops was conducted to develop individual people leaders, which subsequently led to work to develop high-performance teams. Workshops focused on concepts such as 'trust, healthy conflict and accountability' and teams were supported with practical tools and activities to support them through behavioural change and methods of assessing their relative success. Recruitment agencies were briefed on the goals of the organization and encouraged to focus on interviewees exhibiting the right kinds of behaviour, resulting in improved time-to-hire statistics and a more personal connection to EnergyCo's values: 'One of the reasons why I was interested and took the role, [was] because I am a strong advocate for that kind of thinking that doesn't sit in silos'.

EnergyCo's efforts to embed sustainability into the organization paid dividends during Covid-19, as employees clearly understood the company's vision and were emboldened to make swift decisions in line with the vision.

3.2.2   Embedding long-term goals into the strategic-planning process

Following the Covid-19 outbreak, comments from one manager indicated that the longer term three-year planning process that had recently been introduced had helped to 'ground' the company in terms of overall strategic planning, as business units were still working towards the longer term targets and had them in their sights, even though the immediate focus was on scenario planning for the next 12 months. Improved relationships between departments based on an expanded business partnering model also improved the flow of information and made the move to online working smoother.

At EnergyCo, the business planning process for 2019/20 had been done in reference to the organizational vision and the five strategic pillars which represented a ten-year plan for value creation. This was the first time that sustainability had been so formally incorporated into the planning process, and this helped to create awareness and formulate strategies for sustainability (Galbreath, 2010). Business units, supported by finance business partners, developed three-year capex and operating profit plans aligned with the vision and pillars. By the end of June, the board approved a three-year plan, communicated using an 'A3 scorecard' containing financial and non-financial measures for the whole company and supported by individual scorecards specific to each business unit.

This focus on linking the planning to ten-year vision statements helped to embed a shift in thinking from capital-led decision making to outcome-led decision making:

> There has been a metamorphosis – we have moved away from 'So you spent x last year, so in this year you will need "x plus a bit"' ... towards 'So what are you going to do? What is your activity set, and then we'll shape your finances to fit your activity set'.

Another initiative aimed at breaking down the culture of business-unit silos was the expansion of business partnering throughout the company. EnergyCo describes its business units, which produce power and sell to both wholesale and retail markets, as 'verticals'. Supporting these are the 'lateral' functions which include people and performance, finance, corporate affairs and information systems. As EnergyCo started to focus on Integrated Thinking, this distinction started to shift: 'Over the last few years we have moved a lot of the support functions, be they accountants or analysts etc., out of those businesses in the verticals ... and put them into lateral functions to work across the organization'.

The expansion of business partnering improved the flow of information and also made the finance function more aware of business unit issues and opportunities for knowledge sharing and problem solving.

3.2.3   A culture of collaboration and trust

In the interviews during the Covid-19 lockdown, one manager indicated that the transition to working from home would have been far more difficult had it happened 12 months earlier, before the company had begun to focus so heavily on the importance of successful teamwork. The interviewee expressed surprise at how smoothly the transition to working from home had gone, and how many benefits were being realized by improved collaboration and productivity through technology with employees working remotely. Other interviewees observed that EnergyCo's recent focus on 'ways of working' had been considerably more important than its pre-Covid-19 physical move into a new centralized office, which was now described by one interviewee as a 'white elephant'.

The organizational vision discussed earlier in this chapter was underpinned by significant developments in EnergyCo's corporate culture, with a strong focus on collaboration and developing an enterprise-level mindset. Firm culture represented an important social control for EnergyCo (Malmi and Brown, 2008), representing the collection of beliefs, values and assumptions which defined the extent to which its business was conducted responsibly (Schein, 1996).

The most visible example of EnergyCo's dedication to cultural change was the combination of several offices (including the former head office) into a single central office. The new building was carefully designed by both employees and external contractors to encourage collaborative working, with employees having lockers rather than fixed desks, for example, being encouraged to work in different, less traditional meeting spaces and to use collaborative tools such as OneNote and OneDrive. The move had been presented to employees as a change to their ways of working, rather than just a physical move: 'It is really not about the building; it is actually about how we work together and the way in which we work'. EnergyCo's new office served as a way of reinforcing a broader, more integrated organizational perspective for employees, which was generally well received: 'We've got all the tools we need here and it's got a nice positive vibe to it .... I think everybody being within one building helps to "de-silo" people'.

Another key initiative to improve internal collaboration prior to Covid-19 was the formation of an 'enterprise leaders team' comprising approximately 80 senior people managers who meet a few times a year. The team has no hierarchical function, but acts to encourage cross-functional discussion at an enterprise-wide level and to discourage the silo thinking that is a recognized issue with the traditional business-unit structure (Feng et al., 2017; Guthrie et al., 2017). This helped with appreciation of the wider business goals and the importance of collaboration: 'In the last four years we have had a massive push around what we call "sharing and connecting", and breaking down this culture of "This is my stuff and I'm not going to play with you" ... notions of territory ... are not cool anymore'.

Employees were also more likely to share their successes with one another in these enterprise leadership sessions, with a focus on benefits to the entire company: 'An example being sharing of maintenance lessons at one [power] station being applied to save money and time on decisions made at an adjacent one, whereas in the past that may not have happened'.

Interviewees attributed improved decision making directly to these teams, which provided employees with a safe environment to voice their concerns (Schein, 1996):

> There was a history of some projects that had been over time and over budget, potentially because people weren't signalling early if something was potentially going off track ... whereas now there is a lot more 'Well, I see something going wrong I'm going to call it', and things are being addressed more quickly.

EnergyCo's tangible measures of Integrated Thinking included an employee feedback survey conducted every year which provided lead indicators in key areas, indicating positive results for efficient working and addressing conflict. In addition, EnergyCo was using employee-led storytelling to capture success stories resulting from improved teamwork, for example improved time taken to complete projects: 'We measure the impact and have evidence to show that it is adding the value needed to drive the business forward ... we are actually being more efficient ... we are making better smarter decisions faster'.

In addition to internal benefits, interviewees mentioned that the benefits of teamwork within the company were also starting to be recognized by external stakeholders, with potential long-term economic benefits in terms of contract renegotiations: 'Anecdotally we have heard [that] instead of normal contract negotiations with a supplier it has been about people sitting down and getting to know one another, because it is all about relationships and trust'.

Following the Covid-19 outbreak, top management was keen that the treatment of external stakeholders continued to meet EnergyCo's commitment to its five pillars. Conversations with suppliers and customers were focused on enabling them to continue in business with EnergyCo's support, with a focus on preservation of customer and supplier relationships rather than on credit limits and contractual obligations.

The focus on the cultural environment and on enabling collaboration both inside and outside the organization shows the potential for informal controls such as culture and teamwork to deliver positive economic outcomes and to be of considerable importance in the adoption of Integrated Thinking. The coordinated commitment of the CEO, the establishment of cross-functional teams and an increase in business partnering was also critical in this case.

4.   DISCUSSION

EnergyCo did not adopt Integrated Reporting and Integrated Thinking in order to navigate a crisis, nor could any organization have foreseen the level of unprecedented disruption caused by Covid-19. However, it is notable how the work that EnergyCo undertook to embed Integrated Reporting and Integrated Thinking helped it to navigate some early challenges of the pandemic. As Integrated Reporting and Integrated Thinking are recent developments in the corporate reporting landscape, the evidence presented in this case represents one of the first tests of the usefulness of Integrated Reporting and Integrated Thinking in a crisis situation outside of Al-Htaybat and von Alberti-Alhtaybat's 2018 study, set in a war zone.

There are three key features of the EnergyCo case which could apply to any organization regardless of their adoption of Integrated Reporting and Integrated Thinking: clarity of overall organizational goals, embedding sustainability into strategic planning processes and the development or enhancement of an organizational culture of trust.

Firstly, employees at EnergyCo were clear about the overarching goals of the organization, and the focus and constant communications around these goals remained constant despite the disruption. The employees of EnergyCo knew to focus on their five pillars despite the short-term disruption. Supporting struggling customers rather than chasing for payment provides a clear example of this focus on social capital, where formal controls such as credit limits were overridden by more informal social controls such as organizational culture.

The second feature of the EnergyCo case is the embedding of the goals of the organization into the strategic planning process over a longer timeframe.

Despite the short-term disruption, managers were still focused on a three-year strategic plan, supporting an overarching ten-year plan for the firm.

The third feature is that there needs to be an organizational culture of trust and transparency in order for the long-term goals to be realized. Employees at EnergyCo felt safe to acknowledge problems and challenges in order for them to be dealt with effectively. This was evident in EnergyCo both before and after the crisis, and may also have contributed to employees making a relatively smooth transition to working from home.

It was notable in this case that although there were some formal controls used to embed these new ways of working, many of them were achieved informally, particularly through the development of a culture of trust, which in some cases overrode more informal policy controls. This again reinforces the importance of people, and how 'informal cultural, personnel, and action controls, if they are internally consistent and hence functional, form a substitute for the need to adopt more formal control systems' (Sandelin, 2008, p. 339). The case shows how a continued investment in people and teams paid dividends.

5.   CONCLUSION

The case of EnergyCo illustrates how a New Zealand company's adoption of Integrated Reporting and Integrated Thinking helped it to subsequently navigate the challenges of Covid-19 and to continue to align internal decision making, even in a crisis period, with its overall organizational purpose. The study represents one of the earliest tests of the effectiveness of using Integrated Thinking principles during a crisis.

Although this is a single company case study, the simplicity of the six capitals model and the clear resonance of this approach with EnergyCo employees make Integrated Reporting and Integrated Thinking an interesting approach for managers of any organization to consider. The three key learnings explored above are applicable for many organizations. In particular, it is notable that many of the benefits were achieved through investment in people and in clear and consistent communication strategies.

Of course, many organizations already carefully consider similar capitals for their decision making, even if they do not reference them specifically. However, even for these organizations, deliberately articulating the importance of such capitals and communicating them clearly both internally and externally may help to clarify their position with external stakeholders and also encourage employee buy-in. Ensuring a focus on organizational culture and people development is also likely to help to maintain the social capital of the organization by reinforcing the importance of internal and external relationships.

Although many early adopters of Integrated Reporting and Integrated Thinking are large, listed companies, the benefits of the simple six capitals approach, alongside a focus on Integrated Thinking, can be applied to small and medium-sized businesses, family firms and not-for-profits. Indeed, the broader the stakeholder base, the more useful this approach may be. Many organizations are adapting or even thriving as a result of the pandemic, and this approach may also help to ensure sustainable value creation from new business models designed in response to the Covid-19 pandemic.

NOTES

1. EnergyCo is a pseudonym in accordance with the wishes of the organization and the interviewees.
2. Tessier and Otley (2012) consider managers to have social controls (those that appeal to employee emotions, such as values, beliefs, norms and symbols) and technical controls (those that consider rules, procedures and standards that govern day-to-day decision making) at their disposal.

REFERENCES

Al-Htaybat, K. and L. von Alberti-Alhtaybat (2018), 'Integrated Thinking leading to Integrated Reporting: Case study insights from a global player', *Accounting, Auditing & Accountability Journal*, **31** (5), 1435–60.

Black Sun (2014), *Realizing the Benefits: The impact of Integrated Reporting*, accessed 11 December 2020 at https://integratedreporting.org/resource/realizing-the-benefits -the-impact-of-integrated-reporting/

de Villiers, C. and W. Maroun (2018), *Sustainability Accounting and Integrated Reporting*, New York, Oxford: Routledge.

de Villiers, C., P.K. Hsiao and W. Maroun (2020), *The Routledge Handbook of Integrated Reporting*, London: Routledge.

de Villiers, C., L. Rinaldi and J. Unerman (2014), 'Integrated Reporting: Insights, gaps and an agenda for future research', *Accounting, Auditing & Accountability Journal*, **27** (7), 1042–67.

Dimes, R. and C. de Villiers (2020), 'How management control systems enable and constrain Integrated Thinking', *Meditari Accounting Research* (forthcoming). doi: 10.1108/MEDAR-0880.

Elkington, J. (1998), 'Accounting for the triple bottom line', *Measuring Business Excellence*, **2** (3), 18–22.

Esch, M., M. Schulze and A. Wald (2019), 'The dynamics of financial information and non-financial environmental, social and governance information in the strategic decision-making process', *Journal of Strategy and Management*, **12** (3), 314–29.

Feng, T., L. Cummings and D. Tweedie (2017), 'Exploring Integrated Thinking in Integrated Reporting – An exploratory study in Australia', *Journal of Intellectual Capital*, **18** (2), 330–53.

Galbreath, J. (2010), 'Drivers of corporate social responsibility: The role of formal strategic planning and firm culture', *British Journal of Management*, **21** (2), 511–25.

Gond, J., S. Grubnic, C. Herzig and J. Moon (2012), 'Configuring management control systems: Theorizing the integration of strategy and sustainability', *Management Accounting Research*, **23** (3), 205–23.

Guthrie, J., F. Manes-Rossi and R.L Orelli (2017), 'Integrated Reporting and Integrated Thinking in Italian public sector organisations', *Meditari Accountancy Research*, **25** (4), 553–73.

International Integrated Reporting Council (2013), *The International Framework*, accessed 11 December 2020 at https://integratedreporting.org/wp-content/uploads/2013/12/13-12-08-THE-INTERNATIONAL-IR-FRAMEWORK-2-1.pdf

Kaplan, R.S. and D.P. Norton (1996), *The Balanced Scorecard: Translating Strategy into Action*, Boston, MA: Harvard Business School Press.

Knauer, A. and G. Serafeim (2014), 'Attracting long-term investors through Integrated Thinking and reporting: A clinical study of a biopharmaceutical company', *Journal of Applied Corporate Finance*, **26** (2), 57–64.

Malmi, T. and D.A. Brown (2008), 'Management control systems as a package – Opportunities, challenges and research directions', *Management Accounting Research*, **19** (4), 287–300.

Oliver, J., G. Vesty and A. Brooks (2016), 'Conceptualising Integrated Thinking in practice', *Managerial Auditing Journal*, **31** (2), 228–48.

Rowbottom, N. and J. Locke (2016), 'The emergence of IR', *Accounting and Business Research*, **46** (1), 83–115.

Sandelin, M. (2008), 'Operation of management control practices as a package – A case study on control system variety in a growth firm context', *Management Accounting Research*, **19** (4), 324–43.

Schein, E.H. (1996), 'Culture: The missing concept in organization studies', *Administrative Science Quarterly*, **41** (2), 229–40.

Schorger, D. and K. Sewchurran (2015), 'Towards an interpretive measurement framework to assess the levels of integrated and integrative thinking within organisations', *Risk Governance & Control: Financial Markets & Institutions*, **5** (3), 44–66.

Simnett, R. and A.L. Huggins (2015), 'Integrated Reporting and assurance: Where can research add value?', *Sustainability Accounting, Management and Policy Journal*, **6** (1), 29–53.

Tessier, S. and D. Otley (2012), 'A conceptual development of Simons' Levers of Control framework', *Management Accounting Research*, **23** (3), 171–85.

12. Exploring the effects of interorganizational collaborations during the Covid-19 pandemic: the case of drug development

Jose Brache, Deanna Norgrove and Kenneth Husted

1.   INTRODUCTION

Innovation is widely recognized as a contact sport relying on collaborative activities within and across institutional barriers. In particular, technology and research-driven innovation tend to rely on global collaboration to access key innovation inputs or opportunities. Covid-19 has radically impacted some of the essential practices of collaborative innovation – meetings, collaborative spaces, travel and, in essence, every practice which involves personal contact. In the longer term such a radical change in how firms can engage in collaborative innovation may have formative impact on key decisions about how and when to collaborate. However, the immediate effect of Covid-19 would be on how already-established collaborative innovation projects adjust and introduce new ways to foster and organize collaborative innovation.

The topic of interorganizational collaboration has been explored from multiple perspectives including: strategic alliances (e.g., He et al., 2020), interfirm cooperation (e.g., Lyu et al., 2020), networks (e.g., Argyres et al., 2020), open innovation (e.g., Leckel et al., 2020), knowledge sharing (e.g., Husted et al., 2013; Lyu et al., 2020), mathematical biology (e.g., Nowak, 2006), international joint ventures (e.g., Gong et al., 2007), and others. Despite this attention, the particular effects of context on cooperative engagements have been overlooked (Brache and Felzensztein, 2019). We argue that context is essential to understanding cooperation behaviours. The Covid-19 pandemic is accentuating this because of its potential for changing the incentives driving cooperation projects.

Drawing on the literature of open innovation and interorganizational cooperation, we explore how special context settings influence interorganizational collaboration. In this respect, biopharma displays numerous characteristics that make it a unique domain for studying collaborative projects. Among those characteristics are the focus on technology transfer (Madhok and Osegowitsch, 2000), rising technology intensity (DeCarolis and Deeds, 1999), and intertwined connections with diverse stakeholders. This contributes to creating an ecosystem where direct and indirect interactions with the innovation network can be interpreted as a strategic asset for organizations (Salman and Saives, 2005).

This chapter investigates the following research question: how is Covid-19 changing the way organizations in knowledge-intensive sectors, such as the pharmaceutical industry, collaborate to discover, develop, and bring a solution to market? As a contribution to knowledge, it illustrates the impact that unique and distinct complex contexts (such as Covid-19) can have on innovation-oriented interorganizational collaborations.

Initially, we introduce the concept of open innovation and discuss previous studies on interorganizational collaboration in the pharmaceutical industry. Later, we explain the methodological approach used in this study and present our findings. Finally, implications for managers and policy makers are discussed.

2.   OPEN INNOVATION IN THE DRUG-DEVELOPMENT ECOSYSTEM

One widely used strategy for boosting innovation activities in firms is the open innovation (OI) approach. OI is 'a distributed innovation process involving purposive knowledge flows across organizational boundaries for monetary or non-monetary reasons' (Chesbrough, 2020, p. 411). OI argues for accessing and using information and knowledge from both internal and external sources in an environment where organizations exhibit permeable knowledge boundaries. Inbound and outbound flows of knowledge and innovations are an essential part of interorganizational collaborations under this premise. External and internal paths to market are encouraged (Chesbrough, 2003; Ovuakporie et al., 2021).

The biopharmaceutical ecosystem comprises a diverse set of organizations that perform research, manufacturing, development, and commercialization of pharmaceutical solutions. In particular, this ecosystem has integrated many OI practices as a response to an increasingly dynamic competitive setting and constant technological progress in drug development. Following a managerial perspective, Fetterhoff and Voelkel (2006) structure the OI value chain in the biopharmaceutical industry in five phases: (1) identifying and pursuing opportunities, (2) evaluating market fit and innovativeness, (3) partnering for the collaborative development of the opportunity, (4) value capture through commercialization, and finally, (5) innovation expansion.

The framework proposed by Bianchi et al. (2011) captures how biopharmaceutical firms conduct OI to discover, develop and bring a new drug to market. Their framework contemplates the relationships between types of partners, phases of R&D processes and organizational modes of collaboration considering the two dimensions of 'inbound' and 'outbound' OI. Inbound OI refers to 'the practice of leveraging the technologies and discoveries of others' while outbound OI 'is instead the practice of establishing relationships with external organizations to which proprietary technologies are transferred for commercial exploitation' (Bianchi et al., 2011, p. 24.).

However, the models proposed by Fetterhoff and Voelkel (2006) and Bianchi et al. (2011) do not account for contextual effects such as the unprecedented levels of disruption attributable to the Covid-19 pandemic, which has affected the way that businesses and consumers behave (Donthu and Gustafsson, 2020). The pandemic environment has the potential to impact innovation collaboration in several ways, such as introducing partners at stages of the drug-development process where their presence is unexpected, changing the ways that collaborative partners engage in the collaboration given travelling restrictions, providing opportunities to develop novel organizational collaborative structures, and ultimately modifying the motivations for partner selection and collaboration modes. Operation Warp Speed: a US-led project with the objective of manufacturing and delivering about 300 million doses of a Covid-19 vaccine, which has available funding of more than ten billion US dollars, exemplifies the magnitude of the impact of the Covid-19 pandemic context on interorganizational collaboration for drug development. The project is a partnership between the Department of Health and Human Services, the National Institutes of Health, the Centers for Disease Control and Prevention, the Department of Defense and the Biomedical Advanced Research Development Authority with the inclusion of multiple firms such as Johnson & Johnson, Moderna, AstraZeneca, Pfizer as well as many other companies and US government agencies.

Addressing the ongoing relevance of the Covid-19 context, Chesbrough (2020) underlines two significant OI lessons from the pandemic. At one end, there is an unprecedented mobilization of government agencies, scientists, and pharmaceutical firms in an effort to deploy an effective countermeasure to the pandemic. At the other end, the amount of information and knowledge that is currently being shared about the virus is unparalleled. Some of the efforts in the area of knowledge sharing include the alliance of the Gates foundation, the Chan-Zuckerberg foundation, and the White House Office of Science and Technology Policy with the aim of publishing (in machine-readable format) all of the scientific literature on the Covid-19 virus. These lessons from the pandemic reveal that OI and interorganizational collaborations are at the centre of the current scientific responses to the crisis.

3.   DATA AND METHODOLOGY

The empirical investigation followed Max van Manen's pragmatic methods, which allows equal attention to both the phenomenon and the research question, aiding the researchers in theme identification (Neubauer et al., 2019; van Manen, 2007).

3.1   Research Sample

Purposive sampling was employed to select participants. The focus was on experts in the pharmaceutical industry with experience in drug innovation both pre- and during Covid-19. Participants were identified as experts by their role in their organization and their history in the pharmaceutical industry.

Fourteen interviewees representing organizations with operations in New Zealand, Australia, the US, Switzerland and China were included in the research. These interviewees were from various organizations involved in drug-discovery, -development, and -marketing, including large and small pharmaceutical companies, biotechs, universities and academic research institutes, university spin-outs, crown research institutes, contract research organizations (CRO), clinical trial organizations, venture capital firms, industry associations, partnering firms and government funding agencies. Given the nature of the pharmaceutical industry, many of these participants' experiences included a background in different countries, like the United Kingdom, as well as practices across different types of organizations. Table 12.1 provides an overview of the experts interviewed.

Sample size was determined by theoretical saturation, also known as information redundancy (Ando et al., 2014) when no new concepts of interest, relative to the research question, arise from the interviews (Ando et al., 2014).

3.2   Data Collection

Participants' experiences of collaboration during drug innovation were collected via a single interview of approximately one hour. Due to international and national lockdowns, consequent to the Covid-19 pandemic, 13 of 14 interviews were conducted via Zoom. One interview, the first to be conducted, was in person before lockdown. All interviews were audio recorded and transcribed.

Table 12.1   Description of industry experts in the pharmaceutical industry

Interviewee	Current organization	Prior & other organization/experience
1	NZ biotech	International biotechs
2	NZ consultant	International big pharma
3	Aust biotech	International CRO, research institute
4	NZ pharma	
5	NZ/Aust pharma partnering consultant	
6	NZ govt funding agency	Contract manufacturing organization
7	US biotech & NZ academic institute	NZ start-ups
8	Big pharma search & evaluation Asia Pacific	International research institutes, biotechs
9	NZ govt funding agency	International biotech, research institute
10	NZ/Aust pharma partnering consultant	Multi-industry
11	NZ regulatory consultant	International regulatory consultant
12	Aust/NZ venture capital firm	Multi-industry
13	Aust industry association	UK big pharma, consultant
14	NZ industry association	Multi-industry

We aimed to understand the experiences of the participants as they were connected to the contextual forces that shaped their experiences (Bynum and Varpio, 2018). Hence press releases, news articles, industry reports, and relevant journal articles were collected and analysed as secondary data, to triangulate between the primary and secondary data, and maintain the inter-connectedness between the participant experiences and the emerging Covid-19 pandemic.

3.3   Data Analysis

Data analysis was conducted using Max van Manen's ([1990] 1997) thematic analysis. Our stance recognizes the inclusion and influence of the researcher's own experiences on the research and understands the analysis as a dynamic and iterative process of interpretivism and reflection (Bynum and Varpio, 2018; Neubauer et al., 2019).

4.   FINDINGS

4.1   Collaboration and Speed are Necessary

The development of a vaccine is a costly and lengthy process (Lurie et al., 2020). As a result of the urgency introduced by the need to provide a rapid solution to the pandemic, the Covid-19 context has required a swift approach to the development of interorganizational collaborations in the biopharmaceutical sector. This urgency in developing countermeasures to the virus potentially impacts resource allocation, organization structures, process sequences, partner selection, collaboration governance, and trust dynamics in collaborative projects. The participants in the research study expressed:

> something I'd say is it's the level of collaboration, it's the speed that has definitely gone up. It is breath-taking, how quickly the companies are managing to go through the clinical trial processes. (Interviewee 14)

> the collaboration needed to be ridiculously fast. (Interviewee 10)

> So, there was a real drive around speed. So that was the first noticeable difference. (Interviewee 6)

Moreover, our results show that interorganizational collaborations in the Covid-19 scenario should preferably involve multistakeholders because of the advantage generated by diversity in perspectives and knowledge. The following statement captures a widely held view among the participants:

> And this is such a fast-moving project where you need different infrastructure and skills of different forms. And it makes sense to outsource different tasks out. (Interviewee 1)

From the perspective of collaboration incentives, the idea of not missing the opportunity window is an essential motivator for collaboration. But this motivation only activates if the organization already has something valuable to offer to the Covid-19 solution portfolio, such as specific, often advanced knowledge or other resources essential for the discovery process. Some participants explain:

> So large pharmaceutical companies, if they have some existing expertise in that space, then they'd be mad not to be involved. If they have indicated that they are a leader in vaccines, then for them not to have to reach an alliance would be rather odd. If they're not a leader in vaccines, then that sort of leadership position cannot be developed overnight. (Interviewee 13)

> We don't have all this bunch of later stage assets that we can badge with the Covid badge. So, it's not changing my research. (Interviewee 3)

Finally, the change in context seems to have a 'hit-closer-to-home' effect. The incentives to collaborate affect people on a personal level, which creates motivations toward cooperation that go beyond profit maximization and increases the overall propensity to pursue collaboration opportunities. And while the drives to make a financial profit or improve the public relations positioning remain, humanitarian reasons gain momentum under this novel scenario. Some participants explained:

> It's a real and present danger. Meaning that everybody in the world knows what it does. It's not like having to explain … some neurological disease, it's actually in our headlines. (Interviewee 10)

> This time there's other people we can actually help, you know, people with Covid-19 and people in NZ love doing it because it's a Kiwi project. So, there's that emotion to it. (Interviewee 1)

4.2   A Multistakeholder-led Response is Required

The role of government seems fundamental in driving interorganizational collaborations in knowledge-intensive sectors such as the pharmaceutical industry. This is mostly due to the government's capacity to provide substantial amounts of funding to pharmaceutical projects. This availability of financial resources mitigates the risks of failure in the development of virus countermeasures. This is evidenced by the following statements from participants:

> So, yes, there was a, there was a response to Covid, most notably with the NZ Govt Fund 5. (Interviewee 6)

> That we see huge government funding from everywhere. Particularly the US but actually China is the same. So, you can't go wrong. I mean, it's not going to cost them that much. It will cost them a lot when it fails …. That's the risk they're taking. But you know, but that risk is being cautioned at the moment by enormous amount of government money. (Interviewee 5)

> Notwithstanding the key role of government, leading a response to a crisis situation such as the Covid-19 pandemic cannot wait for perfect incentives and low-risk conditions. Some stakeholders in the pharmaceutical industry did not wait for government guidance, quickly owned the problem and started delivering a market-coordinated response. One example of this is: 'I mean, but you know, a number of the companies started the process and didn't get a bean from the government, And now, some of the governments are coming to them to sort of try and collaborate'. (Interviewee 14)

4.3   Global Covid-19 Lockdowns are Levelling the Playing Field

Regular operations in the pharmaceutical ecosystem require intensive business travel and the development and maintenance of personal relationships. This can be something of a disadvantage for actors located geographically distant from major pharmaceutical industry clusters (as in the case of New Zealand). Also, competing for the attention of potential partners can be a challenging task. In this new context, collaboration flows faster as everyone is operating remotely. The following assertion from a participant exemplifies our finding:

> So, proximity is less of an issue for us now, I feel, because whenever we're calling our colleagues in the US, they're usually calling from their home. And so, everybody's remote. So, everybody's equally disadvantaged or so, yeah, actually proximity with virtual type meetings, you know, Microsoft Teams and Zoom and what forth ... so it really comes down to the quality of the science and the asset that really, really counts now. (Interviewee 4)

But, despite being on the same level, organizations can only cooperate if random conditions allow for the organization to be 'open for business' when the partners require them. This is certainly a unique and distinct effect of the Covid-19 crisis because pandemic lockdowns impact cities in differentiated ways. On some occasions London might be in lockdown while Auckland is not. And because of New Zealand's effective policy in addressing the virus, this issue has actually become an advantage for New Zealand-based actors. The participants asserted:

> Our competitive advantage was that we didn't. You know, we were not under lockdown. So, we could do a lot of stuff that was not impossible, because they would be essential workers, but difficult in other locations. So that was the advantage. (Interviewee 6)

> Because they're all shut down. We've doubled and redoubled the things that we're doing for many of our clients and have actually grown 25 per cent or so even in the time of Covid in the last six months. (Interviewee 3)

Finally, working remotely has its limitations. Participants indicated that managing relationships online can be done effectively if the people involved already know each other in real life. Otherwise, building trust becomes a challenge. The following statements provide evidence in that respect:

> But there's a part of that, again, where you really need the person in the room. (Interviewee 8)

> So, given you and I have met before in person, this interview is probably easier because of that, right? I think that where there's a relationship in place. It's meant that we don't need to meet as often. But I think in the longer term for new relationships, I suspect that for me to do my job, I need to get face to face. There's a lot of things that we do that we never get face to face with people, you know, like sending drugs to the other side of the world for testing. You know, the best we do is a Zoom

call. Yeah. So, it's not totally unusual, but I do think that we will be more efficient with how we rely on face to face. (Interviewee 12)

4.4   Collaboration is Not New, but Collaboration at This Scale Is

Our results indicate that while there are partnerships of 'never-seen before' proportions, the OI model and the knowledge-sharing practices that it entails were already present in the biopharma ecosystem previous to the Covid-19 pandemic scenario. In this sense, the processes that lead to interorganizational collaborations and the procedures to manage the collaborative relationships are not novel per se but are being taken to a novel scale. The participants affirm:

> So, drug development is already a global thing .... So, the concept of global drug development isn't up to Covid. (Interviewee 2)

> There's a lot more collaboration between other stakeholders that we haven't seen engage in a collaborative fashion before. (Interviewee 14)

> So, in some ways, I'd say there's a lot more collaboration going on, but it's nothing new, you know, the model for that is ... not new. It's just the intensity of it. (Interviewee 9)

4.5   Processes have Changed and Become More Adaptable, Focuses Have Not

The participants indicate that multiple processes have been adapted to the new environment in order to facilitate the speed of drug development. That is the case for government regulations, which in turn impact the speed of operation of interorganizational collaborations, regulations around intellectual property protection, and data sharing. The participants specify:

> Because it's a well, not only national emergency, but a global emergency, the regulators were more interactive. But just looking at them [the Covid-19 drugs] in a different way. (Interviewee 6)

> There was more open sharing of data in the pandemic, because nobody was really competing, it was an unusual situation and that if someone you know ... and virtually daily or weekly, there would be new information coming out. So that was all shared very quickly and easily. (Interviewee 6)

Despite this, the research focus of organizations has not changed. On this topic, data from Biomedtracker on partnership deals by therapy area show at least a doubling of partnerships for infectious disease in 2020 (which should be expected). Nevertheless, it also shows at least a doubling of partnerships for oncology. Ultimately, every single therapy area has increased its level of partnership in 2020 when compared with 2019 (Giglio and Riordan, 2020). This finding confirms the idea that an increase of overall interorganizational collaboration is possible without producing a collaboration trade-off. One participant commented:

> What it didn't do was it didn't derail business as usual ... a big pharma one still needs to maintain their revenue on allergy and oncology and all of those things. (Interviewee 10)

4.6   Covid-19 may Teach us Some Lessons Going Forward in the Fields of Cooperation and Operations

Most participants perceive that the current context will leave important learnings that will modify the way in which biopharma interorganizational collaborations operate in the future. The following statement serves as an example:

> But what it does highlight is – and that is going to be important for the future – I think what these big companies are seeing is, 'Oh, geez, you know, we can collaborate and things move fast. So why can't we do this in other areas, you know, oncology or infectious diseases?' (Interviewee 5)

4.7   Scepticism of Collaboration is Present

Our results also show that, even in situations of crisis, when the need of collaboration urges organizations to engage and people respond on a personal level to the threat posed by the circumstance with a higher motivation towards cooperation, the cloud of scepticism around the true motivations of cooperation remains present. Some participants indicated:

> I think there's a lot of lip service in it ... people talk about being collegial but they don't really, they don't really. They want to be the first one. (Interviewee 8)

> So, the situation and the unprecedented level of collaboration is probably unique to such an emergency situation, called the pandemic, in this case. So, you know, I don't think that will be the norm in the future. This is a very artificial situation. (Interviewee 5)

5.   CONCLUSION, IMPLICATIONS, AND LIMITATIONS

This study explores how the Covid-19 pandemic fosters faster and more efficient cooperation between actors in the biopharma OI environment. In doing so, our findings extend and complement the previous studies of the biopharma innovation process from Fetterhoff and Voelkel (2006) and Bianchi et al. (2011).

Our results indicate that the sense of urgency created by the pandemic demands collaboration at levels of speed and scale that are unprecedented in the biopharmaceutical industry. Some of the motivations behind the need for speed rest at the organizational level (e.g., the necessity to capitalize on the opportunity) while others are rooted at the personal level (e.g., the pandemic is perceived as a personal threat). Interorganizational collaboration processes should adapt to these changes and leadership in the coordination of a response must come from government and industry (with government maintaining the forefront as it can facilitate a wider extent of resource allocation).

Our findings also highlight that the biopharma ecosystem has been able to respond to this 'context call' because it had already developed and implemented a wide range of OI practices. As a clear lesson from our research, managers from other industries should consider OI practices as a risk-reduction mechanism in crisis times.

For New Zealand organizations, in particular, the appropriate handling of the pandemic by national authorities has become a welcome competitive advantage, giving stakeholders the opportunity to develop collaborations more efficiently since they have experienced less frequent lockdowns.

But not all findings point at a collaboration increase in this study. New ways of online work and scepticism around the motivations of collaboration could become barriers in the development of interorganizational collaborations in contexts similar to the Covid-19 pandemic. Such barriers persist even when remote work is levelling the playing field for collaborating stakeholders and when collaboration is increasing in every single therapy area.

Our findings therefore suggest that more pathways for stakeholder engagement must be developed in times of crisis. Funding must target the development of drug solutions and the construction of multistakeholder networks simultaneously. Government and industry should lead this effort with a focus on facilitating new technologies and platforms that can deliver the most efficient knowledge-sharing mechanisms required by the ecosystem at the accelerated speed demanded by the novel context.

This study is being conducted while the Covid-19 pandemic is going through its first and second wave in most countries of the world. Thus, it will only be able to identify changes in the OI behaviours of the biopharma innovation ecosystem in a limited time range. Future studies should continue the exploration of the effects of context in a wider timeframe. This effort will ultimately expand the knowledge of OI ecosystems portrayed in previous studies.

REFERENCES

Ando, H., R. Cousins and C. Young (2014), 'Achieving saturation in thematic analysis: Development and refinement of a codebook', *Comprehensive Psychology*, **3**, Article 4.

Argyres, N., J. Bercovitz and G. Zanarone (2020), 'The role of relationship scope in sustaining relational contracts in interfirm networks', *Strategic Management Journal*, **41** (2), 222–45.

Bianchi, M., A. Cavaliere, D. Chiaroni, F. Frattini and V. Chiesa (2011), 'Organisational modes for Open Innovation in the bio-pharmaceutical industry: An exploratory analysis', *Technovation*, **31** (1), 22–33.

Brache, J. and C. Felzensztein (2019), 'Exporting firm's engagement with trade associations: Insights from Chile', *International Business Review*, **28** (1), 25–35.

Bynum, W. and L. Varpio (2018), 'When I say… hermeneutic phenomenology', *Medical Education*, **52** (3), 252–53.

Chesbrough, H.W. (2003), *Open Innovation: The New Imperative for Creating and Profiting from Technology*, Boston: Harvard Business Press.

Chesbrough, H. (2020), 'To recover faster from Covid-19, open up: Managerial implications from an open innovation perspective', *Industrial Marketing Management*, **88**, 410–13.

DeCarolis, D.M. and D.L. Deeds (1999), 'The impact of stocks and flows of organizational knowledge on firm performance: An empirical investigation of the biotechnology industry', *Strategic Management Journal*, **20** (10), 953–68.

Donthu, N. and A. Gustafsson (2020), 'Effects of COVID-19 on business and research', *Journal of Business Research*, **117**, 284.

Fetterhoff, T.J. and D. Voelkel (2006), 'Managing open innovation in biotechnology', *Research-Technology Management*, **49** (3), 14–18.

Giglio, P. and M. Riordan (2020), 'Biopharma partnering and financial trends H1 2020', *Informa Connect*, accessed 2 October 2020 at https://informaconnect.com/biopharma-partnering-and-financing-trends-h1-2020/

Gong, Y., O. Shenkar, Y. Luo and M.K. Nyaw (2007), 'Do multiple parents help or hinder international joint venture performance? The mediating roles of contract completeness and partner cooperation', *Strategic Management Journal*, **28** (10), 1021–34.

He, Q., M. Meadows, D. Angwin, E. Gomes and J. Child (2020), 'Strategic alliance research in the era of digital transformation: Perspectives on future research', *British Journal of Management*. https://doi.org/10.1111/1467-8551.12406

Husted, K., S. Michailova and H. Olander (2013), 'Dual allegiance, knowledge sharing, and knowledge protection: An empirical examination', *International Journal of Innovation Management*, **17** (06), 1340022.

Leckel, A., S. Veilleux and L.P. Dana (2020), 'Local open innovation: A means for public policy to increase collaboration for innovation in SMEs', *Technological Forecasting and Social Change*, **153**, 119891.

Lurie, N., M. Saville, R. Hatchett and J. Halton (2020), 'Developing Covid-19 vaccines at pandemic speed', *New England Journal of Medicine*, **382** (21), 1969–73.

Lyu, C., J. Yang, F. Zhang, T.S. Teo and T. Mu (2020), 'How do knowledge characteristics affect firm's knowledge sharing intention in interfirm cooperation? An empirical study', *Journal of Business Research*, **115**, 48–60.

Madhok, A. and T. Osegowitsch (2000), 'The international biotechnology industry: A dynamic capabilities perspective', *Journal of International Business Studies*, **31** (2), 325–35.

Neubauer, B.E., C.T. Witkop and L. Varpio (2019), 'How phenomenology can help us learn from the experiences of others', *Perspectives on Medical Education*, **8** (2), 90–97.

Nowak, M.A. (2006), 'Five rules for the evolution of cooperation', *Science*, **314** (5805), 1560–63.

Ovuakporie, O.D., K.G. Pillai, C. Wang and Y. Wei (2021), 'Differential moderating effects of strategic and operational reconfiguration on the relationship between open innovation practices and innovation performance', *Research Policy*, **50** (1), 104146.

Salman, N. and A.L. Saives (2005), 'Indirect networks: An intangible resource for biotechnology innovation', *R&D Management*, **35** (2), 203–15.

van Manen, M. ([1990] 1997), *Researching Lived Experience: Human Science for an Action Sensitive Pedagogy* (2nd ed.), London, Ontario: The Althouse Press.

van Manen, M. (2007), 'Phenomenology of practice', *Phenomenology and Practice*, **1** (1), 11–30.

13. Special characteristics for technology commercialization: exemplars of New Zealand and global impacts

Peter Lee

1. INTRODUCTION

New Zealand has a burgeoning innovative and entrepreneurial ecosystem contributing to a high-technology component of our economy. It is the fastest growing and currently the third-largest contributor to New Zealand's export earnings. New Zealand has been ranked first in the world for ease of doing business in a World Bank (2019) report.

Auckland, with a population of approximately 1.4 million people, is New Zealand's largest city. It accounts for 38 per cent of the nation's GDP. An inflection in the current growth rate of Auckland's entrepreneurial ecosystem occurred in October 2000 with the Catching the Knowledge Wave project jointly sponsored by the University of Auckland and the New Zealand government (Hood, 2001). The objective was to identify elements of the national strategy which were needed to enable New Zealand's transition from a country solely reliant on primary production to a competitive knowledge-based society. In the intervening 20 years, the experience base for recognizing the potential value of research outcomes and how to realize this potential in practice has grown and matured. This maturity manifested itself in New Zealand's collective response to the Covid-19 pandemic by government, startup companies and academia.

Unlike many regions, New Zealand was able to see the virus coming early and take urgent and robust action to contain its spread. The outcome was the early elimination of community transfer in New Zealand and an opportunity for economic activity to begin to adapt to a new normal following the Covid-19 pandemic. This fast start in adapting commercialization practices post the pandemic occurred while most of the world was still experiencing the disruptive effects of the rapidly spreading pandemic on social and commercial activities.

Covid-19 upended many of the prevalent demand patterns among both consumers and businesses. It caused a sudden contraction in demand among many traditional sectors and created new opportunities for the adaption and development of products to address the needs of emerging markets. The following effects were identified in a survey by McKinsey & Company (Ray et al., 2020):

- ensuring workplace safety as an initial priority,
- investing in innovation directed at the new priorities to emerge in a post-Covid-19 environment,
- being agile in the identification and capture of new opportunities quickly and gaining a first-mover advantage,
- shifting from in-person interactions to digital sales with new e-commerce solutions, and
- finding ways to help customers during their transitions to build long-term relationships.

The following analysis of the three components of our innovation system (i.e., government, academia and startups) will exemplify these principles in a New Zealand context. Innovation in New Zealand will be described as it existed before and during the early stages of recovery from the Covid-19 pandemic. Finally, conclusions and recommendations will be provided for the response of innovation systems for both the future of New Zealand and other similar economies.

Despite the relatively sudden nature of the crisis, articles have begun to report about its impact on regional innovation. Kawamorita et al. (2020) highlighted the main challenges faced by entrepreneurial universities among Middle Eastern nations, and Salamzadeh and Dana (2020) have investigated the main challenges faced by Iranian startups. This chapter reports on ways the innovation system in New Zealand has addressed these challenges during the early stages of recovery from the crisis.

2.   THE ENTREPRENEURIAL ECOSYSTEM IN NEW ZEALAND BEFORE THE COVID-19 PANDEMIC

Malecki (2018) has defined entrepreneurial ecosystems as the dynamic local social, institutional and cultural processes and actors that encourage and enhance new firm formation and growth. His article provides a recent review of the literature, concepts and operationalizations of entrepreneurial ecosystems.

Etzkowitz (2020) developed the triple helix model to describe a national innovation system. The model provides a format to explain the effects of academia, industry and government and their interactions on a knowledge economy. It provides a suitable basis for introducing New Zealand's innovation system and the impacts of Covid-19. In this chapter, I will focus on the high-technology startup sector of our local industry.

The Venn diagram in Figure 13.1 represents the triple helix of academia, government and high-technology startups. Three intersecting circles represent the components, and the areas of overlap between these circles illustrate their relationships.

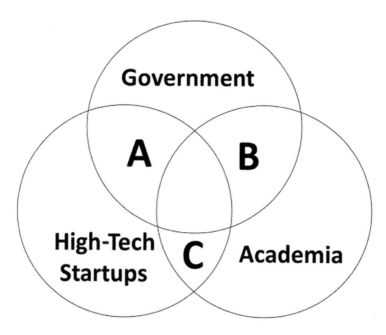

Figure 13.1   Triple helix for New Zealand's innovation system

The interactions change in response to fluctuations in the system's operating environment. The term 'helix', which implies a continually evolving set of interdependencies, reflects this dynamism. This chapter shows how the extent of the overlaps increased, and the form of the overlaps adapted rapidly to changing circumstances.

The space designated as A in Figure 13.1 represents the interactions between the government and the community of high-technology startups. The government has historically deployed multiple policies and practices to support the growth of our high-technology startup community. These include:

- Supporting the early-stage capital market by investing in the Elevate NZ Venture and Aspire funds, both managed by New Zealand Growth Capital Partners. The Aspire fund coinvests along with angels and other venture capital (VC) investors in early-stage companies to fill the investment gap for entrepreneurs needing capital to get their business underway.
- New Zealand Trade and Enterprise (NZTE), the government's international business development agency, helps exporters of all sizes make better decisions and connect to the right partners and investors, through its extensive knowledge and global networks.
- The Ministry of Business, Innovation and Employment (MBIE) through its agency, Callaghan Innovation, provides a range of innovation and research and development support to businesses including R&D funding, R&D tax incentives, R&D loans, project grants, internships, expert advice, networking and the development of design skills. Also, it offers specific support for startups, including a network of technology incubators and accelerator programmes.
- Cosponsoring, through several government departments, along with prominent New Zealand businesses, the Kiwi expats association, Kea. Kea has established and maintains a network of global citizens and friends of New Zealand who are actively engaged and passionate about the future of their country. New Zealand has a larger proportion of highly skilled people living in other countries than nearly any other nation, with approximately 1 million New Zealanders living and working [located] abroad in a broad array of regions, industries and functions. The diaspora is a source of trusted intermediaries among individuals and companies in New Zealand and potentially useful overseas contacts. Someone, somewhere in this dispersed diaspora, is likely to have the knowledge, influence and access needed to reach potential customers.

The space designated as B in Figure 13.1 represents the interactions between the government and academia as it affects entrepreneurism and commercialization. MBIE is the primary source of government funds for precommercial research and development. The funding for research is strongly influenced by its potential to contribute to outcomes useful for business. The government administers this funding through a variety of mechanisms including:

- The Endeavour Fund, an open, contestable fund with a focus on both research excellence and a broad range of impacts significant to New Zealand, including economic growth;

- The Strategic Science Investment Fund which supports a system of seven Crown Research Institutes to conduct R&D supporting New Zealand's primary industries;
- A set of National Science Challenges which aim to tackle the most significant science-based issues and opportunities facing New Zealand. Challenges bring together the country's top scientists to work collaboratively across disciplines, institutions and borders to achieve their objectives;
- A PreSeed Accelerator Fund and Commercialisation Partner Network which support embryonic commercialization prospects that result from publicly funded research or research capability and advance these commercialization projects to the point of investor readiness;
- Technology incubator programmes funded through Callaghan Innovation which find and commercialize complex intellectual property from universities to create deep-tech startups in New Zealand that can attract follow-on investment and create jobs for highly skilled individuals; and
- Government support for universities to attract world-class entrepreneurial academics into New Zealand to stimulate innovation within high-potential areas of research.

The space designated by C in Figure 13.1 represents the interactions between high-technology startups and academia.

- Technology Transfer Offices (TTOs) at the research providers facilitate the transfer of the outcomes of academic research to business. TTOs form many of the early-stage and high-technology startup companies which develop the results of R&D into commercial value. They either grow to become independent companies or are acquired by more established companies. The TTOs work collectively with business and government to adapt and improve their transfer practices.
- Executive Educational Programmes provide advanced degrees, short courses and customized learning to support specific needs of businesses.
- The graduates of these academic institutions provide a comprehensive range of human resources to enable innovation and realize its benefits in our society.

3.   POST-COVID-19 RESPONSES

The national innovation system experienced a rapid adjustment following the early and rigorous lockdown period due to the Covid-19 pandemic. The consequences of the responses by government, academia and four substantial high-technology startups will be reviewed using the following examples.

3.1   Government

The New Zealand government quickly instigated a range of new initiatives for individuals and businesses to cope with the consequences of the pandemic and to build on the existing support programmes mentioned previously. The objective was to support the local economy through the period of disruption and in particular sustain the relatively fragile high-technology startups it had been nurturing.

The additional support took many forms broadly available to most businesses, including the introduction of wage subsidies, cash-flow loan schemes, finance guarantees, commercial leases and mortgage deferrals. Also, there were initiatives explicitly directed at the high-technology startup community with the belief that this community was most capable of rapidly adapting to and flourishing in a post-Covid-19 environment. This targeted support for R&D intensive companies included:

- The New Zealand government quickly established a Covid-19 Innovation Acceleration Fund to provide immediate, short-term support to New Zealand-based entities to develop and deploy a range of new products. The fund has enabled and encouraged researchers in academia and business to adapt their work to address all aspects of a Covid-19 response including detection, prevention and treatment.
- Callaghan Innovation provided low-interest R&D loans to support continued R&D by business.
- The Inland Revenue Department changed the existing R&D Tax Incentive scheme to provide extra cash for R&D-performing businesses by qualifying more loss-making companies to have their R&D tax credit refunded in cash.
- The Kea organization supported the repatriation of tens of thousands of Kiwis seeking the relative safety and stability available in New Zealand by providing linkages between their skills and the needs of local businesses, thereby creating economic benefits. Our boarder entries have been restricted and slowed this repatriation. However, some critical skills have been imported and this is likely to accelerate as boarders open further.
- Auckland Tourism, Events and Economic Development (ATEED), the region's economic development agency and an Auckland Council-controlled organization, responded with support for the upsurge of inquiries from overseas companies wanting to relocate to New Zealand. The same boarder restrictions which have hampered individual relocations have hampered businesses in some cases. However, some enterprises have begun establishing their businesses in New Zealand anticipating increased access in the future.

Non-financial support provided by government agencies was as equally impactful and included networking events, best-practice sharing, professional services and training. The government's response to the Covid-19 crisis was rapid, evidence-based and put people first. This example set the tone for the reactions of both academia and business.

3.2   Academia

The government and business looked to universities for objective and factual information about the appropriate response to the Covid-19 outbreak in New Zealand. Scientists from a diverse array of disciplines, including epidemiologists, virologists, immunologists and statisticians provided expert advice to inform national plans to eliminate the virus.

Universities had to adapt their teaching and research practices in the new environment while maintaining the safety of their students and staff. As a result of their closed doors during the lockdown, teaching was conducted online, which accelerated initiatives for asynchronous web-based education. Laboratory-based work was temporarily restricted but quickly recovered. The results of this academic research were essential to inform both national policies and commercial innovation.

These abrupt changes occurred against a background of a longer-term strategic adjustment as universities were planning for a more digital future, public demand for greater relevance and more international competition.

The University of Auckland is an example of the research-based tertiary education system in New Zealand. The University of Auckland was ranked No.1 globally in the *Times Higher Education* university *Impact Rankings 2020*, maintaining its top position from the previous year's inaugural rankings. A part of this assessment relates to the university's impact on economic development.

UniServices Company is the TTO for the University of Auckland. It incorporated in 1995 and has a long history of commercializing the outputs from academic research. Some of the existing business practices for commercialization, such as the internal processes for informing and assessing the research providers, the cost structure and incentivization schemes, were found still to be appropriate and were maintained. The creative capabilities of the researchers were mostly unaffected. However, many essential aspects of the business environment had changed rapidly, and other parts of the commercialization process needed urgent attention.

The organization had recently and effectively managed its response to the global financial crisis (GFC). There were many similarities between the GFC and the Covid-19 pandemic, and these experiences provided valuable lessons for addressing the Covid-19 crisis. In both cases, there was a return to basics and a focus on the stability of underlying long-term trends such as improved education, sustainable production, clean energy sources and efficient consumption.

A survey by the Innovation Research Interchange (2020) found that, as a result of the Covid-19 crisis, many companies reduced research investments and external partnerships substantially. However, a few companies with the resources and vision saw innovation as a key to their success post the crisis. These few innovative companies looked to the universities, research institutes and their high-technology spin-offs for promising new approaches to address the disruption facing their businesses. UniServices resegmented its markets to provide timely expert analysis and advice to address the needs of these future-oriented businesses. New working relationships were established with business to allow for greater shared risk, such as the formation of consortia of companies and universities to collaborate in the development of new technologies and intellectual property. The university established an Inventors Fund to support the further development of precommercial technology and reduce its risk for angel and venture capital investors.

Initiatives to counter the underlying economic trends and their consequences were derived with an entrepreneurial mindset to find a new way of conducting business in a disrupted environment. The University of Auckland reassessed its core capabilities, and the researchers changed the direction of their discovery towards these new demands.

Examples of these changing relations with society, customers and regional markets included:

- Operations research, customarily applied to increase the efficiency of industrial processes, was repurposed to improve the efficiency of distribution and delivery of health supplies, including the anticipated vaccines.
- Modelling of complex systems and networks was repurposed to model the transmission of the Covid-19 virus in New Zealand.
- Pedagogy was deployed in developing nations with the support of international aid.
- The technology for contactless power transfer was adapted to charge electric vehicles in response to the rapid growth of this industry.

4.   FOUR STARTUPS

The responses of four local startups provide positive examples of the potential for early-stage and high-technology businesses not only to survive but flourish in crises. All companies reported here demonstrate the principles of effective recovery identified previously by McKinsey & Company (Ray et al., 2020).

A brief introduction of each company is provided firstly followed by an account of how they each uniquely practised the principles of recovery.

4.1   Soul Machines

Soul Machines is a New Zealand and San Francisco startup based upon academic research at the University of Auckland. This company has become the world leader in humanizing artificial intelligence (AI) to create Digital People. Its Digital People have a Digital Brain which contextualizes and adapts in real time to situations similar to human interactions. As a result, the company's Digital People provide an emotionally authentic human face to AI engines with the ability to interpret a wealth of knowledge according to the needs of the individual. Many business leaders are moving quickly to elevate the human aspects of digital technologies and AI. In the process, they are reimagining customer experience and increasing the mental, physical and digital availability of its brands. Soul Machines, with its Digital People, was well aligned with the accelerated shift from in-person to digital interactions caused by the Covid-19 crisis.

Soul Machines entered the Covid-19 era, having just completed its Series B round of funding. It had the means to take a long-term view of its future post-Covid-19. Its immediate priority was for the well-being of its employees located in Auckland, Melbourne, San Francisco and Tokyo and enabling them to continue to work safely. Soul Machines quickly established a safe environment, including the ability to work remotely, and then turned its attention to helping its customers to overcome their problems; many of these problems related to people's safety. There were many opportunities, and selecting clients with the motivation and means to innovate in this environment was essential.

Soul Machines is an excellent example of a company finding ways to help customers during their transitions. The company was agile in the identification and capture of new opportunities and quickly developed a series of Digital People as avatars that are particularly relevant to the current and post-Covid-19 environments.

For example, an avatar named Bella helped people in business navigate the new environment, with up-to-date Covid-19 guidance, using information from multiple business sources and inspiration from leading thinkers across all walks of life. Soul Machines (2020) created Bella in a month as a digital helper explicitly designed for New Zealanders to access critical information related to Covid-19.

The company created another avatar named Florence for the World Health Organization (WHO) as a healthcare assistant. Florence was teamed up with resources from Amazon Web Services and Google to quickly provide the support needed by WHO (2020) to assist in sharing life-saving information in multiple languages during the Covid-19 pandemic and combat misinformation.

Both Bella and Florence were provided free of charge. They delivered a powerful and visible demonstration of the value of avatars to offer personalized information at scale, particularly in healthcare settings. Soul Machines found ways to help customers during their transitions and to build long-term relationships. The overall effect of these positive examples was a rapid acceleration of business as the ability of Soul Machines to build relations in a more digitally connected world became apparent.

4.2   Cirrus Materials Science

Cirrus Materials Science designs novel surface-coating technologies based upon core IP and supported by academic research in the New Zealand science system. Cirrus is a world leader in developing novel coatings for Global Fortune 500 manufacturers who need innovative, challenging and sustainable surface finishing chemistries for high performance in harsh conditions. Its product is know-how and intellectual property that can be adapted quickly and exported for a variety of applications. Cirrus has a specialist functional coatings design facility in Auckland, where it develops and tests its materials solutions for global clients.

All of the senior management at Cirrus Materials are serial entrepreneurs who had experienced the GFC and, although the specific circumstances of the Covid-19 pandemic are different, the company applied many of the underlying disciplines of crisis management.

The initial focus of management was to ensure the well-being of staff and restore safe laboratory operations following lockdown. Work-from-home assignments, shift operations and stringent laboratory cleanup procedures all assisted with the transition from the initial period of full lockdown to the less restrictive operating environment following the elimination of Covid-19 from the community. Although its laboratory quickly resumed operations, many regions of the world, where it conducted business, were still experiencing the Covid-19 pandemic. Most of its existing customers had the scale and mix of business to survive and adapt to the pandemic but were unable to maintain progress as planned.

The response to Covid-19 among the markets it served varied, with positive developments in markets with strong underlying drivers related to lower energy costs, reduced carbon emissions and increased consumer and regulatory demands for sustainable materials and manufacture. There were positive developments in consumer devices, space vehicles, electric vehicles and clean energy, which received increased R&D focus. Concurrently, there were adverse developments in internal combustion cars, construction and aircraft, from which resources were diverted. It also initiated new R&D into the development of novel coatings to address emerging priorities, such as antiviral surfaces. The company is an excellent example of agility in quickly identifying and capturing new opportunities and gaining a first-mover advantage by adapting its market focus and value proposition.

Contact with customers was essential to understand their problems and then to design, develop and deliver customized solutions. Cirrus Materials not only needed to maintain contact with its existing customers but also grow its longer-term value by continuing to build relationships with new customers. Its previous reliance on conferences, trade shows and face-to-face meetings to connect with potential new customers ended abruptly with the closure of international borders and the imposition of restrictions on air travel. The company identified digital marketing as a growing and beneficial trend and management responded by redirecting its travel budget to the development and implementation of a digital marketing campaign.

NZTE organized a national programme to support and fund the transfer of best practices in digital marketing. For business-to-business organizations, this involved understanding how potential customers sought and validated solutions to their problems online, presenting their products and credentials in a suitable digital format, providing this information in appropriate online venues and connecting through digital media. Early results were promising and suggested this new approach would positively impact the rate of new customer development in scope and reach. Like many of New Zealand's businesses, Cirrus found digital marketing reduced some of the competitive disadvantages it faced because of geographic remoteness and levelled the playing field with international competitors. The greater reach of the digital marketing campaign has been effective in identifying applications in areas not otherwise recognized.

At the onset of Covid-19, Cirrus Materials was still building business and spending more than it was earning. The company expected delays in growth and predicted a delay in revenue income of between 3 to 6 months. The anticipated revenue delay was a significant part of its remaining cash runway. It sought help from the New Zealand government, which was quickly forthcoming in a variety of ways including a wage subsidy, a low-interest loan for R&D, early refunding of the R&D Tax Incentive scheme and an extension to an existing R&D grant. It also needed to approach investors for additional financing sufficient to bridge the projected delay in revenue. This request was proposed as a convertible note with favourable terms for a future Series A round to avoid suggestions of devaluation in a challenging market. Investors, although cautious in the uncertain business environment, responded positively to the new management and market initiatives.

Cirrus is an excellent example of a company identifying and capturing new opportunities quickly and gaining a first-mover advantage.

4.3   NanoLayr

NanoLayr produces commercial quantities of non-woven fabrics from nanofibres utilizing its proprietary processes and formulations. It has been developing this technology since its formation in 2009. The company can profitably export large quantities of these almost weightless, gossamer-like fabrics from New Zealand to global markets.

The fabric format enables nanotechnology to be used effectively with a wide range of materials and provides a platform capability for diverse applications. The company has recently focussed on being a significant roll manufacturer of four high-technology product lines: filter media, reinforcement layers for fibre composites, sound absorption and skincare. All product lines had exhibited growth before the Covid-19 outbreak.

The New Zealand government granted NanoLayr an essential supplier status during the lockdown to enable it to produce high-performance filters for face masks. This required NanoLayr to quickly provide a safe working environment for its staff while increasing its manufacturing capacity. Teams worked in isolated shifts and adhered to strict standards of personal and workplace hygiene. Stress and fatigue were monitored and managed carefully as employees put in extra hours and effort.

The company had completed a significant financing round just before the Covid-19 outbreak to accelerate commercial opportunities in key offshore markets, and to invest in additional production capability. Also, the government awarded the company a grant from the Covid-19 Innovation Acceleration Fund to support the rapid expansion of nanofibre film production and additional antiviral capability for personal masks.

With its applications spanning a diverse set of industries, it was able to adjust quickly to the Covid-19 pandemic and take advantage of the rapidly changing demands for its core products. The nanofibre filter media, which can efficiently capture microscopic airborne particles such as allergens, bacteria and viruses, experienced overwhelming demand from international producers of face masks used for personal protection. At the same time, the skincare product line experienced strong market pull from distributors of health and beauty aids, particularly from online sales in Asia. The urgent need for more production caused the investment in increased manufacturing capacity to be accelerated. The company hired and trained additional staff for production, maintenance and quality control. The original team of ten employees quickly grew to 40. The company carefully selected the new employees from a large pool of available talent based upon their alignment with a set of core values the company had developed.

It became necessary not only to predict the extent and durability in demand for filtration media but also to allow for the growth in the other product lines.

Predicting demand was a complex calculation heavily dependent on insights available from existing and potentially new customers in international markets. Existing contacts and distribution partners in other countries provided valuable insights into local market demands. Maintenance of existing relationships and the development of new commercial networks were vital. The company expanded its marketing and sales resources accordingly. Much of this market intelligence relied on digital communications.

The company did not increase prices despite the overwhelming demand for filtration products. Instead, it has begun to develop a reputation as an ethical supplier, and new customers were selected based upon their potential to contribute to long-term company growth. The company applied for, and the New Zealand government awarded it, the use of the coveted FernMark trademark, which is officially recognized and endorsed by the New Zealand government. The FernMark embodies the New Zealand values of authenticity, integrity, ingenuity and is a proud connection to New Zealand.

Nanolayr is an excellent example of a company finding ways to help customers during their transitions and build long-term relationships.

4.4   Utility Asset Management

Utility Asset Management (UAM) is a US corporation that is 100 per cent owned by a New Zealand holding company Volt Holdings Limited. UAM has built its business on a proprietary ultrasonic measurement device, developed in New Zealand, and an analytics package to non-destructively evaluate the strength and internal integrity of wooden power poles. The ultrasonic scans are capable of not only detecting existing decay but also incipient decay inside wooden structures. It is a technology that is disrupting the traditional testing methods which rely on a combination of impact soundings and destructive drilling. Sales increased rapidly and did not slow during the Covid-19 crisis because this crucial infrastructure, which conveys electricity and broadband information, must be tested routinely.

Prior to Covid-19 UAM had been able to effectively operate throughout North America from its headquarters in Denver, Colorado. At the onset of the Covid-19 pandemic, management took several steps to mitigate the risks posed by Covid-19 to its operations. These included changing travel routines to focus on driving versus flying, creating 'bubbles' of workers and renting Airbnb housing instead of hotels. UAM also took advantage of its proven ability to conduct business remotely by relocating management to the relative safety of New Zealand. Quick decisions enabled the company's management to return before boarder access became more restrictive. With the management move to New Zealand, one of the country's largest utilities has decided to use the toolset for a local pole inspection project. UAM's return is an example of a recent trend among tens of thousands of highly qualified New Zealanders. Its return has the potential to invigorate the local economy and invigorate its innovative ecosystem.

5.   NEW ZEALAND-SPECIFIC LEARNINGS AND THEIR RELEVANCE ELSEWHERE

New Zealand relied heavily on the entrepreneurial leadership that has been developing in New Zealand for the last 20 years to respond effectively. The experiences of the recent GFC were fresh in the minds of many serial entrepreneurs in leadership positions within the local innovation and commercialization ecosystem at the time. These experienced leaders exhibited resilience and confidence in how they effectively developed practical solutions to the new challenges. The government supported these adjustments based on a strong and long-held belief that growth in our economy depends upon the effectiveness of the high-technology sector.

The three components of the innovation infrastructure in New Zealand (i.e., government, academia and high-technology startups) quickly ringfenced their strengths in commercialization and concentrated on addressing their weaknesses. The issues faced by a burgeoning but not yet self-sustaining high-tech industry, including remoteness from international markets, the small scale of most local markets and the relatively limited availability of domestic venture capital funds, were all quickly acknowledged and addressed. The existing strengths of national unity, extensive global diaspora, a relatively healthy government financial condition and strong leadership all contributed to a successful response.

There was an immediate acknowledgement of the crisis following the outbreak of Covid-19. The strategies identified in the survey by McKinsey & Company (Ray et al., 2020), and introduced at the beginning of this chapter, are strongly represented in the early responses of New Zealand's innovation system to the Covid-19 crisis.

In New Zealand, the initial priority at a national and organizational level was the health and well-being of citizens and employees. Once measures were in place to effectively contain and eventually eliminate the virus from the community, New Zealand was able to concentrate on economic recovery.

All of these companies acted aggressively to capture market share early in the emerging new economic reality rather than wait for a full recovery. Their agility, combined with a focus on customer value, provided the opportunity to create many first-mover advantages in the new normal. Flexibility proved essential in product design and positioning to address the emerging set of new priorities following the crisis, which included a resurgence of interest in environmental issues, personal safety and connectivity. They continued to invest in innovation and adapt their development of priorities accordingly.

There was an inherent belief that companies which sought to help rather than take advantage of their customers during the crisis would strengthen long-term relationships. Which is to say, the benefits expected from the eventual sales growth would be more valuable than the temporary costs of supporting customers during their time of crisis. The approach was consistent with government leadership and our national brand.

The need to shift away from in-person sales and the importance of digital and remote sales quickly became apparent, accelerated many emerging trends and served to reduce the inherent tyranny of distance for many New Zealand companies. Early indications are that the new go-to-market models are likely to outperform the traditional reliance on personal contacts.

6.   RECOMMENDATIONS

These New Zealand responses to the Covid-19 crisis occurred in the context of a world where most countries have continued to struggle.

The issues of scale, remoteness and fragility of emerging startup communities are not unique to New Zealand. Every region will have its own set of characteristics, and there can be no universal solution to a crisis. However, elements of the New Zealand response to this latest crisis can inform the development of these other local solutions. Other small nations and regions within larger developed economies, such as the USA, Europe and China, can apply a subset of our local solutions to inform their responses to Covid-19.

The examples demonstrate the value of regional unity, government support, digital marketing, product adaption, market realignment and collaboration among participants to develop a new normal for commercialization practices in response to Covid-19 and future crises.

The long-term effects of these early approaches to recovery by government, academia and high-technology startup companies will depend not only on these local initiatives but also upon the extent and duration of the effects of the Covid-19 crisis on the global economy. The results reported here are early in the recovery from the Covid-19 crisis, and continued diligence is required. Some opportunities to build on accomplishments locally include:

- All participants in the innovation system should maintain the behaviours of collaboration and caring support for others, including employees, business partners and customers.
- Startups should continue to deploy the newly learned skills of innovating during a crisis to track emerging trends and accelerate future adaptation.

- Startups should extend the digital initiatives learned during the Covid-19 crisis beyond marketing to other aspects of international cooperation such as teamwork, secure communications, open innovation and research collaboration.
- All companies, regardless of size, should observe, learn from and deploy the principles of crisis management demonstrated during the Covid-19 crisis by the high-technology startup community.
- The government should support the newly returned ex-pats to remain and succeed beyond the current crisis.

There will be further unexpected developments, but the resilience derived from the experience, agility and innovation demonstrated here will put New Zealand and others who take some of the same initiatives in good stead to prevail.

REFERENCES

Etzkowitz, H. (2020), *The Triple Helix: University–Industry–Government Innovation in Action* (2nd ed.), Abingdon, Oxon: Routledge.

Hood, J. (2001), 'The knowledge wave … creating Kiwi prosperity', accessed 6 December 2020 at https://cdn.auckland.ac.nz/assets/uabsknowledge/English/uabr-archives/2001-volume-3-issue-2/v3i2-knowledge-wave.pdf

Innovation Research Interchange (2020), 'Community Forum, June 23, 2020' accessed 6 December 2020 at https://www.iriweb.org/articles/community-forum-q-what-impact-Covid-19-your-organizations-investments-external-sponsored

Kawamorita, H., A. Salamzadeh, K. Demiryurek and M. Ghajarzadeh (2020), 'Entrepreneurial universities in times of crisis: Case of covid-19 pandemic', *Journal of Entrepreneurship, Business and Economics*, **8** (1), 77–88.

Malecki, E.J. (2018), *Entrepreneurship and Entrepreneurial Ecosystems*, Wiley Online Library, https://doi.org/10.1111/gec3.12359

Ray, M., S. Redaelli, D. Rudich and A. Wong (2020), 'A post-Covid-19 commercial-recovery strategy for B2B companies', accessed at https://www.mckinsey.com/industries/advanced-electronics/our-insights/a-post-Covid-19-commercial-recovery-strategy-for-b2b-companies

Salamzadeh, A. and L.P. Dana (September 2020), 'The coronavirus (covid-19) pandemic: Challenges among Iranian startups', *Journal of Small Business & Entrepreneurship*, 1–24. https://doi.org/10.1080/08276331.2020.1821158

Soul Machines (2020), 'Meet Bella', 14 April, accessed at https://www.soulmachines.com/2020/04/meet-bella/

Times Higher Education (2020), *Impact Ratings 2020*, accessed at https://www.timeshighereducation.com/rankings/impact/2020/

World Bank (2019), *Doing Business 2019*, accessed at https://www.doingbusiness.org/content/dam/doingBusiness/media/Annual-Reports/English/DB2019-report_web-version.pdf

World Health Organization (2020), 'Quit tobacco today!', accessed at https://www.who.int/news-room/spotlight/using-ai-to-quit-tobacco

14. Higher education transformation and management during Covid-19

James Metson and Cate Roy

1.   INTRODUCTION

Among the many business and operational models disrupted by Covid-19, tertiary education would be high on the impact list for many countries. Not only have institutions faced a rapid transition to alternative modes of delivery of their core operations, they have also had to confront the crisis of a long-established business model being almost instantly overturned. For research-led institutions, the rising dependence of this model on export education, particularly over the last decade, has been starkly exposed by closed borders and the collapse of international travel.

Covid-19 has impacted on almost every dimension of university operations. The immediate reaction to the health crisis, with border and campus closure, coupled with the simultaneous failure of the economic model, has required a major reorganization of many institutional activities. The speed of this transition has placed huge demands on staff and presented significant leadership challenges for university management.

Despite the recent turmoil wrought by the global pandemic, higher education has proved remarkably resilient. Doubts around the value of a university education have been dispelled as society has made it clear that it values deeply the role of universities. While the pandemic has legitimized the role of online education, students and faculty have reinforced the importance and value of direct interaction and the stimulating effect of a relational based higher education system. The pandemic has also underscored the huge contribution of global research and science, the critical importance of collaboration and the significant potential for higher education to contribute to tackling other major societal issues such as climate change.

Even with the emerging prospect of viable vaccines, the sector will not return to a new equilibrium anytime soon. Universities and the global tertiary education landscape have been reset and can expect to evolve to look radically different over the next decade. Drawing on the experience of the University of Auckland, New Zealand's largest comprehensive university, this chapter endeavours to take an overview of what will be needed to reinvent the university in response to the global pandemic but also in the face of the other societal challenges. The pandemic has accelerated trends already underway, including the restructuring of the global economy, shifting geopolitics, the rise of the education technology industry and digital transformation. How universities respond and adapt to these major societal shifts and accompanying demands and expectations will be critical in shaping community perceptions and attitudes towards higher education.

2.   THE IMMEDIATE RESPONSE

New Zealand's swift and decisive response to the Covid-19 pandemic had an instant impact on the nation's higher education sector. With national lockdown initiated in late March 2020, campus closure was immediate other than for critical and especially Covid-19-related research. Community lockdown and locked out campuses imposed an immediate challenge to course delivery, a situation that persists in many parts of the world. The shift to online delivery platforms, coupled with the pastoral care of a very large and dispersed community of staff and students, placed enormous and ongoing demands on systems and people. Campus closure was then progressively lifted, starting some six weeks later as the country moved down through alert levels to full access by early June.

In the immediate response, the university's capacity to instantly accelerate the digital transition already underway has been critical. This shift to alternative modes of delivery occurred with relatively few ripples, reflecting devolved decision making, the empowerment of the academic workforce and the availability of critical technologies. These changes in delivery modes have indeed been foreshadowed in the technology-enabled, student-centric model of the universities of the future (Cawood et al., 2018). As with many examples of technological evolution, the trends are known but it is far more difficult to predict the disruptive changes that drive them. Post-pandemic, strong interest in online learning, or a hybrid of on- and off-campus learning, is likely to remain. These shifts will require evidence-based design and rigorous evaluation to ensure optimum learning outcomes for all students.

The pandemic has accelerated trends in online higher education. The expansion of new modes of learning globally is a consequence of advances in technology, growth in demand for new modes of higher education and financial pressures facing the tertiary sector. Traditional boundaries are blurring between professional development, occupational credentialing and formal higher education, resulting in a growing appetite for a diverse range of credentials (Gallagher, 2016). Universities have not been immune to the growing trend towards 'unbundling': a process of disaggregating educational provision into its component parts, often with external providers (Czerniewicz, 2017). Reduced state support for higher education in many national contexts coupled with the accelerating cost of institutional operations have placed financial pressures on many institutions. Increasingly, institutions are under pressure to do more with less, resulting the growth of unbundling. Proponents of unbundling note that offering low-cost models of higher education opens up higher education opportunities to populations that have previously lacked access. However, there are also risks associated such as limited pedagogical interaction, access to resources and the enrichment activities associated with broader campus life (McCowan, 2017).

While many aspects of teaching and learning were able to move near seamlessly to new modes of delivery, research continuity has been another matter. The largest impacts flow from the lockdown of laboratories and places of experiment, especially in those areas involving contact with people as research subjects. In some extreme cases, whole programmes such as clinical trials have been lost. The pandemic response has also exposed a vulnerable workforce. Research staff on fixed-term contracts (often early career researchers) are impacted most as the workforce contracts in response to the tightening financial position and the loss of projects through lockdowns and restricted movement (Levine and Rathmell, 2020; Saxe, 2020)

University research is also critically dependent on the movement of people. Research students move through advanced degrees and on to a range of pathways such as further study, employment and research fellowships at home and abroad. Similarly, students and research fellows are attracted from abroad to regenerate and invigorate the domestic research ecosystem. In a shrinking system, with closed borders, this global research workforce is increasingly stranded in place.

This career interruption particularly impacts early career researchers within the university where the opportunities to travel, meet colleagues and build research networks have all but evaporated (Levine and Rathmell, 2020). Universities have increasingly been focusing efforts on supporting this community, and particularly those most impacted by lockdown, for example through carer responsibilities.

In the midst of the initial response, New Zealand universities have rediscovered the role of the university as a social institution, serving local, national and global communities. New Zealand universities have contributed a network of expertise and science advisers to government through which advice has been effectively channelled and filtered (Freshwater, 2020; Ministry of Business, Innovation & Employment, 2020). The role of epidemiologists, infectious disease specialists, modellers, engineers and others has provided not only the knowledge critical to decision making, but also communication of these concepts to a fearful and knowledge-hungry public (Baker et al., 2020). At the University of Auckland, many staff have also provided direct assistance in the Covid-19 response in the establishment of testing capacity, the fabrication of face shields and other PPE, and providing significant support in areas such as community mental health.

Globally, the collaborative efforts in Covid-19 research have created a series of viable vaccines in less than a year. This reflects an unprecedented international science collaboration between universities, institutes and industry (United Nations, 2020). Higher education has sustained and further validated its central social role during the pandemic and will need to continue to adapt and evolve in order to meet the requirements and expectations of the communities it serves.

3.   RECOVERY

Mirroring broader society, the university shifted rapidly from navigating through the initial, and in many cases subsequent, waves of campus disruption, to tackling the medium- and longer-term future of the university and indeed of the whole international tertiary landscape. As with the societies universities reflect, the pervasive mantra in the pre-Covid landscape has been an economic model that optimized supply chain efficiency in the generation and delivery of goods and services, including higher education and research. The highest margin activity has invariably been the education of international students and this has provided much of the revenue needed for investment in areas such as research and campus development.

The lack of resilience in this approach has been comprehensively exposed by Covid-19. The reset needed, to both find and transition to a more resilient model, is urgent; however, at a time when such significant change is demanded of the university, the shortcomings in the economic model mean resources to undertake this realignment are in short supply.

Outside of Europe, universities in most of the Western world have steadily evolved over the past 50 years, with decreasing levels of direct government support and increasing dependence on revenues generated by research, philanthropy and – especially – as outlined, high-margin, fee-paying international students (Horne, 2020; Newsome and Cooper, 2016). The model has been sustained by relentless growth of the international education sector essentially funding both the current operations and aspirations of institutions. This has been accompanied by a shrinking demographic of domestic students as static levels of school leavers and participation in tertiary education have limited growth.

The expectations of students have also changed with a growing emphasis on graduate outcomes, employability and a return on investment (Tran et al.

2020). The evolution of universities from social enterprises to what is often described as a more corporate model, anchored by this business model, has brought greater independence and differentiation, but increased risk (Parker, 2012). For a number of countries, Covid-19 has brought an abrupt end to this model, removing the discretionary cashflow from international student tuition fees.

Over several decades, the social contract means governments have demanded growth in access and steadily increasing operational efficiencies though shrinking public funding of institutions on a per capita basis (OECD, 2020). This increases the burden on the student 'consumers' of the services and on institutions to seek more diverse funding sources – research, commercialization, consultancy, philanthropy, etc. In teaching and learning, the student view of a return on investment model has led to a focus on so-called 'work ready' graduates, raising challenges for the very survival of a comprehensive university. It builds tension between two roles – the liberal arts approach to a broad education, compared with producing students who are technically useful to the demands of the contemporary society and economy. The rise of employability as a central metric is now well embedded in global university ranking systems and increasingly in the public's judgement of the value of a university (Tomlinson, 2017).

The export education market has been underpinned by both the significant earning premium conferred by a higher degree, particularly from a top-tier university, and the strong global market for quality tertiary qualifications, especially for students from emerging economies. This also reflects that higher education is increasingly viewed as being for the economic benefit of the individual rather than being for the collective benefit of a society of educated individuals that John Henry Newman envisaged (Newman et al., 1996). The excessive focus on a return on investment model has some questionable consequences. In mid-2020, the amount of outstanding student loan debt in the United States had reached $1.6 trillion, owed by a collective 44.7 million borrowers (Bustamante, 2020). It is now accepted that a proportion of these students will never recoup their initial investment (*Economist*, 2014). On the other hand, many tertiary institutions have benefited from the demand-driven market. Over the past few decades, inflation in the cost of a university education, particularly in the USA, has even outstripped that of healthcare (Koch, 2019).

Universities have not led the charge in the adoption of this more utilitarian, corporate model supported by export education revenues, but rather it reflects the increasingly commercial and individual values of the societies in which they are embedded. This has also been reflected in the retreat of the state as the dominant funder of these institutions. For research-led universities this model is especially fragile as, particularly in Australasia, international students have provided the significant discretionary income needed to support institutional research endeavours (Marshman and Larkins, 2020).

As the recovery phase has begun, there has been a rapid redistribution of student destinations based on access. Borders have remained closed to destinations like Australia and New Zealand where virus elimination has been the national strategy; on the other hand, international student enrolments at UK universities are up by 9 per cent (Adams, 2020). International education is still highly valued with 56 per cent of respondents in a recent study suggesting they would defer their studies rather than other options such as online delivery or seeking a different destination country (QS, 2020).

The impact of international students on host societies reaches well beyond the walls of the provider institutions and the immediate economic impacts on host communities (Hughes, 2019). Post-study work rights is a major driver of international education, with many nations benefitting from the skills, knowledge and international networks of international graduates (Berquist et al., 2019). For research-led universities like the University of Auckland, international students contribute to the domestic talent pool, via spin-off companies, research translation and commercialization, significantly boosting the innovation economy in host countries (Chellaraj et al., 2005). For example, it is not unusual to see international students disproportionately represented amongst the founders of spin-out companies from university research. However, in New Zealand and elsewhere, Covid-19-triggered unemployment has dramatically shifted and reduced the social licence for such work rights (Fry and Wilson, 2020). An unintended consequence is an unwitting throttling of the thriving international talent and cultural exchange that international student migration has enabled. This talent movement is therefore a crucial and underestimated contributor to research performance with significant and untold impact on broader society and the post-Covid recovery.

4.   REINVENTION

Well before Covid-19, debate about the future of higher education had begun to intensify. Higher education has become as mass enterprise. Globally, around 40 per cent of the world's youth population now enter tertiary education, rising to 80 per cent in many countries (Callender et al., 2020). These students reap the multiple benefits of higher education through systematic engagement in knowledge and social relations. The result is a massified system of higher education across the globe that is no longer the preserve of the elite (Altbach, 2016).

Despite considerable success in expanding access, there are strong arguments for the need to transform, adapt and innovate higher education. This might range from refreshing core academic activities and exploring and innovating new modes of operation, through to a new type of university operating in a mode yet to be conceptualized. Diverse models will ensure universities not only remain relevant and accessible, but will be positioned to take a leading role in helping society understand, navigate and shape the future.

Under labels such as Education 4.0, or even Universities 4.0, efforts have been made to map the digital future of the university onto the framework of Industry 4.0 and examine the impacts of the cyber-physical world of the future on higher education (Dewar, 2017). These studies foreshadow an environment of student-centred learning delivery where content and interaction can be sourced across a multitude of platforms and across many timescales. Although content and assessment processes are far from optimized for this environment, development of the platforms has been essential to the Covid-19 response. Notably, the role of the educational technology industry has moved from the fringes and is now deeply embedded in the higher education sector globally. The pandemic has served to accelerate developments already under way and the arrival of new kinds of services and platforms means that practice is well ahead of research into emerging trends in many cases.

Accelerating digital transformation has been a Covid-19-response enabler, for example, through online course delivery and new modes of research collaboration. However, it has also heightened inequities already apparent in higher education with students from disadvantaged backgrounds often lacking access to technology and infrastructure. In New Zealand, many tertiary students lacked both a device and adequate internet required to study at home, with Māori and Pacific students disproportionately impacted (RNZ, 2020). Equity issues loom large and redistributing opportunity at scale requires a significant retooling of our digital environment and skills development to address disadvantage, irrespective of the mix of modes of learning that will characterize the university of the future.

Although the University of Auckland has largely shifted back to on-campus delivery of teaching, some institutions have committed their future to being fully online in course delivery. While this effectively mitigates risk and reaches a distributed and increasing diverse student body, deeper questions remain over how the nature of the cocreation of knowledge which lies at the heart of the learning process (Bovill, 2020) will evolve in such a differentiated system. Fully online delivery provides only part of the deep learning leading institutions aspire to deliver. The campus experience is not only a proven forum for the cocreation of learning, but aids in the development of critical interpersonal skills and the moral and ethical framework that guides our lives.

For many universities, Covid-19 has also precipitated a very rapid reconsideration of the physical requirements of the future campus. If part of the sector will stay permanently online for course delivery, or offer multiple teaching modes, particularly for large undergraduate classes, then the need for traditional, monolithic lecture theatres is reduced. The misfit between physical assets (buildings and amenities) and digital assets is already apparent and is likely to accelerate. Universities are typically 'bricks and mortar' rich but the assets are highly illiquid, leaving few degrees of freedom in the redeployment of resources. This is a rapidly emerging challenge for university leadership as a Covid-19-induced reshaping and sizing of institutions needs to be undertaken.

In contrast, many areas of research activity are far less amenable to a similar model of mixed-mode delivery. For research-intensive universities, the dependence on physical plant such as laboratory, clinical and workshop space will remain and indeed increase. This suggests the overall university estate in such cases will increasingly reflect this function.

The future campus is therefore likely to reflect this move away from monolithic teaching spaces, coupled with more emphasis on smaller, flexible, technologically infused learning spaces and specialized research spaces. This will be accompanied by an increased emphasis on student and staff amenities to enrich the on-campus experience and complement the balance of purely online delivery of teaching and learning. This campus is also likely to merge more into its environment in several ways. In locations where this is feasible, shared facilities with community and industry will be more common, making more effective use of capital investments and enriching the learning and research experience.

5.   THE FUTURE

At the same time as the economic model of the university has been upended, nations are looking to higher education to drive economic and social reinvention. The closure of international borders has resulted in universities re-orienting their focus on their local communities. There is a greater emphasis on servicing local communities and industries with more education and training, and research partnerships that promise knowledge-led socioeconomic transformation (Coates et al., 2020). Beyond the expertise needed to inform and support the Covid-19 response is the need to reskill and upskill a displaced workforce. The arrival of micro-credentials, digital badges and stackable certificates is evidence of the unbundling of higher education and a trend towards more granular certified learning (Oliver, 2019). New actors are emerging, sometimes in partnership with universities, to provide and deliver content. There is a growing emphasis on employability, digital skills and meeting the requirements of a rapidly evolving labour market. Many countries are amending their national qualifications frameworks to include micro-credentials and formally recognize them (Oliver, 2019). In the face of continued global economic uncertainty, universities will need to prove how they add distinctive value by producing talented graduates, promoting innovation and developing productive, reciprocal relationships with their communities (Coates et al., 2020).

One could again argue this represents a partial reversion to the social enterprise model, but to date the contribution from such activities in most jurisdictions still leaves institutions far short of a sustainable economic model. As universities struggle to meet the demand to rapidly build and offer packaged, skills-based learning through vehicles such as micro-credentials and diplomas, new actors (for profit and not for profit) enter the higher education field. Relatively little is known about their influence and effect on the repurposing of higher education, and major questions remain about the transformative potential of these new modes of higher education.

While unbundling promises to transform teaching and learning, university research and innovation will be central to a green and inclusive economic recovery from the Covid-19 pandemic. Similar to many other nations, New Zealand has laid out its plan for inclusive prosperity and a transition to a low-emissions economy (New Zealand Labour Party, 2020). Achieving this ambition will require a strong commitment to technology and innovation (Productivity Commission, 2020). New Zealand, as with many mature Western democracies, has a persistent productivity deficit (Nolan et al., 2019). Indeed, the country is one of a small number of OECD countries with both a low level of labour productivity and low productivity growth. This points to the dominance of a labour-intensive primary-sector economy and relatively few 'frontier' companies (Productivity Commission, 2020). Prioritizing and investing in research and innovation is critical to lifting growth and productivity.

Universities are uniquely placed to provide the innovation needed to catalyse a more knowledge-rich economy and generate the productivity gains that are essential to address some of the more pressing social and wealth inequality issues faced by our communities. The New Zealand government has committed to an economy that is productive, sustainable and inclusive with a focus on combatting climate change, reducing waste and supporting green energy. Innovation is central to achieving this vision and universities will play a pivotal role in the innovation-led recovery. The experience of other small, advanced economies highlights the critical role of researchers, innovators and the pipeline of highly educated graduates, as well as the importance of fostering collaboration between universities and industry. In the New Zealand context, finite government resources are likely to be focused on a small number of high-potential areas reflecting existing and emerging strengths and capabilities. An innovation-led recovery will require upgrading the research and innovation ecosystem and building deep networks between industry, researchers and government (Productivity Commission, 2020).

However, responding to major societal challenges such as climate change also has the potential to create a more utilitarian view of the role of the university and a steadily increasing focus on the STEM (science, technology, engineering and mathematics) disciplines. This has been reflected in the recent recasting of university fees in Australia (Visentin, 2020) to lower fees in the STEM disciplines and education, and raise costs in the arts and humanities. In terms of research, this may mean focusing on core strengths and building up programmes where the institution has a natural advantage. The result can be positive with gains in research productivity, new lines of inquiry being discovered and institutions with limited resources assuming leadership roles in new disciplinary fields (Gilbert et al., 2018). However, there is also the risk of reducing the breadth and diversity to which comprehensive institutions are deeply committed at a time when interdisciplinary collaboration is required to address 'grand challenges' or 'wicked problems' facing society (Holm et al., 2013; Pohl et al., 2017). The value of interdisciplinary research has been showcased during the pandemic with experts from a wide range of disciplines working on the Covid-19 response. By maintaining a breadth of disciplines, universities are home to the intersection of ideas that offer the most profound opportunity to address global issues such as climate, sustainable development and global inequality in resources and opportunity.

6.   CONCLUSIONS

The Covid-19 pandemic has generated an extraordinary range of challenges for the global community. In many countries it has reshaped, and continues to reshape, the operational models and expectations of the tertiary education sector. In New Zealand, the pandemic has led to a fundamental change in the nature of the relationship between universities and the wider communities in which they are embedded. The value of the expert and indeed the contest of experts, has in part been rehabilitated. This is undoubtedly helped by the limited degrees of separation in a relatively small society and the well-formed and trusted structure of science advice to government (Gluckman, 2014). This is contrasted with the rapid rise in populism globally and the proliferation of misinformation and 'fake news', and underscores the important role of universities in civil society.

Of equal significance in New Zealand, and indeed in many countries, has been the agility that universities have displayed in their response to Covid-19. The ability to pivot rapidly and find new solutions in modes of working and delivery of teaching and learning, and in research, has been remarkable. This speaks to an ability to manage change and uncertainty that has not typically been associated with universities which remain one of society's most enduring institutions.

What universities offer – the ability to interact with their communities and catalyse an exchange of knowledge and contest of ideas – is somewhat better understood, even in the polarized age of Covid-19. This role as 'honest broker' must be used with care as communities have a well-developed antenna for the detection of self-interest over national interest. The role of the university as a social institution committed to serving local, national and global communities has never been more important. How the university of the future delivers on that role is likely to be significantly different, through a process of change much accelerated by Covid-19. Although the attraction of the physical campus endures, growth will be through a much larger digital footprint, with the capacity to deliver both teaching and research though a broad range of platforms to a wide and diverse range of audiences.

REFERENCES

Adams, R. (2020), 'UK universities recruit record numbers of international students', *The Guardian*, 24 September, accessed 14 December 2020 at https://www.theguardian.com/education/2020/sep/24/uk-universities-recruit-record-numbers-of-international-students

Altbach, P.G. (2016), *Global Perspectives on Higher Education*, Baltimore: JHU Press.

Baker, M.G., A. Kvalsvig, A.J. Verrall, L. Telfar-Barnard and N. Wilson (2020), 'New Zealand's elimination strategy for the COVID-19 pandemic and what is required to make it work', *The New Zealand Medical Journal* (Online), **133** (1512), 10–14.

Berquist, B., R. Hall, S. Morris-Lange, H. Shields, V. Stern and L.T. Tran (2019), *Global Perspectives on International Student Employability*, International Education Association of Australia (IEAA), accessed 14 December 2020 at www.ieaa.org.au

Bovill, C. (2020), 'Co-creation in learning and teaching: The case for a whole-class approach in higher education', *Higher Education*, **79**, 1023–1037. https://doi.org/10.1007/s10734-019-00453-w

Bustamante, J. (2020), 'Student loan debt statistics', accessed 14 December 2020 at https://educationdata.org/student-loan-debt-statistics

Callender, C., W. Locke and S. Marginson (eds) (2020), *Changing Higher Education for a Changing World*, Bloomsbury Higher Education Research Series, London and New York: Bloomsbury Academic.

Cawood, R., J. Roche, A. Ong, D. Sharma, A. Mulder, L. Jones, D. Ta and J. Kirkhope (2018), *Can the Universities of Today Lead Learning for Tomorrow? The University of the Future*, Australia: Ernst & Young.

Chellaraj, G., K.E. Maskus and A. Mattoo (2005), *The Contribution of Skilled Immigration and International Graduate Students to US Innovation*, Washington, DC: The World Bank.

Coates, H., Z. Xie and X. Hong (2020), 'Engaging transformed fundamentals to design global hybrid higher education', *Studies in Higher Education*, **46** (1), 166–176.

Czerniewicz, L. (2017), 'Unbundling and rebundling higher education in an age of inequality', *Educause Review*, 29 October, accessed 14 December 2020 at https://er.educause.edu/articles/2018/10/unbundling-and-rebundling-higher-education-in-an-age-of-inequality

Dewar, J. (2017), 'University 4.0: Redefining the role of universities in the modern era', *Higher Education Review Magazine*.

Economist (2014), 'Is college worth it?', 5 April 2014, accessed 14 December 2020 at www.economist.com/united-states/2014/04/05/is-college-worth-it

Freshwater, D. (2020), 'What universities bring to the Covid recovery', *Newsroom*, 5 August, accessed 14 December 2020 at https://www.newsroom.co.nz/ideasroom/what-universities-bring-to-covid-recovery

Fry, J. and P. Wilson (2020), *Could do Better: Migration and New Zealand's Frontier Firms. NZIER Report to the New Zealand Productivity Commission*, accessed 14 December 2020 at https://nzier.org.nz/publication/could-do-better-migration-and-new-zealands-frontier-firms

Gallagher, S. (2016), 'From micromasters to nanodegrees', *University World News*, 12 August, accessed 14 December 2020 at https://www.universityworldnews.com/post.php?story%20=20160809133730588

Gilbert, C.G., M.M. Crow and D. Anderson (2018), 'Design thinking for higher education', *Stanford Social Innovation Review*, accessed 14 December 2020 at https://ssir.org/articles/entry/design_thinking_for_higher_education

Gluckman, P. (2014), 'Policy: The art of science advice to government', *Nature News*, **507** (7491), 163.

Holm, P., M.E. Goodsite, S. Cloetingh, M. Agnoletti, B. Moldan, D.J. Lang … and R.W. Scholz (2013), 'Collaboration between the natural, social and human sciences in global change research', *Environmental Science & Policy*, **28**, 25–35.

Horne, J. (2020), 'How universities came to rely on international students', *The Conversation*, 22 May, accessed 14 December 2020 at https://theconversation.com/how-universities-came-to-rely-on-international-students-138796

Hughes, J. (2019), 'Why international students are so important to their host countries', accessed 14 December 2020 at https://www.academiccourses.com/article/why-international-students-are-so-important-to-their-host-countries/

Koch, J.V. (2019), *The Impoverishment of the American College Student*, Washington, DC: Brookings Institution Press.

Levine, R.L. and W.K. Rathmell (2020), 'COVID-19 impact on early career investigators: A call for action', *Nature Reviews: Cancer*, **20**, 357–358.

Marshman, I. and F. Larkins (2020), 'Modelling individual Australian universities resilience in managing overseas student revenue losses from the COVID-19 Pandemic', Melbourne: Centre for the Study of Higher Education, accessed 14 December 2020 at https://melbourne-cshe.unimelb.edu.au/__data/assets/pdf_file/0009/3392469/Australian-Universities-COVID-19-Financial-Management.pdf

McCowan, T. (2017), 'Higher education, unbundling, and the end of the university as we know it', *Oxford Review of Education*, **43** (6), 733–748.

Ministry of Business, Innovation & Employment (2020), *New Zealand's COVID-19 Research Response*, accessed 14 December 2020 at https://www.mbie.govt.nz/dmsdocument/11621-new-zealands-covid-19-research-response-pdf

New Zealand Labour Party (2020), *Labour's 2020 Election Manifesto*, accessed 14 December 2020 at https://www.labour.org.nz/news-labour_2020_manifesto

Newman, J.H., G.P. Landow, J.E. Newman, F.M. Turner, M.M. Garland and S. Castro-Klaren (1996), *The Idea of a University*, New Haven, CT: Yale University Press.

Newsome, L.K. and P. Cooper (2016), 'International students' cultural and social experiences in a British university: "Such a hard life [it] is here"', *Journal of International Students*, **6** (1), 195–215.

Nolan, P., R. Pomeroy and G. Zheng (2019), 'Productivity by the numbers: 2019', New Zealand Productivity Commission, accessed 14 December 2020 at www .productivity.govt.nz

OECD (2020), *How has Private Expenditure on Tertiary Education Evolved Over Time and How Does it Affect Participation in Education?*, Education Indicators in Focus, No. 72, Paris: OECD Publishing. https://doi.org/10.1787/6b7ded53-en

Oliver, B. (2019), 'Making micro-credentials work for learners, employers and providers', accessed 14 December 2020 at https://www.voced.edu.au/content/ngv:83922

Parker, L.D. (2012), 'From privatised to hybrid corporatised higher education: A global financial management discourse', *Financial Accountability & Management*, **28** (3), 247–268.

Pohl, C., B. Truffer and G. Hirsch Hadorn (2017), 'Addressing wicked problems through transdisciplinary research', in R. Frodeman, J. Thompson Klein and R.C.S. Pacheco (eds),*The Oxford Handbook of Interdisciplinarity*, pp. 319–331.

Productivity Commission (2020), *New Zealand Firms: Reaching for the Frontier*, accessed 14 December 2020 at https://www.productivity.govt.nz/inquiries/frontier -firms/

QS (2020), *International Student Survey 2020 Report – Volume 3: Defining the Student Experience*, accessed 14 December 2020 at https://www.qs.com/portfolio -items/international-student-survey-2020-report-volume-3-defining-the-student -experience/

RNZ (2020), 'AUT helps Māori and Pasifika students with computers and internet', 27 April accessed 14 December 2020 at https://www.rnz.co.nz/international/pacific -news/415198/aut-helps-maori-and-pasifika-students-with-computers-and-internet

Saxe, J.P. (2020), 'Introductions to the community: Early-career researchers in the time of COVID-19', *Cell Stem Cell*, **26** (5), 627–628.

Tomlinson, M. (2017), 'Forms of graduate capital and their relationship to graduate employability', *Education and Training*, **59** (4). doi:10.1108/ET-05-2016-0090

Tran, L.T., M. Rahimi, G. Tan, X.T. Dang and N. Le (2020), 'Post-study work for international graduates in Australia: Opportunity to enhance employability, get a return on investment or secure migration?', *Globalisation, Societies and Education*, **18** (5), 495–510.

United Nations (2020), 'Scientists optimistic about COVID-19 vaccines for all', accessed 14 December 2020 at https://news.un.org/en/story/2020/12/1079322

Visentin, L. (2020), 'University fees are changing. How will it affect you?', *The Sydney Morning Herald*, 17 October, accessed 14 December 2020 at https://www.smh.com .au/politics/federal/university-fees-are-changing-how-will-it-affect-you-20201009 -p563ib.html

PART IV

Concluding management perspectives on
Covid-19

15. Concluding management issues, associated learnings and social resilience

Kenneth Husted and Rudolf R. Sinkovics

The Covid-19 pandemic has been seen as a wicked problem, which creates unique policy and governance challenges (Sahin et al., 2020). Besides being associated with uncertainty and a wide range of consequences for an extensive range of stakeholders, a defining characteristic of a wicked problem is the difficulty in framing and formulating the essence of the very problem at hand. Therefore, wicked problems are considered ill-structured (Simon, 1973; Baskerville, 2008). For the purposes of this book, we framed the Covid-19 pandemic problem by introducing three distinctive sets of dichotomies. The first is around proximity and distance, a key feature of the NZ geographical and economic position in its regional and global networks. The second dichotomy relates to centralisation and decentralisation in decision making. The third dichotomy is associated with collective versus individual learning.

To look back at the chapters that comprise the present book, we now reflect on them in a structured way by drawing on the meta-capability policy framework developed by Menzies and Raskovic (2020). We depict this framework in Figure 15.1 and then connect the chapters and their stories to basic resilience dimensions.

Resilience is here seen as a capability to address adverse effects and recover from these through positive adaptation (i.e., bouncing back) or even emerge stronger and thus bounce beyond adversity (Hoegl and Hartmann, 2020). Underpinning fundamental resilience dimensions as in Menzies and Raskovic's (2020) framework and building on the conceptual work of Saja et al. (2019) as well as Obrist et al. (2010), we posit that bouncing back and beyond Covid-19 is a function of basic capabilities and developing meta-capabilities. Basic capabilities can be categorised into geography and physical environment capital (gc), economic capital (ec), social capital and institutions (sc), cultural capital (cc) and leadership capital (lc).

The 14 chapters in this book address key management issues from a unique NZ perspective. Table 15.1 provides a detailed overview of these

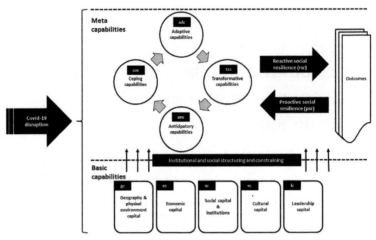

Source: Adapted from Menzies and Raskovic (2020).

*Figure 15.1   Meta-capability social resilience framework to mitigate
                 Covid-19 disruption*

key issues and the specific learnings derived both for the domestic NZ and
the wider international context (see the "learnings" column). Each chapter
further elucidates how individuals and members of companies/organisations
have responded to fundamental resilience challenges. In the table, we build
connections between the various chapters in the book and how these relate
to specific NZ characteristics. For instance, three chapters – by El-Jahel and
MacCulloch (Chapter 2), by Maani (Chapter 3) and by Fiedler et al. (Chapter
6) – refer to geographical and physical capital. The particular way NZ has
quickly shielded its population against the novel external threat by isolating
the island nation thoroughly through a swiftly implemented early travel ban
from China signifies how the country's geographical and political location was
instrumental in the slowdown of negative health implications. The chapters
by El-Jahel and MacCulloch (Chapter 2), by Dimes and DeVilliers (Chapter
11), by Lee (Chapter 13) and by Metson and Roy (Chapter 14) connect the NZ
economic environment to its ability to recover quickly and provide platforms
for swift economic redevelopment. Despite a long-standing productivity gap in
NZ, which is also referred to in Chapter 2 by El-Jahel and MacCulloch, NZ's
entrepreneurial and innovation-friendly environment provided the government
with confidence that with support of a wage subsidy scheme, and a reasonably
flexible workforce, the economy would be able to recover from a national strict
and demanding lockdown.

Almost all book chapters refer to social capital and institutions, which can be explained by the fact that NZ has a strong focus on health and well-being and features prominently in the Better Life Index (OECD, 2019). Furthermore, the "team of 5 million" spirit invoked by Prime Minister Jacinda Ardern and permeated throughout the country with a well-functioning civil service and supportive workforce, enacted and reinforced a widely lauded community spirit, buttressed by Māori values.

The chapters by Plester (Chapter 7), by Jindal and Boxall (Chapter 8) and by Wolfgramm, Houkamau and Love (Chapter 10) in Part II of the book expand on the social capital and institutions theme by addressing issues of cultural capital around themes as diverse as humour, job crafting and Māori cultural values and practices respectively. These chapters also provide fascinating insights into how cultural capital as an important dimension of basic capabilities translates into meta capabilities that help to mitigate Covid-19 disruption through social resilience.

Nine out of the 14 chapters relate to and/or address leadership capital. Chapter 4 by Carroll looks into that issue from a meso/macro level perspective, highlighting the view that expert leadership in NZ is widely recognised through a frame that goes beyond the technical and rational aspects of expert knowledge; it is rather invoked through relational and distributed and collaborative leadership. Chapter 5 by Ott and Michailova picks up this theme through the lens of talent management, where NZ is now in the enviable position to have reversed its human capital and leadership drain into a terrain that is highly attractive to both domestic and international talent. Fiedler et al. (Chapter 6) demonstrate in their empirical study how the export managers have swiftly moved on to learning about export markets through digital technologies. Benson-Rea, Erakovic and Watson (Chapter 9) relate their chapter to the leadership capital issue through the lens of boards and board governance, which provides learnings in terms of more fuzzy boundaries between senior management and board members and the ensuing ability to facilitate emergency strategies and economic contagion effects. In Part III of the book, three out of the four chapters take this basic capability up as well. Chapter 14 by Metson and Roy focuses on the higher education sector, where the disruption has supported a much more federated decision making than ever before, and many observers hope that the top-down fiat structures may be a fad of the past. Brache, Norgrove and Husted (Chapter 12) show how leadership capital enables R&D collaboration to adjust to and experiment with new practices.

Table 15.1 also enumerates how the various chapters in the book connect to the development of meta-capabilities. This follows the logic of institutional theory (e.g., Kostova et al., 2008) or how social mechanisms of institutional and social structures guide and constrain actors' behaviour, in our case NZ firms and organisations, managers or workers. For instance, NZ's recent experience with disasters has strengthened its anticipatory capabilities. In addition, high levels of trust have strengthened social compliance related to wearing face masks and thus limited the spread of illness, which in other countries proved to be more difficult (Menzies and Raskovic, 2020).

Darkow (2019) suggests that organisational resilience essentially rests around avoiding crises before they happen and containing the scope of crises once these are unfolding. Drawing on this perspective and connecting it with the meta-capability social resilience approach of Menzies and Raskovic (2020), we can pinpoint how the book's 14 chapters connect the basic capabilities to the meta-capabilities and thus proactively or reactively support the development of social resilience. Anticipatory capabilities (anc) are defined as capabilities that allow us to foresee and plan for disruptions. The chapters by Haworth (Chapter 9), by Carroll (Chapter 4), by Jindal and Boxall (Chapter 8), by Benson-Rea et al. (Chapter 9), by Wolfgramm et al. (Chapter 10) and by Dimes and de Villiers (Chapter 11) lucidly describe the contexts and conditions which have fostered societal and managerial processes that allowed NZ actors to benefit from these meta-capabilities during the unfolding of Covid-19. Coping capabilities (coc), on the other hand, refer to the ability to deal effectively with adverse events and/or significant change (Duchek, 2020). Twelve of the 14 chapters connect with this type of meta capability. The underpinning basic capabilities and the significant catastrophic events of the past seem to have helped develop better personal coping and resilience, as outlined in the chapters.

Adaptive capabilities (ac) refer to the ability to adapt and self-renew through innovation (Hoegl and Hartmann, 2020). NZ's SME context, its unique embeddedness in the Māori indigenous culture and a relatively flexible and innovative organisational system have arguably fostered swift and uncomplicated positive adjustment under challenging conditions. Ten chapters refer to this meta-capability, supporting the notion that this particular meta-capability has been successfully leveraged at a country level. Transformative capabilities (tc), on the other hand, refer to "how we learn and transform behaviours after an initial disruptive shock by bouncing beyond adversity". The "Kiwi let's roll up our sleeves and just get on with it" mentality (Menzies and Raskovic, 2020, 3) is a prime example of the ability of firms and individual actors to respond by bouncing back and beyond.

As the chapters in this book illustrate, there are unique learnings from the NZ context for organisational and political economy actors outside the country and the Oceania region. As the world is still going through various experiences in policy and individual actor responses, we hope that the NZ experience of Covid-19 reduction and elimination of community transmissions offers valuable insights. This book's ambition is to contribute to the debates about management responses to Covid-19 and improvement of preparedness and resilience regarding future shocks. These are probably not far away.

Table 15.1   *Key management issues of the book chapters, associated learnings and their relationship to the meta-capability of social resilience*

Part I	Key issues addressed	Learnings	Relationship to basic capabilities					Relationship to meta-capability development					
			gc	ec	cc	sc	lc	anc	coc	adc	trc	rsc	psc
Haworth	Adoption of 'go hard, go fast' approach, coupled with emphasis on community engagement, effective national communication and generous economic interventions No stipulation of a 'best response' to Covid-19, but emergence of 'just in time' response	Flexibility in the government response, built on institutional trust and national policy leadership with consistent communication Potential to leverage expert recognition internationally regarding expert leadership and trade (especially APEC)				X	X	X	X	X			
El-Jahel and MacCulloch	NZ implemented on of the world's strictest lockdown regime Approach of 'gross national happiness' to the pandemic	Significant success regarding the stringent lockdown and prioritisation of health and well-being outcomes in the short term. Challenges to realise long-term economic growth under continuing lock-down regime and tightened border controls.	X	X		X			X	X			

	Key issues addressed	Learnings	Relationship to basic capabilities					Relationship to meta-capability development					
---	---	---	gc	ec	sc	cc	lc	anc	coc	adc	trc	rsc	psc
Maani	Shifts in operations, sectors and workforce due to restrictions Designation of essential work, technology-facilitated remote work, contactless retail and wage subsidies	Relative swift return to 'normality' due to stringent government response Role and value of 'essential' work with ramification for future living wages	X		X				X	X			X
Carroll	NZ pandemic experts understood themselves as leaders rather than policy makers/advisers Experts hold constructive relationship with science	Expert leadership can be recognised through leadership frame beyond the technical and rational knowledge Relational, distributed and collaborative leadership is vital for crises response			X		X	X	X		X	X	X
Part II	Key issues addressed	Learnings											
Ott and Michailova	Covid-19 has unexpectedly transformed brain drain issues into (domestic) brain gain	NZ national culture and organisational culture supported through trust and unity			X		X				X		X

			Relationship to basic capabilities			Relationship to meta-capability development			
Fiedler, Fath, Sinkovics and Sinkovics	Physical distance to export markets shielded NZ early on in the crisis. As the pandemic unfolded, building new market knowledge, new networks became more important.	Digital technologies and connectivity improve operations and business model reconfiguration. New forms of learning are required to offset disadvantages due to physical distance and closed borders	X			X	X	X	X
Plester	Boundaries between work and home became porous due to Covid-19. Humour supports coping under lockdown conditions	Informality of workplace interactions and kindness, source of strength in turbulent times. Humour as positive coping strategy	X	X		X	X	X	X
Jindal and Boxall	Covid-19 triggered new forms of job crafting, i.e. ways in which employees shape and transform their jobs, to make them meaningful. Collegiate NZ workplace culture makes job crafting more likely	Due to pandemic turbulence, it is sensible to support flexible, hybrid model of working. Job crafting leads to higher levels of satisfaction and commitment	X	X	X	X	X	X	X

			Relationship to basic capabilities					Relationship to meta-capability development					
Benson-Rea, Eraković and Watson	The disruptive nature of the pandemic challenged CEOs, board chairs and directors in handling the crisis	Blurring of internal boundaries between boards and senior management to enable emergent strategy implementation Considering stakeholders benefits the organisation itself			X		X	X	X	X	X		
Wolfgramm, Houkamau and Love	Covid-19 put spotlight on already existing health and socioeconomic disparities in the society	Māori cultural values and practices provide effective communal responses by enabling recovery and fostering resilience			X	X		X	X	X	X	X	X
Part III	Key issues addressed	Learnings	gc	ec	sc	cc	lc	anc	coc	adc	trc	rsc	psc
Dimes and de Villiers	In a crisis like Covid-19, business should focus both on short-term decision making and cash generation and long-term goals for sustainable value creation	Integrated Reporting and Integrated Thinking improve organisational communication, collaboration and trust Firms with Integrated Reporting and Integrated Thinking are even in a crisis situation able to balance day-to-day decisions with long-term sustainability objectives		X	X		X	X	X	X	X		

		Relationship to basic capabilities			Relationship to meta-capability development			
Brache, Norgrove and Husted	Covid-19 calls for collaborative R&D effort At the same time the pandemic has disrupted long-established practices for R&D collaboration	New practices also have to accommodate speed of discovery Global Covid-19 lockdowns are levelling the playing field for actors in the ecosystem		X	X	X	X	
Lee	NZ's triple helix and entrepreneurial model is resilient in the pandemic context	Following focus on health and well-being the entrepreneurial ecosystem supported adaptation and innovation towards recovery	X	X		X			X
Metson and Roy	Near instant transition to online learning Changes to business model as the global movement of students have been curtailed	The value and use of expert knowledge has in part been rehabilitated Universities can be agile in their response	X	X	X			X	

Note: gc = geography and physical environment capital, ec = economic capital, sc = social capital and institutions, cc = cultural capital, lc = leadership capital, anc = anticipatory capabilities, coc = coping capabilities, adc = adaptive capabilities, trc = transformative capabilities, rsr = reactive social resilience, psr = proactive social resilience.

REFERENCES

Baskerville, R. (2008), 'What design science is not', *European Journal of Information Systems*, **17** (5), 441–443. doi: 10.1057/ejis.2008.45

Darkow, P.M. (2019), 'Beyond "bouncing back": Towards an integral, capability-based understanding of organizational resilience', *Journal of Contingencies and Crisis Management*, **27** (2), 145–156. doi: 10.1111/1468-5973.12246

Duchek, S. (2020), 'Organizational resilience: A capability-based conceptualization', *Business Research*, **13** (1), 215–246. doi: 10.1007/s40685-019-0085-7

Hoegl, M. and S. Hartmann (2020), 'Bouncing back, if not beyond: Challenges for research on resilience', *Asian Business & Management*. doi: 10.1057/s41291-020-00133-z

Kostova, T., K. Roth and M.T. Dacin (2008), 'Institutional theory in the study of multinational corporations: A critique and new directions', *Academy of Management Review*, **33** (4), 994–1006. doi: 10.5465/amr.2008.34422026

Menzies, J. and M.M. Raskovic (2020), 'Taming covid-19 through social resilience: A meta-capability policy framework from Australia and New Zealand', *AIB Insights*, **20** (3). doi: 10.46697/001c.18165

Obrist, B., C. Pfeiffer and R. Henley (2010), 'Multi-layered social resilience: A new approach in mitigation research', *Progress in Development Studies*, **10** (4), 283–293. doi: 10.1177/146499340901000402

OECD (2019), *OECD Economic Surveys – New Zealand, Focus Well-being*. Paris: OECD.

Sahin, O., H. Salim, E. Suprun, R. Richards, S. MacAskill, S. Heilgeist, … C.D. Beal (2020), 'Developing a preliminary causal loop diagram for understanding the wicked complexity of the covid-19 pandemic', *Systems*, **8** (2), 20. doi: 10.3390/systems8020020

Saja, A.M.A., A. Goonetilleke, M. Teo and A.M. Ziyath (2019), 'A critical review of social resilience assessment frameworks in disaster management', *International Journal of Disaster Risk Reduction*, **35**, 101096. doi: 10.1016/j.ijdrr.2019.101096

Simon, H.A. (1973), 'The structure of ill structured problems', *Artificial Intelligence*, **4** (3), 181–201. doi: 10.1016/0004-3702(73)90011-8

Index

'Management Perspectives on the Covid-19 Crisis: Lessons from New Zealand *by Kenneth Husted and Rudolf R. Sinkovics is a timely and most important addition to the literature. At a time when the world is experiencing the most disastrous disruption in modern history, organizations, governments and communities are all struggling to come to grips with the repercussions of the global health pandemic, and responsible and impactful actions that can be taken. The experience of New Zealand in this context is like no other. As many countries failed to respond effectively to the disruption, best practice illustrations from New Zealand government and businesses have been most welcome. In this book where knowledgeable authors provide perspectives on responsible and impactful responses, the reader is treated to numerous insights along the lines of fresh conceptualizations, organizational activities and management implications. Husted and Sinkovics have assembled an amazing inventory of case studies and illustrations all of which should prove productive and informative to all of us.'*
S. Tamer Cavusgil, Fuller E. Callaway Professorial Chair and Professor of International Business, Executive Director CIBER, J. Mack Robinson College of Business, Georgia State University, USA

'*We know a great deal about virology and managing a healthcare during Covid, but this book highlights the contribution of management scholars to the workplace issues resulting from this pandemic. Leading management researchers explore the impact of remote working, building resilience at work, the impact of technology, organisational leadership and many more relevant topics. It is an outstanding collection of management research insights that will help in creating 'the new workplace' post-Covid. A must read for all interested in organisational behaviour and change.*'
Sir Cary Cooper, CBE, 50th Anniversary Professor of Organizational Psychology & Health, Alliance Manchester Business School, The University of Manchester, UK

'*The unpredictable, permeable and deathly threats of COVID-19 have confounded nations and their experts in tackling the unprecedented public health crisis that has impacted the economy, society and even mental state of their citizens. New Zealand has stood out as a classic example of defying the pandemic through prudent and responsive management at macro, meso and micro levels. That citizens and institutions – formal and otherwise – collaborated with perseverance and wisdom are amply evidenced in the absorbing chapters of this rich volume edited by Husted and Sinkovics. This is an inspiring volume not merely in management but what the co-editors term as 'social resilience'.*'
Keshab Das, Professor of Economics, Gujarat Institute of Development Research, Ahmedabad, India

'*This book is an extremely valuable source for politicians and business leaders in countries that, in light of being hit hard by the second wave of the pandemic and new mutations to the virus, try to switch to the Covid Zero strategy as applied by New Zealand.*'
Christoph Dörrenbächer, Professor of Organizational Design and Behaviour in International Business, Berlin school of Economics and Law, Berlin, Germany

'*I am recommending this book because there is not any comprehensive volume in the market that captures such rich and in-depth contextual approaches and strategies required to deal with the Black Swan crises such as COVID-19.* Management Perspectives on the Covid-19 Crisis: Lessons from New Zealand *by Husted and Sinkovics provides a solid account of the social resilience strategies needed to deal with external prolonged shocks by drawing key lessons from New Zealand.*'
Zaheer Khan, Professor in Strategy and International Business, The University of Aberdeen, Business School, UK

'*This volume offers an exciting perspective into how actors in New Zealand have been dealing with the Covid-19 crisis, turning perceived disadvantages of the country into unexpected strengths from which all countries can learn about becoming more crisis resilient.*'
Peter Knorringa, Professor of Private Sector & Development, Institute of Social Studies, Erasmus University, Rotterdam, The Netherlands

'*This is a very interesting and appropriate book for the current global pandemic situation caused by COVID-19 virus. This unprecedented situation has had a global impact and has transformed business logic in all countries. New Zealand's particular situation deserves special attention given its ability to manage the COVID-19 crisis in an exemplary manner. Undoubtedly, the contribution of this book edited by Professors Husted and Sinkovics is a welcome contribution not only to learning from an academic point of view, but also from a business point of view. Anyone interested in deepening the international management of COVID-19 crisis should read this book.*'
Francisco-Jose Molina-Castillo, Professor of Marketing, The University of Murcia, Spain

'*Husted and Sinkovics pick a great subject and the timing is perfect for this book. NZ is a success story on Covid, although how much of that is due to political leadership or other factors is difficult to separate. The chapters do a great job to delineate macro-level issues through NZs 'go hard, go fast' strategy from meso-level job-market and critical worker issues to micro-level human resources, innovation and exporting issues. As the themes covered in*

*this book indicate, leadership, the well-being agenda and personal charac-
teristics play a central role in explaining the response. Thus, this book is of
interest not only to management scholars but also behavioural economists
and scholars in fields of politics, sociology, international political economy
and development studies.'*
Khalid Nadvi, Professor of International Development, Managing Director
and Head, Global Development Institute, School of Environment, Education
and Development, The University of Manchester, UK

*'Countries in the Asia-Pacific, New Zealand in particular, have been highly
effective in dealing with the COVID-19 pandemic. This book by Kenneth
Husted and Rudolf Sinkovics provides a timely and precious source of knowledge in the field of management to understand the successful responses of
New Zealand in tackling COVID-19. There are unvaluable lessons that New
Zealand can teach to the world, particularly to countries such as Brazil and
the USA, that performed poorly. The authors were able to put together an
authoritative group of experts in the field of management that could bring
new insights on how to deal with wicked problems, such as COVID-19 and
future crises. It is a text that everyone must read to understand that success
requires capabilities and leadership to make the right decisions and manage
crises like these, and those do not emerge overnight. Capabilities and effective leadership need to have the right environment to flourish and be built
overtime to be deployed when needed.'*
José A. Puppim de Oliveira, Professor, FGV - Fundação Getulio Vargas
(FGV EAESP and FGV EBAPE), Brazil

*'This timely book edited by Husted and Sinkovics elaborates on and inte-
grates theories and perspectives from various realms in order to elucidate
the daunting challenges in coping with COVID-19 crisis as a multifaceted
intriguing topic, and provides novel and significant insights to both scholars
and executives on how to tackle the pandemic-related issues in the particular
context of New Zealand. It is a solid and authoritative source for anyone
interested in exploring the resilience – and its outcomes - while dealing with
one of the greatest challenges facing humanity nowadays.'*
Shlomo Tarba, Chair in Strategy and International Business, Fellow of
the Academy of Social Sciences, Co-Editor-in-Chief of British Journal of
Management, The University of Birmingham, UK